T0375027

 Getting By in Postsocialist Romania

New Anthropologies of Europe

Daphne Berdahl, Matti Bunzl, and Michael Herzfeld, founding editors

Getting By

in

Postsocialist Romania

Labor, the Body, & Working-Class Culture

David A. Kideckel

Indiana University Press

Bloomington & Indianapolis

This book is a publication of

Indiana University Press
601 North Morton Street
Bloomington, IN 47404-3797 USA

http://iupress.indiana.edu

Telephone orders   800-842-6796
Fax orders   812-855-7931
Orders by e-mail   iuporder@indiana.edu

© 2008 by David A. Kideckel

All rights reserved

No part of this book may be reproduced or utilized in
any form or by any means, electronic or mechanical,
including photocopying and recording, or by any
information storage and retrieval system, without
permission in writing from the publisher. The
Association of American University Presses'
Resolution on Permissions constitutes the only
exception to this prohibition.

The paper used in this publication meets the minimum
requirements of American National Standard for
Information Sciences—Permanence of Paper for
Printed Library Materials, ANSI Z39.48-1984.

Manufactured in the United States of America

Library of Congress Cataloging-in-Publication Data

Kideckel, David A., date
    Getting by in postsocialist Romania : labor, the body, and
working-class culture / David A. Kideckel.
        p. cm. — (New anthropologies of Europe)
    Includes bibliographical references and index.
    ISBN-13: 978-0-253-34957-6 (cloth : alk. paper)
    ISBN-13: 978-0-253-21940-4 (pbk. : alk. paper) 1. Roma-
nia—Social conditions—1989- 2. Post-communism—Romania.
I. Title.
    HN643.5.K53 2007
    305.5'620949809049—dc22
                                                    2007043959

1 2 3 4 5   13 12 11 10 09 08

To the memory of Dorel Racolţa and that of my parents, Ben and Ida Kideckel, for their commitments, strengths, and spirits.

The distinction between violent words and intellectual exercises is built into the subject of bodies. The choice has to be made every time a body is represented: Will the pictured body express discomfort or pain, even if that pain is only spiritual? Or will it be something clever, something *thought-out* rather than felt? Will it be a picture of violent death, or an abstract mathematical body? The same choice between feeling and thinking appears in everyday life. A headache or a broken bone exists in two states: in one, we feel it, and often we cannot think of anything else; and in another, we think of it, and feel nothing.

James Elkins, *The Object Stares Back: On the Nature of Seeing*

Contents

Preface

One day in a Jiu Valley restaurant, the proprietor introduced me to two of his old university professors who were eager to learn about me and my work. So I told them about my research on workers' lives and health. After my brief but animated description, the more voluble of the two, a mathematics emeritus, cocked his head and looked at me disapprovingly. "What are you," he said, "a communist?"

* * *

Workers' lives are discomfiting subjects in East-Central Europe today, and workers' bodies are *terra incognita.* Much as my interlocutor dismissed the substance of my interest, seeing instead only political motivation, many others avoid these subjects entirely or focus exclusively on macro aspects of industrial labor. In a few short years industrial workers have gone from paragons of socialist virtue to near-pariahs of postsocialist uncertainty. Scholarly and political indifference to their large-scale, long-term unemployment, rough physicality, demographic distress, falling standards of living, and mass emigration only heightens workers' problems and lessens the likelihood that serious, systematic efforts will be made to solve them. Workers are visible only when they threaten and protest. Until then they are ignored or used to mark socialism's failures.

Rejecting this general disregard, this book maintains that workers' lives, and especially their physical states and embodied perceptions, have special meaning in the postsocialist world. We can only understand the true trajectories and structures of the societies created on the ruins of forty-plus years of communist control and socialist economics by close examination of the condition of industrial workers, especially those employed by the remnants of the large, state-controlled industrial complexes. Though the former socialist states have made remarkable strides in developing political institutions, in raising standards of living for many of their people, and in integrating themselves into global institutions and relationships, all these developments are cheapened by the struggles demanded of large sectors of their population. To correct this oversight, this book pays particular attention to workers' words and thoughts: about themselves, their work, their families, their societies, their fears and dreams.

This book's title highlights and queries the characteristic processes of "getting by": the diverse practices, legal and illegal, by which people in East-Central Europe and Romania make do under difficult circumstances. That people in these regions do get by and manage somehow has been generally unquestioned. However, postsocialism has produced a new order of political economy and a different set of challenges such that—for workers, at least—getting by, *descurcare*, is uncertain at best and fraught with physical pain and embodied alienation. "Getting by" also implies acting in one's own interest. However, postsocialist pressures on labor and bodies produce what I call a "frustrated agency." The burden of labor, embodied distance, and demographic decline undermine the possibilities open to today's workers and their families. Their plans for their future have largely been put on hold, and present-day practices of getting by end up as strategies for mere survival instead of actions aiming at significant social transformation, whether at individual or collective levels. Such crabbed lives are an essential feature in the decline of many East-Central European workers, and must be placed front and center in any work concerned with postsocialist realities and committed to their transformation.

This work has benefited from extraordinary assistance and forbearance by a great number of individuals and institutions. Special mention must be made of the International Research and Exchanges Board (IREX), which has been so generous to me over the years and without whose assistance my research in Romania and East Europe would have never been possible. IREX funding was provided through the U.S. National Endowment for the Humanities and Title VIII. Additional funding was also provided by the U.S. National Council of Eurasian and East European Research (NCEEER), with funds provided also under authority of a Title VIII grant from the U.S. Department of State. I also thank the Wenner-Gren Foundation for Anthropological Research and Central Connecticut State University for their support of various aspects of this research. None of these organizations or the United States government is responsible for the ideas and conclusions expressed here.

A great number of colleagues, friends, and family also assisted in many ways with this project, though they also are not responsible for its final form. David Ost and Stephen Crowley were in at the beginning. The conference they organized on the state of labor and unions in East-Central Europe, in Warsaw, Poland, in May 1999 set out many of the questions I consider here. Vintilă Mihailescu, the late Trăila Cernescu, and Mircea Baron provided important social and historical information on labor in Romania. Dorel Abraham and colleagues at the Center for Urban and Rural Sociology helped translate surveys used in the research. Florentin Olteanu, Cornel and Stela Teulea, Gabriela and Sorin Miloiu, Pitiu Braitigan, and Gabriel and Teodora Dolea provided creature comforts and friendly advice in both the Jiu Valley and Făgăraş. Enikö Magyari-Vincze read parts of the book and was also a gracious host during my time in Cluj. In the Jiu Valley, Gigi, Daisy, and Ana Nicolau also regularly hosted me and put up with my odd hours and needs. Bianca Botea, Raluca Nahorniac (who helped in all phases of this project), and Vasile Şoflău ably assisted with the field research. I am certain I learned more from them than they from me. Alin Rus also helped prepare and administer surveys and assisted with interviewing in the latter stages of the research. Alin also encouraged me to enlarge this project by producing a film on the Jiu Valley miners: *Days of the Miners: Life and Death of a Working Class Culture.* Although our work on the film delayed my completion of this book, the opportunity to graphically portray miner lives added valuable perspective to it. Finally, the officials, union leaders, and functionaries who contributed opinions and assistance are too numerous to mention. This work would be considerably impoverished without their help.

A number of other colleagues also assisted in various ways. Gerald Creed was particularly insightful and encouraging along the way. Abigail Adams also offered helpful comments, as did Gene Hammel and Jane Schneider in the early phases. Chris Hann and Michael Buchowski read and commented on an early draft. Diligent library and Internet research by Doina Lechanu provided a steady stream of new ideas that required me to reexamine received wisdom. Sam Beck and Steve Sampson were their usual supportive, humorous, and interesting selves. I would also like to thank an unnamed reader and the supportive staff at Indiana University Press, Rebecca Tolen, Shoshanna Green, Miki Bird, and Laura MacLeod for their efforts in this project. Their patience is much appreciated.

I also owe my children, Mimi Brunelle (and John, Simon, Max, and Liza Jane) and Zachary and Caitlin Kideckel, special thanks for putting up with me and my travel for this project over the years. My sister, Allene Kideckel, also was supportive at critical moments. The deaths of my parents, Ben and Ida Kideckel, bracketed this project.

My father died in late 2000, my mother in summer 2004. My parents provide a classic example of people who got by and prospered in the process. Raised poor in the Depression, they learned the sanctity of labor and the blessings of practicality and crafted a life replete with friends, family, and strong community ties. They are always an inspiration.

Finally I owe special gratitude for the assistance, friendship, advice, intervention, and criticism provided by Dorel Racolţa, late president of UMetal, Romania's largest union of workers in nonferrous metals, and founder and member of the board of Cartel Alfa, one of Romania's major labor confederations. I met Dorel in May 1999, just as this project got underway. In the brief time I knew him his good humor, larger-than-life presence, and *joie de vivre* in service to Romania's workers were ready reminders of both postsocialist possibilities and unkept promises. Dorel was a constant source of optimism and forward-looking practice, but his untimely death in July 2004, hastened by constant labor and inattention to health care, illustrates some of the conditions that crush workers' bodies and spirits. I only hope this book will help bring his dreams to public consciousness, and perhaps fruition.

Getting By in Postsocialist Romania

Map 1. Romania and the Jiu Valley
and Făgăraş regions.

1   **Getting By in Postsocialism**

Labor, Bodies, Voices

> A major preoccupation in the Western tradition has to do with the incommunicability of pain, its capacity to isolate sufferers and strip them of cultural resources, especially the resource of language.
>
> —**Arthur Kleinman, Veena Das, and Margaret Lock,** *Social Suffering*

> The propensity to speak politically, even in the most rudimentary way . . . is strictly proportionate to the sense of having the right to speak.
>
> —**Pierre Bourdieu,** *Distinction: A Social Critique of the Judgment of Taste*

Variations on a Theme of Despair

Constantin Moldoveanu paced the floor of his small living room. Out of work for the last year, he mainly left home to register for unemployment benefits at the Work Directorate office. Moldoveanu's physique belied his deteriorating mental health. He was tall, muscular, and youthful and healthy-looking in short shorts and a tight knit shirt. Still, though physically impressive, he acted more like a nervous schoolchild than like the accomplished former miner he was.

Moldoveanu's two-room apartment was impeccable, though located in the midst of the crumbling buildings and garbage-strewn grounds of the "Eighth of March" Petrila neighborhood. A large display cabinet (*super de sufragerie*) stuffed with porcelain figurines dominated the living room. Courtesans comported with dwarves as panthers and tigers wandered through glass flowers. Two rolled and tied Persian rugs sat atop the cabinet, unused since being purchased with Moldoveanu's severance pay from the Lonea Mine. "It looks like we have a lot," he said, pointing at the *super*, "but everything here we bought when Ceauşescu was in power." As he paced, he waved his arms agitatedly and beseeched me for help. "I haven't slept a whole night since I quit work," he said, the dark shadows under his eyes supporting this statement. "I've never been like this. I can't eat. My wife and I haven't made love in six months. I yell at the children."

Moldoveanu arrived in the Jiu Valley in the early 1980s, sent to the Petrila Mine by the Romanian army. In Petrila he met his future wife, whose father sorted coal at the Petrila Preparation Facility. Unlike many soldiers, he took to mining right away. Though he returned to Moldavia with his wife after his term in the military, he wasn't happy "behind the plow." He gladly returned to mining when his father-in-law, arguing that "it is not right for a woman to live so far from her family," asked him to.

> I started as an unqualified worker and always had good relations with the guys in the mine. My closest friends were two brothers: Sandu was an explosives expert [artificier] and Petrica was a brigade chief. They helped me, taught me things, and protected me while I learned to be a miner. From Petrila I was transferred to the Lonea Piler Mine, which was a new mine and a highly regarded place to work. Everyone wanted to work there, but only the best were sent there. I was lucky to get a permanent job there and lots of people wondered how me, an unqualified worker, could do that. Basically it was luck. One day I had to report to the mine director that the cement for the new mine shaft had been delivered. His name was Constantin, like mine. That day also just happened to be the name day of Saints Constantin and Elena. So, he asked me why I was there, and I said that I came to work with the cement for the shaft. But I guess he liked the way I looked and acted, so he gave me a permanent job to celebrate our common name, and I worked there until I left last year in the buy-outs [disponibilizare].
>
> I never would have signed up for the buy-out if I had known the truth. However, the woman from the coal company who got people to sign up told me I could return to work in a year or so. That was a lie just like the rest of it. They said that there would be houses for miners in Sibiu, houses left vacant by Saxons, and that the mayor of Sibiu had offered over a hundred jobs. I know some people who went, and the houses weren't there and neither were the jobs. I don't even know why they closed the Dâlja Mine. There were three hundred meters yet to dig in the main gallery and they still closed it. I understand that unproductive mines should close, but why should they close good ones? I think, over the next five

years, the government will close all but one or two mines. But the mines are the foundation of people's lives in the Jiu Valley . . . so if the mines close they will die. Miners were such hard workers, and now they are nothing but debtors. I got 16.5 million lei in severance plus nine months' unemployment and eighteen months' welfare, and now we have nothing.

DAK: What did you do with the money?

I paid 3.5 million lei for the *super,* bought those two rugs for 600,000 each, and bought a pig for 1.2 million. The rest we just used to live on . . . Now my health is really bad. This month I've already had three colds, and my family is sick too. I am nervous and have had insomnia for the last few years. Not everybody is like me, but everybody suffers one way or another. The town offered me a job sweeping streets, but all that work for such little pay is not worth it. Costs of living are especially high. I have two girls at school. I have to pay two million lei for each to begin the school year, and I have to pay one million for my little boy for kindergarten. I didn't send him since I couldn't afford it. The school asks for even more. They don't have desks, so you have to send stools with the kids. You have to contribute to the class fund. Fifth graders need special notebooks that cost forty thousand each and you need two or three of those. The only way we get by is with help from our parents. They bring us things from the village when they come or we go there. I am lucky my mother is still alive. Before, when I worked for the mine, rent was free and electricity costs were reduced because of the eight tons of coal that I got free from the mine every month and gave to the apartment association in exchange for hot water and heat. Now we only get hot water twice a week, and for five people, for cold water alone we have to pay fifty thousand for each person. This summer I took the kids to the countryside to escape some of these payments.

DAK: Well, are there any particular parties to blame for this crisis?

Who can be guilty but the government? They're the ones. We don't know at all what's going to happen with this country. I voted for Iliescu the last time, but even he's no good. The guy who really did us in was Ciorbea.[1] All he did was give us rope to hang ourselves. Still, I am lucky compared to some of my buddies. God has given us healthy children. I have silicosis and would go for treatment if I could, to Geoagiu,[2] but to get accepted there you have to give a bribe, too. Now I do nothing but sit around here. Just a few years ago I was very active, and played soccer and handball all the time. We are all sick now in our family.

"Yes," Moldoveanu's wife, Maria, said vehemently. She was listening to our conversation from the kitchen and chimed in about her health. "I have back problems and a kidney stone and they have done nothing for me." Constantin continued:

I took her to the emergency room [*urgenţa*] at the hospital a few times, but she needs real treatment and that costs money. So we only go to the urgenţa, where it is free. Also, since I've been laid off, except for two visits to the mine clinic, I've not gone to the doctor or even to the urgenţa. They can do nothing for me.

Everything is worse. People who've been laid off fight much more with their spouses. I know one guy whose wife kicked him out of his house because he couldn't find another job.

Maria interjected, "Look what they do to men here. I heard women in Hungary make 2.5 million lei a month growing mushrooms and here a man can't even make a million. Women can get jobs now, but women can't work like men and shouldn't have to."

> CM: Yes, I was a hard worker. Once when we had to make our quota I worked three shifts in a row [eighteen hours]. I really made money then. Hey, for money, who wouldn't do that kind of work? But now us poor folks can only shut up and swallow what they send us, while the big shots complain they are also starving. I can inherit some land from my mother, but only after she dies. I'll have a one-hectare garden and a quarter share of 2.5 hectares of arable land, shared with my siblings. So that's it. We live in total poverty and total despair.

* * *

Ioan Popa sat stolidly at his living-room table in Făgăraş's "New Field" (Cîmpului Nou) neighborhood of 1970s apartment blocks. Wearing a flannel shirt, blue work pants, and a sheepskin vest (*cojoc*), he looked as though he had just put down a pitchfork or stepped from a tractor. Still, he has lived in Făgăraş, a city of forty thousand, for over twenty years, since apprenticing as a lathe operator at the UPRUC factory.[3] Popa's home is well appointed. The living room has a large color television, but Popa says it hasn't worked in two years and he can't afford to repair it. "We leave it here to make it appear we have some luxury items." Wooden furniture and decorative objects grace the living room, all designed and made by Popa. He is a skilled craftsman and hoped to study architecture at the University of Bucharest in the early 1980s, but lost his seat because of rigged competition. Popa's life has been one of missed opportunity; for education, for promotion, for emigration to the United States, for a position as a factory union leader. Still, he doesn't grumble. He is thoughtful and temperate, in keeping with his stolid physiognomy. But despite his outward calm, he is as stressed as the "wired" Moldoveanu.

Popa's chief concerns are the same as those animating the Moldoveanus: the insecurities of labor, the cost of living, and their physical and emotional toll. He is especially worried that declining production in his factory will force it to close.

> I don't worry about my job. If the factory survives, so will my job, but who knows if the factory will survive. Before, we worked and had orders. In one shift each month we could manufacture 110 pumps. Now we are lucky if we have orders to make five or ten a month. Our economy is like a closed circle. When one part of the circle is blocked than all activities suffer. Since methane gas has become very expensive, the Făgăraş Chemical Combine doesn't work like it should. And since the Combine doesn't work, it doesn't place orders for pumps. Since it doesn't place orders for pumps, UPRUC suffers. It is very stressful.
>
> DAK: Why stress?
>
> Stress comes from uncertainty. Every day you are unsure what will happen. Stress also comes from demands on our family. My wife works legally at a private shop. She's worked there three years but still earns a minimum salary of 450,000 lei a month for 7.5 hours a day, six days a week. The salary is small, but if no other job is available, even that is good. It affords us some luxuries, like our telephone. The worst thing is that our kids come home from school with no one to watch them. My parents live in Făgăraş, next door to my sister, but they have their own problems and are closer to my sister's kids anyway. When we both work at the same time, the kids fend for themselves. We are afraid something might happen, but we have no choice. All this does is just add to the stress.
>
> The way people are treated makes this worse. My wife works all hours, and on Saturdays there are few customers in the afternoon and evening. So I thought I would bring her a radio to help her pass the time. The shop owner said it was OK as long as he didn't have to supply the radio. So this past Saturday, as my wife listened to the radio, a state fiscal agent came in and requested to see her radio license. We have one for our home, and I thought this was sufficient for the radio at work. However, you need a license for where you listen to the radio, not for the radio itself. Because we didn't have that, the agent confiscated the radio and now we may have to pay a fine, from 700,000 to 7 million lei. If we can't, my wife may have to spend three months in jail. The owner still doesn't know about this, and if we tell him, my wife may lose her job. This country is sad. A woman stole a goose and got four years in jail, but a member of the state intelligence service [SRI] who killed four people in an accident got a suspended sentence. We know we can't do much about this, so we make *haz de necaz* [laugh at our troubles].
>
> DAK: What about your health?
>
> Our section at work is not too bad compared to others. Our biggest problem is that after so many years working in poor light our eyes become very bad. There is not an older worker in our section who doesn't wear glasses. It is also very cold in our section because the directors do not provide enough heat. We also have heart problems and headaches, both caused by stress. I would take medicine if I could afford it. My family's health has also suffered lately, because it is so cold in our apartment.[4] Our

entire family sleeps together in one room, where we have a small space heater. We are lucky, since our apartment is in the middle of the building and not as cold as some on the ends of the building.

DAK: If you are all in one room, can you have a married life?

It is very difficult. We wait until the children are sleeping. We go into the other room, but it is very cold. We make sacrifices to be together. Last month we sent one of our kids on a school trip to Bran Castle. We let him go, but suffered from the cost. Still, I can't complain, since my family does well compared to others. My parents each worked forty years at the Combinat[5] and together their pensions total as much as one base salary. There are even some guys who come to work with only a bit of bread to eat. Think how difficult their lives must be.

Postsocialist Workers as Subject and Object

Postsocialism hurts. As Constantin Moldoveanu and Ioan Popa attest, change today is painfully inscribed on the bodies, in the minds, and in the speech of many living through these uncertain times. This book is concerned with the nature of postsocialist life and labor, how it is understood and expressed by workers, and how such expressions influence workers' conceptions of their physical selves and their consequent ability to act in the world on their own behalf. I discuss the integration of labor, narrative, body, and agency and their combined effects on the lives of two groups of workers in postsocialist Romania, Jiu Valley coal miners and chemical workers in the Făgăraş region. These groups differ in many ways. However, the transformations of their labor, their persons, and their stature in postsocialist society force a common outlook and language upon them. In speaking of their world, workers look both inward on themselves and outward on postsocialist society with fear and alienation. They fear for their health, they fear for their and their families' future, they fear for the continuity of their lives and culture. At the same time, they feel rejected by and isolated from the new society in which they live. They see themselves as different, as outsiders looking in: a complete inversion of their former position in socialism.

Romanian workers, like workers typically (Shilling 1993, 131), are famed for their ability to "get by" (*să descurá*): to make do, perhaps even to prosper, on limited resources and in tough times. Today, though, getting by is made more difficult by embodied feelings of inadequacy that often paralyze workers and magnify their alienation. Tales of getting by, of trickery and guile, are replaced by those of complaint, of injustice unpunished and pain undeserved. This is more existential scream than muffled moan. Romanian workers construct a common language about their decline, one similar to the Russian litanies of woe that Nancy Ries (1997) describes. Their discourses, like Moldoveanu's and Popa's, emphasize the intractability of life, the obstacles that face them, the unlikelihood of escape from their predicament, their poor treatment at the hands of others. Despite having some opportunity for engagement and growth, workers thus conspire in their own repression. My goal here is to understand how different types of workers are changed by the circumstances of postsocialism, how workers express those changes in language and in their understanding of their biological natures, and how those changes contribute to such obstruction and defeatism.

The comprehensive nature of change in East-Central Europe since the end of socialism has inspired an extraordinary range of analyses. These typically focus on the distortions of society and individuals in the remaking of this region. Postsocialist society is a rough place, and postsocialist studies is not a happy genre. Analyses of privatization illuminate the changing and uncertain status of property and ownership and how this is manipulated for power and advantage (Hann 1993; Verdery 2003; Zerilli 1998, 2000). The movement from socialism to market democracy (Stark and Bruszt 1998) produces breathtaking inequalities and spurs the instrumentalization and commodification of basic social relations (Berdahl 2005; Dunn 2004). The weakness of state structures enables mafias to run circles around central governments (Satter 2003), and corruption threatens to overwhelm civil society at every turn (Hann and Dunn 1996; Sampson 2002, 2005; Zerilli 2005). NGOs struggle with or succumb to lack of funds, and the money that comes from foreign assistance is diverted and misused (Sampson 1996; Wedel 1998a). Religious groups compete angrily for visibility and privilege (Hann 1996; Verdery 1999). Gender, ethnic, and national identities are contested, sometimes to the point of violence (Gal and Kligman 2000a; Lemon 2000a; Stewart 1997). Many people emigrate while declines in agricultural markets force many who remain in rural villages to return to subsistence farming (Cartwright 2001; Creed 1995; Rey 1997). The struggles and uncertainties within postsocialist societies even show up in uncertain definitions of postsocialism itself (Humphrey 2002a; Verdery 2002; Verdery and Kligman 1992).

Unhappiness is not without analytic virtues. The structural principles of troubled societies are often sharply highlighted. Postsocialist studies has used this to great advantage to define diverse dimensions of changing human subjectivity and meaning in nations, regions, and systems of interest. The postsocialist project is as viciously modern as they come, and postsocialist studies leads the way in considering the effects of the forced diet of neo-liberalism on populations that fantasized something quite different (Tismaneanu 1998) when the socialist regimes fell (Petrovic 2002). However, the interest in changed human subjectivities has just begun to spur attention to labor, and the lives of workers have been poorly represented even in postsocialist anthropology.[6]

Given their numerical preponderance and their location at the nexus of a range of social problems, work and workers must be afforded greater significance in our understanding of postsocialism. Still, the backgrounding of workers is understandable in societies exorcising decades of socialist class policies and rhetoric, where concern for labor can expose one to accusations of communist sympathies. Workers' lives are also marginalized by national governments and international organizations, although those institutions have produced a plethora of policies and interventions allegedly in workers' interests. Frequently, these efforts are planned, implemented, and sustained without worker input, and are aimed more at political control than political empowerment and economic improvement. It is not odd that they have largely failed to rejuvenate ramshackle worker towns and apartment complexes and remodel worker social relations. Even state laws favoring workers, like Romania's recent labor contract reforms (Rubin Meyer Doru and Trandafir 2003), ostensibly improving job security, seem mainly sops to labor, and are impossible to enforce in any case.

Concern for workers is also contradictory to post–Cold War Western triumphalism and to the related "transition" model that dominated recent social science understanding of East Europe (Lane 1997; Pasti 1995; Snyder and Vachudova 1997). Daphne Berdahl (2000) sees "transition" as an academic representation of triumphalist politics and the intellectual means for capitalist penetration and the elision of labor from the postsocialist project. Transition thus implicitly defines workers as either anachronistic artifacts of failed socialism or obstacles in the march to capitalist prosperity, or even as both. Transition measures the fit between Western capitalism and postsocialist practices or "map[s] institutional changes imposed 'from outside and above'" (Mihailescu 2004). Hence, the transitional approach focuses on Western preoccupations with issues of ownership, market, and the rule of law. Workers' concerns—occupational insecurity, unfair distribution of value, and declining workplace conditions—have until recently been off the table (Dunn 2004; Weiner 2005).

This book takes a different position. I argue that workers, rather than being an anachronistic survival of a bad Marxist dream, occupy a critical position in the postsocialist political and economic landscape. Their lives and possibilities, and the conditions of their spirits and communities, are bellwethers for tracking and managing postsocialist change. Workers, especially in the Jiu Valley, are the canaries in the coal mine of postsocialism. But more than serving as an early warning of society's failings, workers' lives and words testify to the essences of postsocialist structures. Workers both link and are pulled apart by the two systems of socialism and postsocialism. Their structural and historical position between the collectivities of state centralism and the private persons of postsocialism, set loose from those collectivities, intensifies their sense of estrangement, which then magnifies their fears for themselves, their families, their futures.

Undoing the Postsocialist Working Class

Certain analyses of postsocialism argue that the commonalities of class no longer explain the circumstances of labor. Despite disagreements about what constitutes socio-economic class in the first place (Tilly 1999, 3–5; Williams 1976, 60–69), many scholars agree that changes in East-Central European society in the last decade and a half are so vast as to obscure whatever class structure exists (Słomczyński and Shabad 1997) and make its measurement nearly impossible.[7] Furthermore, though East-Central European politics are increasingly responsive to class issues (Szelényi, Fodor, and Hanley 1997), social analyses often see peoples' interests as neither automatically class-responsive nor "tied to their location in the political economic order of the old regime" (Słomczyński and Shabad 1997, 167). Diverse social identities, spurred by new consumption possibilities, allegedly supercede class as the prime mover of postsocialist life. Socialist states celebrated class (as defined by position in a production hierarchy) and enforced a rough equality of consumption within and between classes. Postsocialism defines groups by privileging consumption over labor (Berdahl 2005; Mandel and Humphrey 2002; Patico 2005) and encouraging differentiation over sameness, niche over mass products (Dunn 2004). Where socialism sought to plan the distribution of resources and rewards, thus giving workers collective access to education and upward mobility, postsocialist states show renewed faith in private ownership and markets and leave individuals to make their own way in society. Socialist society was insular and its relationships with other social systems severely restricted, but postsocialist society rapidly integrates into global networks, thus contributing to a confusion of overlapping identities and furthering individual differentiation in the process (Rausing 2004; Verdery 1998).

Postsocialism elides the significance of class not only by defining new relationships between state, society, and the individual, but also by creating those relationships in new ways. Postsocialist systems are characterized by an intense and inherent changefulness which, in itself, facilitates differentiation and a breaking of class boundaries. Change and uncertainty, in fact, seem essential features of postsocialist society, as suggested by Mariella Pandolfi's (2005) oxymoronic, bittersweet idea of "permanent transition." Constant change and the impermanence of social structures especially confound those groups whose identities were closely bound up with socialist social relations and whose key economic and symbolic resources are severely eroded in the current conditions.

However, though class analysis is shot through with holes and the differences between groups may become as significant as their similarities, there is something to be said for recognizing that some groups, including postsocialist workers in formerly socialist enterprises, are especially vulnerable to and disadvantaged by the structure and pace of postsocialist change. In fact, postsocialist change leaves workers, especially, in a no-man's-land of uncertainties. Once labor elites, even if only in name, workers in postsocialism have few landmarks with which to navigate or safe harbors in which to escape the ravages of change. Their identities unraveled as the ideological supports and subsidies of the all-enveloping corporate state were yanked from under them (Borneman 1998). Their current existence is utterly unpredictable, and the future seems largely denied and constantly out of reach. Their industries are restructured, mines shut, and factories downsized (Gâf-Deac 1994; Tulbure and Irimie 1995), as identity-producing labor is replaced by unemployment and falling living standards (Anon. 1994a, 1994b, 1999b; Iordăchel 1993; Pasti 1995; Pasti, Miroiu, and Codinţaa 1996; Ştefan 1997).

Taken together, all these changes foment social difference and worsen both people's objective conditions and the symbolic and ideological referents by which they shape their sense of self and others. However, though class identification may be on the wane, the relevance of class-based experience is not. As class identification has declined in the years since the fall of socialism, and especially in the first years of the twenty-first century, there has been a similar decline in worker labor activism (Ost 2002; Ost and Crowley 2001). This is also the case in Romania, where postsocialist workers had been some of the most militant in East-Central Europe and often lashed out, protesting threats to their position in labor action (Bush 1993; Kideckel 1999, 2001, 2002; Sturdza 1990) and forcing the government to accede to some union demands (Cartel Alfa 1997b; Romania Government 1999b; Rubin Meyer Doru and Trandafir 2003). Though Romania has recently seen an increase in national labor actions, especially in service sectors like education and transport (Anon. 2005),[8] the commonalities of class paradoxically mean that workers now rarely engage in mass action to preserve their declining conditions.

Postsocialist society is not satisfied with workers' staying out of view; it also strives to drown out their voices with an overabundance of rhetoric proclaiming the joys of market democracy (Weiner 2005). Still, when one bothers to speak to those on the sidelines, it is clear that they nurse deep-seated grievances about their circumstances. Although workers are pushed to the sidelines of postsocialist society, and although their ability to plan and act in their own interest is severely compromised, society disregards them at its peril. Ignoring their grievances, whether expressed or not, ensures continued ferment, economic uncertainty, and demographic decline, thus derailing a humane transformation of life in the post-socialist states.

Worker Embodiment, Agency, and Narrative

Despite differences between workers and the weakening of class identities, workers share a common understanding of their lives as stressful, dangerous, and distanced from society and community. This perception manifests itself differently in different states and communities. However, workers generally express, sometimes with laser-like precision and sometimes through a stress-based haze, a belief that, compared to socialism, postsocialism denigrates and disadvantages them. In voicing this belief, workers create obstacles to every possible response to their current condition. As a result, postsocialist workers do not so much practice or plan for the future as they react, embarking on short-term projects to maintain tenuous holds on life, work, family, and community (Rose 1997). Stumbling from crisis to crisis, workers live lives of unmitigated stress and difficulty. In the best case, they escape through emigration. In the worst case, they sicken and die at a frightening pace (Bobek and Marmot 1996; Cockerham 1999; Leon et al. 1997; Stone 2000; Watson 1995; Weidner 1998).

To consider how worker agency is frustrated by narrative and embodied alienation, let me first offer a working definition of agency. Following Mustafa Emirbayer and Ann Mische (1998, 963), I consider agency to be

> a temporally embedded process of social engagement informed by the past (in its habitual aspect), but also oriented toward the future (as a capacity to imagine alternative possibilities) and toward the present (as a capacity to contextualize past habits and future projects within the contingencies of the moment).

Thus, effective agency depends on people's ability to use models of the past to recognize and develop diverse responses to the present, which are also oriented to other, more temporally distant possibilities. All humans are agents. What differentiates us is the extent to which we clearly see the past, are able to use past experience to understand and act in the present, and successfully plan for the future.

Discussions of agency regularly celebrate the resistance strategies of subordinated people (Hegland 1995; Scott 1985), and anthropologists seem almost ritualistically required to identify such possibilities among the marginalized peoples with whom we work.[9] In fact, postsocialist workers, and Romanians in particular, vary considerably in their ability to succeed as agents. Some workers, motivated perhaps by religion or an unshakable desire to succeed in business, are able to push the boundaries of, and perhaps even escape, the systemic constraints of postsocialism. Some seek education, and more try emigration. However, in recent years, worker collective agency and resistance has largely evaporated, and most people's strategies for the future have become narrow, reactive, or absent altogether (cf. Ashwin 1999). Workers often rail at their fate or wait for someone or something to extricate them from their present predicament.

This generalized failure of worker agency is due to a number of factors. First, workers misconstrue the socialist past when defining goals for the present and strategies for the future. Workers today know that socialism reinforced their political subalternity (Bahro 1977) and produced the penury of persistent shortage (Kornai 1980), but downplay these to contrast the past with the tenuousness of work and life today. Speaking of the past, workers—even those scarcely born at socialism's end—frequently ignore their political disenfranchisement and instead say that socialism provided other resources enabling them to succeed. Their discussions reinforce such positive images as social collectivity and shared commitment at work, orientation toward achievement, and confidence in family, if not personal, mobility. Above all, nostalgia for socialism focuses on security: of one's job, of the community, of physical life. However, such selective use of the socialist model is ultimately futile and frustrating for effective agency, as it elevates relations and conditions that are thoroughly discredited today. Collectivist practices make little sense in postsocialist institutional contexts and have little support among either globalizing elites or the hard-pressed, but energetic, middle classes.

Agency is frustrated further by workers' perceptions of alienation from society at large, a perception that grows as their political actions are discredited. From the fall of socialism to the turn of the millennium, the political fortunes of workers steadily declined (Crowley and Ost 2001; Crowley 2004). In Romania, worker power lasted somewhat longer than elsewhere, and through the 1990s workers were a vast and, to many, menacing presence in society. Their militancy ran the gamut from the so-called *mineriade,* the actual and threatened invasions of Bucharest by Jiu Valley coal miners, through periodic national strikes, to a whole range of localized walk-outs and wildcat actions. Romanian unions were also far more visible and militant than their East-Central European counterparts (Kideckel 1999, 2001).[10] Unions represented about two-thirds of 6.5 million potential nonagricultural workers. Union leaders played roles in national politics, had the ear of presidents and prime ministers, and influenced national economic decision-making. One former union leader, Victor Ciorbea, was even prime minister in the right-center government of 1996.

Yet union militancy barely held the line for workers' standards of living, and it contributed to the discreditation of workers' lives and politics and the defamation or pitying of workers by others.[11]

Besides bearing little fruit and promoting denigration of industrial laborers, the constant demonstrations caused the Romanian government to erect a number of obstacles to worker collective action. Thus, a law passed in 1991 required a lengthy process before a strike could be legally declared (Brehoi and Popescu 1991; Bush 1993; Ockenga 1997; Romania Parliament 1991). Though the law is marginally effective,[12] together with workers' fear of job loss it has dampened their senses of the possible. A miner from the Jiu Valley town of Vulcan suggested,

> There is little we can do to change our situation these days. People won't go on strike anymore. Not only are they afraid, but we actually need permission to strike. What kind of a country is it where workers need permission to strike?

Because of the alienation—both imposed and self-inflicted—of workers in post-socialist society generally and Romania in particular, workers have few resources or rationales with which to justify their place at the postsocialist table. They are certainly citizens of a new social order, but decidedly second-class ones. Unlike the diverse peoples of Chernobyl, described by Adriana Petryna (2002), who justify their claim to society's resources by their past victimhood and their current jeopardy, or even women's and ethnic minority groups that bask in international support and interest and have UN work groups and conferences devoted to them, workers feel largely bereft of qualities that could earn them support or power. All they have are their grievances, their memories of former glory, and their numbers. But their large populations are shot through with so much variation and uncertainty in the unraveling class conditions of postsocialism that numerical preponderancy in some ways even limits their potential for individual and group agency.

Frustrated agency and perceptions of fear and distance are particularly pronounced in the way people speak and the kinds of narratives they develop about their changing world and their attempts to deal with those changes. Narratives both structure and provide context for individual understandings of what is likely and possible in one's world (Weiner 2005, 573). To understand the lives and struggles of postsocialist workers and how they conceptualize and thus shape the way they negotiate and get by in their world, we must hear them and give credence to their voices and thoughts. The present work thus gives considerable space to workers' own words. However, the full significance of narratives to the individuals who express them depends on more than words alone. Where and by whom people feel their words are considered (or not) also gives them meaning. Thus, the common thread running through narratives such as Moldoveanu's and Popa's at the beginning of this chapter is not just fear and uncertainty. The speakers' angst is intensified by the knowledge that those in power refuse to hear them and are purposefully unconcerned for their pain and problems. Workers perceive their narratives and concerns to be largely kept out of public discourse, and they begin to see conspiracies out of proportion to reality (see Briggs 2004 for an analogous case). Thus, because those who matter in society turn a deaf ear, workers come to see every aspect of their lives as shaped by conspiracy.

In other words, narrativizing fear and distance, in an atmosphere of unrealistic expectation and rapid, unsettling change, elevates these words and sentiments of stress and struggle as central to worker lives and imposes them across all manner of social circumstances. They are, to use Stanley Tambiah's (1990, 750) notion, focalized and transvalued. Workers are held in thrall to their own words, which manifest across the spectrum of their lives in perceptions and practices related not only to labor, but also to social relationships, to political possibilities, and to changing identity, among other things. Though a variety of practices and conditions characterize each of these transvalued domains, focalization generally demands their being evaluated as threatening, stressful, and problematic. As workers are persistently concerned by the likely negative qualities and results of their conditions and relationships, these stresses and fears are internalized and displayed in changing physical life; stance, appetites, health beliefs and practices, standards of beauty, masculinity and femininity, sexuality, dress, and rates of morbidity and mortality. Narrative, in other words, has physical consequences. Sticks and stones, of course, break bones; but names and words, whether used by others or by people about themselves, also hurt.

Focalized and transvalued, embodied and narrativized fear and distance overwhelm workers' ability to prosper and plan, and thus play havoc with their chances of "getting by." Romanians pride themselves on the ability to make do under difficult conditions, to be *descurcăreţi*.[13] "Getting by" was particularly important in the socialist economy of shortage, under which people cobbled together different relationships, sources of income, and other forms of sustenance to not only survive, but also strive for social mobility. Important as it was in socialism, getting by is more so today. Under socialism one's job and minimal creature comforts were assured, but that is no longer the case. Privatization and the development of a market economy have eliminated shortages, but, along with globalization and economic restructuring, they have reduced people's ability to secure resources. Thus, as postsocialist conditions take hold, the meaning of "getting by" shifts from "manipulating the system in one's interest" to "managing basic survival." This is especially true for the unemployed, but even workers with secure jobs must focus more intensively on meeting their basic needs: food, shelter, health care.

Getting by is also necessary in the postsocialist workplace, though here too it does not mean securing resources, as it did in the past, so much as just keeping one's job. Certainly, shortages of all sorts still characterize postsocialist production, especially in state-owned or -controlled industries like Jiu Valley mining or Făgăraş chemical production. Miners, for example, complain about the poor quality of their tools, often a consequence of corruption in purchasing and maintenance. As in socialist times, workers overcome these shortages by technological cannibalization and other strategies. But more often, "getting by" in labor means putting up with inequities in the workplace, keeping quiet and getting on with the job so that one's position will not be threatened in the inevitable next round of layoffs. This is true also in newly privatized plants, from EU Poland (Dunn 2004) and Hungary (Kurti 2002) to struggling Romania.

Getting by is thus increasingly difficult in every sphere of life. But since there are few ways to overcome postsocialist obstacles, getting by is superceded by collective narratives of complaint about the circumstances of worker lives and labor. In Romania complaint is called "crying," *plângere*. Unlike *descurcare, plângere* has not been elevated to a central Romanian cultural quality; people didn't generally talk to me about "crying," they just did it. Postsocialist complaint links Romanian workers with others in these hard times. A culture of complaint, as Ries (1977) argued in her discussion of Russian discourse and as Rose (1997) suggests generally, is common throughout East-Central Europe. Such verbal expression of suffering is not merely "kvetching." Instead, *plângere* uses narrative to unify concerns about life and health with grievances about superordinates, political officials, and bosses. *Plângere* defines suffering, woe, loss, and grievances small and large, whether at home or in labor.[14]

Plângere grapples with and gives voice to all manner of difficulties: the fears or indignities of unemployment, the desperation of social solitude, the pain of chronic illness. Despite the suggestion by David Morris (1997, 27) that troubled circumstances are often "suffered in silence," Romanian workers readily share their complaints with others, as if they were a badge of postsocialist identity. However, as Charles Briggs (2004) suggests in another context, worker voices and complaints are disregarded by the larger society. Because of this rejection, the conditions that prompt worker complaint in the first place are magnified beyond their actual significance. Complaint is consequently also focalized and transvalued and becomes deep, existential, and redolent with hierarchal tensions. Furthermore, by linking personal problems with workplace struggles, complaint unites the body with the circumstances of social differentiation. Complaint varies across socio-economic strata. Supervisors complain about the poor quality of labor. The wealthy complain about political and economic conditions and poor investment climates. However, workers often see others' complaints as hollow and as testifying to a certain callousness on the part of the dominant toward the real problems of postsocialism—which, of course, are those that afflict industrial laborers.

Getting By in a New World of Goods

Postsocialist workers' focalized and transvalued narratives of fear and distance stand in great rhetorical contrast to expressions of life in the corporate socialist state. The "familistic" state (Verdery 1996) was both controlling and nurturing, and state practices at once overtly threatening and seductively salutary. They expressed both qualities of what Michel Foucault termed state "bio-power" (Foucault 1980), i.e., coercion and care. In its exercise of bio-power the socialist state enabled meritocratic advancement via education, guaranteed at least minimal creature comforts, and protected, while vigilantly monitoring, workers' health, though always in service to the project of the state (Foucault 1978, 144). These desiderata are still available, though individuals must now obtain them in the market. However, though workers (like others) are encouraged to individuate themselves through consumption, postsocialist transformations have largely limited their ability and opportunity to do so. Furthermore, the means they do have, wages and (decreasing) subsidies, are insecure, evanescent, and distinctly pallid compared to those of others. It is little wonder that, as workers give voice to their present predicament, they readily downplay the state's past coercion to look favorably on the security and enabling features of socialism.

Just as narrative shapes consciousness, it also expresses and re-inforces understandings of the physical. Our understanding of bod-ies and physical practice in socio-economic contexts has been enliv-ened by Pierre Bourdieu's notion of the habitus. Bourdieu defines habitus as "a relatively enduring, bodily and personal 'disposition' produced by repetitive experience and reproduced in and as social practice" (1977, 95). That is, in learning habitual bodily practice, individuals inculcate

> the objective structures (e.g. of language, economy, etc.) to succeed in reproducing themselves more or less completely, in the form of durable dispositions . . . Therefore sociology treats as identical all the biological in-dividuals who, being the product of the same objective conditions, are the supports of the same habitus. (85)

Debate about the significance of habitus largely centers on the issue of group versus individual agency: that is, to what extent in-dividuals are "the product of the same objective conditions." Some hold that Bourdieu overemphasizes internal class consistency, thus limiting individuals' ability to act subjectively in their own behalf (see for example Herzfeld 2004, 37–38). However, others (Brubaker 1985, 750–52; Reed-Danahay 2005, 35–36) see habitus as a product of the negotiation, by subjective individuals, of those objective class conditions. Unnoted in this debate, however, is the constructive quality of language and that discussion of "objective conditions," when those conditions lead to similar experiences and are discussed in similar ways, contributes in great measure to the way individuals respond to those conditions. Thus habitus, too, is shaped by narra-tive, which is itself mediated by particular histories, social institu-tions, and work regimes that frame the issues about which people tell stories. Thus, edgy, fast-paced, leather-jacketed Jiu Valley min-ers look, act, and sound very different from stolid Făgăraş, in rough corduroy and padded nylon jackets. Similarly, the two groups make very different choices about diet, drink, sexuality, child-rearing, and a host of other behaviors. Both groups, however, express anger and frustration at their uncertain jobs and falling incomes and both raise the issue of the state's and society's lack of concern for worker circumstances.

Thus workers, in telling stories about themselves and their pres-ent-day circumstances, verbally express three layers of meaning, roughly corresponding to the layered structure of bodies as social entities (Lock 1993, 135; Scheper-Hughes and Lock 1987, 7). As layered phenomena, both narratives and bodies first express workers' individual experiences and practices. Underlying these, however, are their perceptions of themselves and their groups as defined by relationships to society and to others. Finally, the third level of narrative, like that of the body, expresses their and their cohorts' potential for action and agency, whether enabled or disabled by interaction with prevailing hierarchies. Thus, each level of bodily experience and narrative expression is interrelated with the others and shapes physical conditions, perceptions, and practice. Most significantly, as long recognized in class society (Thompson 1963) and as reconfirmed in postsocialist Romanian worker circumstances, the critical links in the formation of bodies, embodiment, and agency are the relationships between different social groups that produce the common experiences and understandings within groups, as expressed in narrative structures.[15]

Changing hierarchies in East-Central European postsocialism shape physical lives and narrative expressions of those lives in ways sharply distinct from those prevailing in the past. Privatization and reintegration into the Western market system discourage East-Central European states from exercising centralized control over their citizens' bodies. But now, as private persons, workers are cut loose from their social moorings and placed at the mercy of new national socio-economic hierarchies. They must look out for themselves within the context of changing possibility. Each postsocialist state is thus truly on its own path out of socialism (Stark and Bruszt 1998). However, each also faces the same task of changing its mix of economic sectors: state and private, service and production, balanced and specialized. This process also shapes the distribution of reward and possibility, which impinge on workers' bodies, their understandings of their physical selves, and the way they speak of these understandings.

Whether these socio-economic transformations are accomplished at great speed or in dribs and drabs, for workers they are always accompanied by unemployment, underemployment, threats to employment, and large-scale change in work contracts and regulations (Crowley and Ost 1999; Earl and Oprescu 1995; Ost 1993). Workers' physical conditions and representations are particularly stressed by these processes and uncertainties. Furthermore, stress on workers is multidimensional and integrated, thus especially harmful. Some processes operate at the level of structure, changing workers' position in labor institutions and their relation to those who dominate such institutions. Some effects are social, precipitating massive change in the relationships in which workers live and reproduce their lives. Others symbolically degrade workers and deprive industrial labor of meaning. Taken together, all these changes provoke an overwhelming sense that the world is loosed on its moorings and that little will change this.

Postsocialist workers' lives, especially in Romania, are diminished even further by the great difference between them and the lives of the "fortunate classes," which has ballooned in the last years. In the midst of their own difficulties, working people see the wealthy resplendent in designer clothes and the pink, wattled flesh of lavish dining. In postsocialist luxury shopping districts, the indolent offspring of business and political elites slouch at the wheels of luxury cars, glaring out their windshields without sympathy for those who cross before them. Young, middle-class professional women wear aerobically toned bodies like "calling cards" (Svendsen 1996, 1997), advertising their modernity and availability. Urbane businessmen (and some few women) stalk through airports with multiple cell phones. Even though workers' lives vary from state to state and region to region, the great differences between them and the wealthy and powerful make workers feel clearly distinct from, and placed in opposition to, other groups in society, and challenge them to distinguish themselves in some more proactive way (Bourdieu 1984).

In Romania, in particular, workers' living conditions are significantly different from those of others. Heat in workers' flats is often irregular and water, when available, is frequently brackish and unhealthy. Shards of window glass litter children's play areas. Health care is also increasingly unavailable. Where once every socialist worker could count on at least minimal care at factory or mine clinic, today those clinics are shuttered or operate on greatly reduced schedules. For many, medical care is a luxury, as food and housing take most of their pay. To their credit, many worker families combat their arduous conditions any way they can. Apartments I visited were almost always clean and well maintained. Sacrifices are made for children's health care and schooling. Diverse strategies for living are formulated and reformulated. However, degraded housing and health conditions are systemic and often beyond individual remediation. Health problems, attested to by falling birth rates and life expectancies (Bobek and Marmot 1996; Cockerham 1999; Hall and White 1995; Rivkin-Fish 2003) are rampant among post-socialist East-Central European workers and worker communities. Middle-aged men between thirty and sixty, many of whom work or once worked in the large socialist industrial complexes, are especially hard hit by rising morbidity and mortality rates (Leon et al. 1997; Stone 2000; Watson 1995; Weidner 1998). Epidemic diseases like tuberculosis are reappearing in new, more virulent forms and established illnesses like cholera persist with dispiriting tenacity.

Postsocialist economic transformation also contributes to sexual commodification in all its dimensions. Pornography is ubiquitous, and prostitution has grown exponentially throughout the region (Cohen 2000). East-Central Europeans occupy every niche in the international sex trade. The International Organization for Migration estimates that 300,000 Balkan women are trafficked annually into the European Union (Chiriac 2000). West Europeans, meanwhile, venture to the east on sexual forays, such as the neo-colonial gay sex excursions of Austrian men to the Czech Republic described by Matti Bunzl (2000). Not unexpectedly, HIV infection rates are high and rising throughout East-Central Europe (Agence France Presse 2000). The expanded regional sex industry contributes to the sense of disorder among socially conservative postsocialist workers.

In these difficult conditions, workers' bodies sit heavy on their minds and in their talk. Workers vary in their physical appearance, but still perceive great differences between themselves as a group and others and believe that little can be done to turn the tides in their favor. One can't talk too long with people in either region before they pour out their anguish over falling wages, increased unemployment, declining living conditions, poor diets, and other physical challenges. All these conditions affect the ability of workers and their families to make their way in this new world. Not only is their access to basic resources challenged or even restricted, but the lack of these resources is an affront to those who were celebrated by socialism, as were the miners, or at least left to their own devices to work hard and prosper, as were the Făgăraş.

Researching Labor, the Body, and Narratives of Woe in Postsocialist Times

Despite great regional variation, workers' experiences in postsocialism are homogenized in a way that is readily observed in research practice and heard in their words. In George Marcus's formulation (1995), multisited research enables us to define pathways connecting regions and localities of the modern world system. Such connections—through money, migrants, and media, among other things—can be metaphoric or actual. Research in the Jiu Valley and Făgăraş is multisited research within a single country, and it allows us to observe the results of large-scale processes and generalize their effects beyond regional or even national borders.

Thus, despite their differences (including the significant differences between their physical lives in the past), workers' physical and verbal responses to postsocialist conditions are broadly similar. For example, though different causes are blamed, perceptions of ill health are on the rise in both regions, as are sentiments that little can be done to arrest increasing morbidity and early death. Among miners, these sentiments result from their antagonistic relations with medical personnel and the health care system. Făgăraş workers, on the other hand, have greater respect for doctors and the health care system but rarely visit doctors and generally suppress their feelings of ill health until conditions are grave. Sexual identities are also frustrated among both regional populations, though again for different reasons. To generalize, many Jiu Valley men and women are upset at the loose morality of changing dress and comportment codes, while in Făgăraş people are disaffected because of their lack of access to these new morals. Nonetheless, different attitudes still translate into commonalities of embodied understanding.

Unhappily, the groups also share a lack of confidence in their ability to shape their own lives. Both accept the ultimate legitimacy of market democracy and the need to adapt to that system. Furthermore, unlike Romanian workers and peasants in the past, they increasingly recognize that luck and fate play small roles in their lives. Workers have a firm grasp on the reality of postsocialist political economy, but it is this realistic outlook that makes them feel at a loss to develop contingencies for present and future. Regardless of job security, economic condition, family structure, level of education, or other variables, worker communities across the postsocialist world feel overwhelmed by stress and incapacity, and the ubiquity of such feelings requires explanation.

Doing research for this book, and for the documentary film *Days of the Miners: Life and Death of a Working Class Culture,* was, in a word, depressing. People's objective material conditions—their homes, their clothing, their diet—are better than those of many in the developing world, and could often be classified as comfortable or satisfactory. Nonetheless, the emotional content of their lives and discourses was the inverse. Sentiments of fear, anger, stress, resignation, and uncertainty dominated most discussions. High emotion pervaded events like hunger strikes and interviews with tearful, desperate workers losing their jobs. At other times emotion was pushed aside by deep resignation and apathy. As little could be done to address these emotional conditions, discussions often ended in embarrassed silence.

It is true that much of the existential grief communicated by informants in both regions was magnified by interview situations. In narrativizing their conditions, some informants hyperbolized their accounts, since they knew that American audiences might hear of their circumstances. Two recent books on fieldwork in postsocialist venues contain contributions primarily from West Europeans and Americans (DeSoto and Dudwick 2000; Berdahl, Bunzl, and Lampland 2000, 5–7), and these authors often describe their informants confronting them with personal and social dilemmas (Brown 2000) and their own frustration at their inability to assist people (Zanca 2000). My assistants and I faced the same situation in Romania. Like anthropologists the world over, we were often asked for medicines, tools, and the like. However, people more often sought information, an especially valuable commodity in postsocialist uncertainty. Would outside investors target their region? What would be the fate of particular factories or mines? How did one apply for an American, Canadian, or Australian visa? How are Romanian workers treated in foreign countries? Lack of opportunity clearly prompted these requests. Though they clearly defined a sense of worker agency, in the end they only increased workers' frustration, as do conditions in the rest of their world. Informant requests during socialism—say, for meat for a wedding or a critical part for a nonfunctioning automobile—were easy to supply if one had the cash or connections. In postsocialism, the most we could offer was an educated guess and an open ear, neither of which could resolve our interviewees' uncertainty.

We observed life in the Jiu Valley and Făgăraş in various ways. We interviewed people in mines and factories. We visited regional union and unemployment offices and spoke to both officials and workers there. We attended union meetings. We interviewed people in their homes or at the bar. We were on site at hunger strikes and other protests. Additionally, we played backgammon with unemployed and retired miners in Petroşani and Lupeni neighborhoods and parks. Most workers wanted to talk to us and have their story told. However, responses to our questions often outlined in sharp relief critical regional labor and social issues. Interviews were conducted in Romanian. Some were translated into English and transcribed, while others were transcribed in their original Romanian; they were coded and analyzed using Ethnograph 5.0.

Informants spoke to us as if they expected us to bring their stories to the decision-makers who affect their fates. In Făgăraş, for example, before we began observations at the UPRUC factory, both the union leadership and factory management met with us and immediately presented their side of some thorny issues in the factory. Both also mentioned the need to find "white knights" to hasten the involved and contentious process of privatization. In the Jiu Valley, which has a reputation elsewhere in the country as violent, ugly, and anachronistic,[16] many people urged us to develop a correct image of the place, one that would better represent them to others. However, what image was correct depended on the person we were speaking with. Institutional representatives, such as town officials and National Coal Company administrators, wanted to show off the quality of Valley life, the importance of coal production, and the strength of the mining industry. Miners similarly insisted on coal's importance, but wanted to convey how difficult their lives were and how disadvantaged they felt compared to other groups. They especially wanted others to learn that the *mineriade* were not just exercises in mass violence but attempts to gain justice for all Romania's workers. In the Jiu Valley people also regularly talked about how foreign visitors, studies, and interventions come and go, leaving little to show for their activities, implying that we had a responsibility to do things differently.[17]

Research on physical practice and embodied understanding also resulted in a number of discomforting moments. Informants did not see questions about their physical lives as particularly prurient. Questions about sexuality were addressed in a fairly straightforward, if somewhat uncertain, manner; both men and women often first indicated that the topic was not much discussed in their households. Unlike questions about sexuality, however, questions about health elicited a whole range of angry and plaintive responses concerning family problems, changing morals, tense social relationships, and, again, problematic labor. Informant responses continually reinforced the notion that health and the body sat at the nexus of a whole range of postsocialist phenomena, including difficulties of getting by and planning for the future on a declining income.

To honor informant requests, I occasionally raised some of their issues with various state, regional, and local policy makers, office-holders, or administrators at factories, mines, unions, or health care institutions. All of them spoke freely, but were mostly unmoved by the plight of individual workers, let alone by that of the great masses of unemployed and underemployed. The solution to work-ers' problems, according to these authorities, depended either on in-ternational factors (like "Romania joining Europe," receiving aid to better develop its production capacity, or getting better loan terms from international financial institutions) or on individual work-ers themselves, who ought to try starting a business, or move to other regions, or work harder, or stop complaining and accept other jobs as a step toward the future. Some officials, like a highly placed member of the Făgăraş city administration, were critical of worker actions and claims. He argued that much of the country's problems could be traced to

> the many labor actions that slow the economy and frighten investors. La-bor actions are a chain. When they start in one place, they spread easily to others. But the West has to understand that the reasons for the labor actions here relate to some of the things that Western policies have created in Romania. Unless there is labor peace here, there won't be peace there. The West is to Romania like the Romanian upper class is to the Romanian poor . . . i.e. without responsibility, rapacious, living off of them in para-sitic way. When Western states finally understand this, this can change the whole historical process of the end of communism. Consciousness, after all, passes through the stomach.

Other local and regional officials were not terribly sympathetic either. Various staffers at the public health services of both Braşov and Hunedoara counties, the administrative centers of the Făgăraş zone and the Jiu Valley respectively, absolved themselves of respon-sibility in regional change and considered the workers of the two regions partially to blame for their own circumstances. However, another Hunedoara Public Health functionary suggested that the health service responded to miners' health needs only after min-ers threatened political protests. The director's comments were not nearly as pointed, but he still said,

> Part of the problem with Jiu Valley miner health is that people move around a lot . . . and lack skills to manage budgets, They drink a lot and

have many children. We do little with the unemployed. If they ask for a consultation, we give them a day when they can come to the health ser-vice for information, but other than that there is not much we do. Simi-larly, there is nothing that we do for the hunger strikers. We only have so much money. What we do is to provide things to the hospitals that people attend. In fact, the improvement of the general hospitals at Vul-can and Uricani was a direct result of our response to the miner protests [*mineriade*].

Though others blame them for their own plight, many workers maintained a mournful dignity. Some of this was probably simple depression, but some responses clearly showed the extent to which workers recognized the problematic aspects of their lives, the need for something to be done about them, and the uncertainty that this would happen. Political responses had largely disappeared in the last years, because of police actions, fears of job loss, emigration, and poor health. But workers know this situation cannot continue indefinitely. How they respond—with violence, early death, labor activism, torpor and apathy, or intense reengagement with soci-ety—will in great measure determine the strength and health of postsocialist societies.

The Plan of This Book

Above, I established the general relationship of postsocialist condi-tions to workers' embodied senses of dread and distance, the actual physical conditions of workers' lives, and their frustrated agency. Chapter 2 brings this discussion to ground, to specifically consider the declining circumstances of postsocialist workers and their loss of actual and symbolic capital in the changeover from socialism to postsocialism. In detailing this transformation and its influence on changing physical representation, I also consider the origins and de-velopment of the Jiu Valley mining and Făgăraş chemical industries and their working populations. In particular, the chapter traces the way in which workers have become "others" in postsocialist society, their loss of symbolic value, and the specific forces of postsocialism which brought about this change.

The otherness of postsocialist workers is created in their labor, cemented in their politics, reaffirmed in their restricted consump-tion, and subsequently transferred into their domestic and com-munity relationships and identities. Chapters 3 through 6 examine these spheres of workers' postsocialist experience and show how they are systematically interrelated and also produce and reinforce the senses of decline and difference, fear and distance, that workers live with today. Change in labor, considered in chapter 3, sets the pace for the others. Rapid change in the labor market and related labor practices are disorienting and establish baseline conditions for the embodiment of danger and dread among the miners and their chemical worker cousins. Labor was a site for security and fulfillment, and sometimes struggle, in the socialist past. Unsettling change, persistent insecurity, and the perceived ending of a distinct way of life make labor in the present day a confusing, threatening, and ultimately alienating experience.

Chapters 4 and 5 examine the relation of these labor-induced changes to political understanding and practice and changing social relations. Chapter 4 considers the development of worker politics and examines how workers see themselves in relation to the developing state. Again, by way of illustration, miners and chemical workers retain different senses of entitlement from socialism, and this difference is manifest in their particular forms of political protest and labor action, including the *mineriade* of the Jiu Valley miners. However, though they have different opinions on the proper role of the state in their lives and different histories of political involvement, workers of both regions today see politics and political actors as far outside their sphere of influence.

Chapter 5 considers change at the level of family, household, and community. Such personal relationships had always provided workers with a sense of fulfillment, though labor and politics often eroded them. However, as the chapter shows, these relationships, too, become increasingly problematic as a result of postsocialist processes, and they further increase perceptions of decline and fear for continuity and well-being. Family and community life among working people is lived with a constant feeling of having failed even to live up to cultural expectations, let alone satisfied the new demands of children heavily exposed to consumer culture. Institutions thus crumble when the exchanges on which they depend become rare or disappear altogether.

Threatened labor, foreclosed political options, and fraying households and communities echo in changing senses of the individual and of gender identities in particular, the subject of chapter 6. Postsocialist gender relations are typically seen as uncertain and open to a range of possibilities. However, chapter 6 shows clearly that, for workers at least, acting out one's role as man or woman is also increasingly problematic and subject to the same pressures and frustrations as other postsocialist phenomena. Frustrated gender in particular informs and deepens workers' physical confusion and also contrasts greatly with gender practices among other postsocialist groups.

Chapter 7 examines the health circumstances, representations, and responses to health challenges by Valley folk and Făgăraş. Though determining the causes of variations in individual and group health is nearly impossible, this chapter views the decline in worker health as largely a result of the various stresses in their lives, beginning with those emanating from their work, or lack thereof. Chapter 8 concludes the book. Again in the polemic mode, the chapter discusses ongoing interventions in the regions and the extent to which these have made or can make a difference in workers' senses of the possible and their related agentive behavior.

All told, changes in labor, politics, community, gender, and health make getting by, for postsocialist industrial workers, a persistently problematic, frequently joyless, and threatening task. In defining the forces that impinge on the human form in postsocialism, I hope this book offers some insights into the predicaments that characterize the world of postsocialist workers. Many factors underlie the ongoing health and demographic problems of the region. Poor diet, alcohol and tobacco use, struggling institutions, problematic environments all take their toll. However, until they are reintegrated into society as an important and respected social group, the physical degradation and frustrated agency of postsocialist workers will continue, to the great misfortune of themselves, their communities, and their societies.

2   How Workers Became "Others"

Talking Alienation

> The working class, oppressed and exploited
> in the past, without political rights, has now
> become the master of the means of produc-
> tion . . . and fulfills with success its role as the
> leading class of all society.
>
> **—Nicolae Ceauşescu, Speech to the
> Plenary Session of the Central Committee of
> the Romanian Communist Party,
> October 24–25, 1968**

> Workers, workers, workers. People are tired
> of hearing about workers.
>
> **—SL, Bucharest journalist**

Blaming the Victim

In the state socialist societies of Eastern and Central Europe industrial workers were considered paragons, even if that image was often mainly rhetorical lip service. Today, however, those central actors in the socialist project are among the least of social categories,
if they are even considered at all in the debates and discourses of
postsocialist society. What is behind this fall? Why have the images
and symbolic capital of industrial workers, to say nothing of their
actual working and living situations, lost so much ground throughout the postsocialist states? How is this loss reflected in the actual
experience of real working people from the Jiu Valley and Făgăraş,
and what does their experience say about that of postsocialist workers generally?

Examining the emergence, development, and crumbling of the
regions' diverse working populations, and focusing on two exem-

plary groups in this process, this chapter grounds and historicizes the emergence of embodied alienation among postsocialist workers. Many factors that underscore the decline of labor were identified earlier. In particular, the privileging of private over common interests and the celebration of capital and consumption over production reduce the significance of labor in postsocialist society. However, postsocialist change is multidimensional and integrated. So many factors contribute to the anguish of labor, accounting for them all is an endless undertaking. Privatization and unemployment separate workers from their identities and their groups. Inflation robs them of their power in the market, not to mention life's small joys. National policies limit workers' right to strike or diminish state oversight of labor practices. Workers either disappear from national media altogether, or appear only as unrecognizable caricatures. All these factors submerge worker experience, blur particular lives into an undifferentiated mass, and rob workers of their historical variation, not to mention their voice and agency. Workers are pushed far from the center of postsocialist concern and even convinced of their own lack of worth.

The laboring classes began to be erased from postsocialism even as socialism fell apart. The allegedly limited role that workers played in the antisocialist revolutions was a particularly significant factor in the decline of workers' image in the early postsocialist state. East-Central European workers, with few exceptions, were largely defined as absent from the barricades and marches that ended in the fall of socialism (Fuller 1999); the primary exception was in Solidarity, which had early on a very clear working-class identity (Laba 1991) but which quickly metamorphosed from a worker to a quasi-religious movement (Kubik 1994). Czech students, Bulgarian ecologists, East German and Hungarian tourists, Romanian mothers and priests and soldiers have all been credited for the last push that sent socialism over the precipice (Garton Ash 1989). But every one of those groups had a worker background, whether recognized or not. Though workers were not seen as active counter-revolutionaries, as the Jiu Valley miners were in Romania, their symbolic replacement by others as socialism came apart enabled new postsocialist leaders to receive them only tepidly, if at all.

However, to blame workers for their decline at the end of socialism adds insult to injury. Given their subalternity and the political bonds in which they were held, as well as the tendency of socialist politicians in the past to "play the working-class card" to gain state legitimacy, workers were virtually denied their own representatives and voices in socialism and had few effective spokespersons in early postsocialism, despite the frequent and aggressive strikes in the first years after the fall of the socialist state. Furthermore, the "parcelization of sovereignty" that Katherine Verdery identifies in the early socialist state (1996, 207–14) further dismembered whatever unified presence workers might have achieved and turned them into afterthoughts and hangers-on in fragmented and parcelized networks.

The multidimensional role of the West must also be factored in to the decline of labor. Western triumphalism, foreign assistance, globalized institutions, and vast, explosive marketization in particular leave little room for a worker presence in the postsocialist universe. A precise attack against the principles of working-class politics in Western foreign assistance or academic discourse cannot be identified. However, the intense demands to privatize not just industry, but also resources held by states in common for their populations, sent a clear message as to the worth of workers in the political future of the postsocialist world.

Stephen Crowley (2004) provides, perhaps, the most comprehensive evaluation of labor's decline in postsocialism and Western influences on that decline. Evaluating a range of diverse studies on labor's position in postsocialism, Crowley shows an unmistakable weakening of labor, seen in shrinking union membership, declining strike activity, and lack of state support for labor benefits, among others. His most significant conclusion, however, is that the capitalist system developing in the postsocialist states is largely modeled on the American variety, which demands great flexibility from labor while generally failing to provide the social supports and benefits of European-style social democracy. Crowley's conclusions are reconfirmed in a few diverse studies of "actually existing" work institutions (Ashwin 1999; Dunn 2004; Pollert 1999, 2001b).

Thus, workers are beset by a multidimensional onslaught: the celebration of privatized production and the market; declining state support; their manipulation and caricaturization by the media; the disorganization of labor unions, which were already reeling because of their ties to the socialist power structure (Synovitz 1997); real and actual threats of globalization and American-style capitalism; the condescension of the triumphal West; workers' obscurity in the postsocialist revolution; the scars of socialist brown fields; the breathtaking divisions in worker ranks; and the differentiation of consumer "lifestyles." All these erode workers' energy, vision, and identities. Such processes eliminate workers' centrality in the workplace, intensify the insecurity of factory and mine, diminish the importance of workers and their unions in the development of institutions of production, and above all threaten the very identity "worker" in postsocialist society. Even so, workers as a definable social group still predominate through the cities and towns of East-Central Europe, and are still the backbone of the postsocialist economies. Their possibilities and their continued presence demand that we understand how the particular processes that turn "workers" into "others" play out in actual postsocialist lives and transform the subjective understandings of working people and their families and communities.

Labor, History, and Society

The lives and fates of the miners and workers of the Jiu Valley and Făgăraş regions put a face on many of the aforementioned events and processes. These groups are distinct in their history, geography, society, demography, ethnicity, worker identity, and political economy, to name but a few dimensions. Their diverse histories and possibilities, however, come together in the dissolution of socialism, as all those phenomena that rob workers of their symbolic and political economic capital merge like so many streams into a flood of change. A decade and a half after the fall of socialism, the two regions' workers and miners have developed a similar sense of the world and a similarly frustrated agency, daily expressed in narratives and practices.

The worker populations in the two regions developed under different influences. Jiu Valley coal production has long dominated the regional economy, with coal extraction and processing constituting about 90 percent of the region's economic activity during socialism.[1] Industry in Făgăraş (Kideckel 2004c) grew from local peasant cottage and town crafts (Bărbat 1938). Though the Făgăraş chemical industry and the region's working class reached their zenith in socialism, their position in local life was less significant than that of the miners in the Jiu Valley. Făgăraş chemical production generated about 60 percent of the region's total product (Zderciuc 1972, 280). The working populations of the region also differed significantly. The miners were descended from two main waves of immigration, one at the founding of the industry in the mid- to late nineteenth century, and the other after a major antisocialist strike in 1977. Furthermore, miners and their families were demographically concentrated in a number of dense urban settlements. These factors, along with the nature of mining work, contributed to the growth among the mining population of a relatively unified working-class identity that persisted in one guise or another into postsocialism. In contrast, Făgăraş workers emerged from regionally autochthonous town and village populations, and remained dispersed across the region even through socialism.[2] Făgăraşeni are better described as peasant-workers. Even workers newly arrived in the city had interests in both town and village.

These different profiles shaped significant variation among the regions' working populations. Most miners were male,[3] though women played critical roles in early mining communities. Some women ran or worked in small businesses selling household handicraft items. Others marketed produce. Some women sorted coal, and some worked in commerce and small regional factories. Despite all these, however, women never made up more than 20 percent of the Valley work force. In Făgăraş, by contrast, women constituted about one-third of chemical plant workers (Herseni et al. 1972, 243), were prevalent in other industries, and dominated agriculture work during socialist collectivization (Kideckel 1993). This considerable, historically based variability, however, did not survive the emulsifying pressures of postsocialism.

The Origins and Social Conditions of Jiu Valley Coal Mining

Coal is evident everywhere throughout the Jiu Valley. Local upland peasants, termed Momârlani,[4] called it "the stone that burns," and they are said to have set extensive surface deposits ablaze to scare off invading Turks in the eighteenth century. Momârlani also scavenged coal to fire smithies and for cottage industries. The Valley coal industry began when entrepreneurs from throughout the Habsburg Empire, of which the region was a part,[5] opened the first mines in the 1850s, after passage of a law allowing private mine ownership (Baron 1998, 64–65). They built housing complexes (*colonie*) and other amenities in the booming coal towns to attract people from throughout the Empire. Soon the Valley was flooded by Romanians, Czechs, Poles, Slovaks, Magyars, Szeklers, Ruthenians, Italians, Germans, and Jews, many whose working-class backgrounds went back generations. Today many Valley people call the region "Little America" because of this "melting pot" quality (Kideckel 2004b).

Jiu Valley culture in the heyday of mining was characterized by periods of calm interrupted with great moments of ferment and change. The growth of the mining industry to the middle of the twentieth century, and the increasing dominance of socialism, were accompanied by the rapid development of community life and institutions. The private mines offered fairly secure jobs and considerable benefits, and mining quickly became the occupation of choice and a family tradition. Mining companies offered workers minimal, though reasonable, living conditions in the *colonie* built along the Simeria-Petroşani-Lupeni rail line, which brought in supplies and took out coal. Mining shaped local community life. The mines sponsored local bands and theater groups, and spiritual and religious life was also full, given the region's mixed ethnicity.

Ethnicity, in fact, was never an issue. Valley women maintained each group's crafts, cuisine, and confession, and older informants told us that people were only differentiated during holiday seasons. One German-Hungarian miner who mainly worked at the Vulcan Coal Preparation Facility said,

> I never knew I was a minority or even that there were such people as minorities until after World War II. Then, because of my German background, I was deported to Ukraine to work in the Dombas coal mines. Before, I walked on Vulcan streets and greeted people in their native languages. Holidays were best, because different people all had their own celebrations with different food, songs, and decorations. Kids played together and we never gave a thought to our differences. All the people on the street looked out for all the kids and sent them home when they knew their parents wanted them.

The main Valley social distinction was between Momârlani peasants and the diverse outsiders. Momârlani produced cheeses, milk, meats, and vegetables for sale to mining families, whose trading partners they became. Momârlani, however, remained outside the mines until the 1970s, when, under economic pressures of socialism, they too began to go underground, though largely as auxiliary workers and rarely, if ever, to work at the coalface.

Labor in the Jiu Valley was in greater ferment than were regional ethnic and social relations. Population flux was common as production expanded and contracted. Also, when the region became part of "Greater Romania" after World War I, many non-Romanian ethnics permanently left (Baron 1998, 273). Mine mechanization, begun in 1924, also caused the unemployment of great numbers of miners. Thus Jiu Valley mining before socialism was tense and conflictual. Wildcat strikes over pay and working conditions were common (Toth-Gaspar 1964, cited in Friedman 2003, 191), especially as the price of coal plummeted and the world teetered toward depression in 1929. In August of that year a huge strike in Lupeni, which remains ambiguous and contested today (Oprea 1970; Ţic 1977; Velica 1999), resulted in the deaths of twenty-two miners. Communist historiography demonized interwar conservative governments by blaming the deaths on overzealous police action due to right-wing attitudes toward workers' lives and health. However, it now appears that union and non-union miners had also fought amongst themselves (Velica 1999, 32–33); the incident presaged fraying miner unity in times of severe economic trouble.

Change in the presocialist Valley was thus spurred by boom and bust business cycles and vast political transformation. Families came and went, but the uncertainty was not unexpected and miners had a variety of responses. They joined labor unions. They returned whence they had come or migrated to the West, often for jobs in mining (Baron 1998, 276). Some left mining and sought work in other Valley industries or commerce. But this all changed with socialism, when mining became a lavishly supported industrial sector and work in the mines became secure, a condition contrasting so extensively with miners' lives today.

The Origins and Social Condition of Făgăraş Industry

Făgăraş experiences are of a different order. The Făgăraş zone is a clearly defined geographic micro-region distinct from the rest of Transylvania to the north and the Romanian lands to the south. The region was settled by a Romanian-speaking nobility dominating a small-scale Romanian peasantry between the twelfth and fourteenth centuries. From the fourteenth century the area came under Magyar control, and by the seventeenth century it was fully encapsulated in Magyar-dominated feudalism. A distinct division of labor through the mid-nineteenth century restricted Romanians to peasant livelihoods and work as priests and teachers. In the cities, Magyars held most positions of political responsibility while Saxon Germans controlled commerce, banking, and small trades, and were yeoman farmers to the north, east, and west.

After the end of feudal control, regional development suffered from marginal agriculture, overpopulation, and limited commerce. Together these spurred mass emigration; many regional Romanians left for cities to the south or for the developing U.S. industrial midwest (Bărbat 1938; Fekett 1956; Nemoianu 1997, 2001). Magyars in the region also left for Hungary proper and for North America. Many Romanian emigrants returned to their native communities to marry and establish themselves as successful householders. Like the Jiu Valley, the Făgăraş region is also called "Little America" by many of its inhabitants, in recognition of those returned migrants and the influence of those who remained in the West but kept in contact with their families in the region (Kideckel 2004b).

Făgăraş small-scale industry and craftworking intensified, especially after the region's incorporation into "Greater Romania" after World War I. Many businesses were financed or founded by returned migrants. Regional industries included tobacco processing, tanneries, lime production, glassworks, wood processing, sawmills, and dairies. In 1922 the Nitramonia factory was founded to produce chemical fertilizer and explosives, drawing its work force largely from the peasantry and craft workers in surrounding villages (Bărbat 1938, 181). Făgăraş workers were thus chiefly local and not long removed from their village origins. Regional workers comprised landless or land-poor peasants, those who came daily from the peri-urban villages near the city, sons and daughters of urban craftspeople, and even peasant craftworkers. The peasant base of Făgăraş workers, and the petty patron-client nature of regional industrial hiring, kept labor activism in check. Sociologist Traian Herseni,[6] in his study of the Făgăraş Chemical Combine (i.e., Nitramonia) on the occasion of its fiftieth anniversary, though utilizing some Communist Party catchphrases and what Romanians call its "wooden language" (*limbaj de lemn*), spoke of this early Făgăraş and Nitramonia working class:

> At the start of . . . capitalist industrialization, almost all workers had rural origins, with deep roots in their native villages, including keeping small agricultural holdings . . . Most had few advanced sociocultural aspirations, nor organizational capacity, nor clear conception of the historical necessity to develop their socioeconomic demands in a decisive way for political struggle. In these conditions, class exploitation was not faced with many serious obstacles. The union movement was mainly diffused, and only the most advanced members of this group had any knowledge of socialism. (1972, 307)

Thus, in the Făgăraş region, village communities and their web of social relations were critical determinants of individual lives and identities well into the socialist period. Prior to socialism, regional status derived from land ownership, and wage labor only supplemented agriculture. Many poor peasants sought to leave worker ranks as soon as they had sufficient resources to purchase a reasonable estate. Even if they did not manage this, most regional workers had access to rural resources, either through ownership or by labor exchanges with village kin. Women also played critical roles in regional networks and economy. They were mainstays in agriculture and in petty commerce, and also employed early in industry. Early Făgăraş industrial enterprises were frequently family affairs, with owners utilizing the labor of kin, neighbors, friends, and their offspring in the small manufactories. Women's participation in the local economy was also facilitated by a steady decline in the birth rate. Făgăraş went through the demographic transition at a much earlier date and a more rapid pace than most places in Romania. Influenced by the Saxon Germans in and around their region and by persistent land shortages, Făgărăşeni had reduced the average number of children per household to less than three by the interwar period, while before the war it had been five to six.

Dress, attitude, stance, and even diet also developed differently in each region. Făgărăşeni are stolid. Usually heavy of bone and flesh, they are slow and precise in their movements, peasant-like in their dress, ruddy in their complexion. They consider their bodies as suited less for adornment than for hard, steady work. They are initially reserved in their approach to others, but always earnest in their dealings. Mainly taciturn, they give their word infrequently, but keep it assiduously. Făgărăşeni are judicious in movement, in economics, in their social relations. They keep to themselves, such that a "good person" (*un om cumsecade*) is someone who has "no business with others" (*n-are treabă cu nimeni*). Jiu Valley people are mainly thinner and more intense than their Făgăraş cousins. (Work in the mines both sweats off the pounds and tends to select for those more able to squeeze through small passages.) The pace of life in Valley towns, at least among people not idled by unemployment, is quicker. Miners have only so many hours to get things done before their next shift. More children are visible on Valley streets, and clutches of older men play cards or backgammon in apartment complex commons or public parks. Middle-aged people, men and women both, are dressed in more modern styles than in Făgăraş. They contrast with Momârlani men and women, who come to town in peasant garb to sell their produce.[7] Such regional differences persisted throughout socialism as workers in both regions settled into lives that were predictable, and that even offered occasional hope of advancement for themselves and their children.

Socialism and Changing Culture

Socialism left a complicated heritage to Jiu Valley miners and Făgăraş workers, both in the type of social system that formed in each region and in the memories of socialism which people conjure to orient themselves to present-day life. These memories are often rose-tinted. Workers largely gloss over petty and punitive socialist politics, shortages, and the capricious dictator and his power-hungry wife. Instead their talk lauds socialist treatment of labor and the body, and the predictability and relative prosperity of socialist life. Thus, worker narratives are more than just a model of the past. They suggest workers' expectations of the present and the areas of present-day life most troubling and problematic to them. That is, these narratives focalize and transvalue, and thus magnify, workers' frustrated sense of belonging in postsocialist society and their fear that they and their families are rejected by that society.

The "greening" of socialism emerges from workers contrasting the rough equality of the past with today's extraordinary and rapid socio-economic differentiation. Scholars disagree over the extent of class differentiation and its significance in socialist society.[8] Certainly rank in the centralized political economy gave a select few power, wealth, and the means to project them over time. In this system, despite policies equalizing access to some resources and rhetoric lauding workers' achievements and mission, workers were largely subordinated, and social and political differences between them and socialist state and party managers were institutionalized.[9] However, whatever one's take on the extent of socialist class differentiation, workers also remember those policies that modulated its worst aspects, which allows them to believe that more possibilities were open to them under socialism.

Of all the strategies of the socialist state to ameliorate class realities, none stands out as clearly as the rhetorical and symbolic emphasis on the heroism of labor. Romania's "cult of labor" (*cultul muncii*) was one of the most elaborated regimes of worker symbolism in the socialist world. Images of Romania as an industrial society of long duration created worker traditions out of whole cloth and conjured an industrial heritage where one was lacking (Kideckel 1988,

Figure 2.1. Remains of the socialist cult of labor.
Photograph by the author.

1993, 189). Such images encouraged workers to identify their interests with those of the state by emphasizing workers' roles in developing the Romanian state and in Romanian cultural and scientific
achievements (Hoffman, Raşeev, and Ţenovici 1984). Furthermore,
via literary, artistic, and journalistic portrayals of work as the source
of all value and workers as incarnations of all that was heroic, stal-
wart, and socially conscious (Bârgău 1984; Pospai 1978), the "cult
of labor" encouraged a work ethic, labor mobilization, and—not in-
cidentally—social control.

Tales of battles against capitalism and commemorations of important labor events emphasized workers' sacrifice and their role
in the formation of socialist society. According to the socialist history of the 1929 miners' strike in Lupeni in the Jiu Valley, for example, workers striking for better pay and the right to organize,
selflessly defending their interests, were shot dead by the army, on
the command of a Peasant Party prefect (Oprea 1970, 486; see also
Ţic 1977).[10] Similarly, the renowned 1933 Griviţa railway workers'
strike was seen as

the peak of the working people's actions during the years of economic crisis . . . which strongly influenced the social and political situation of Romania . . . and unleashed a broad movement of solidarity of the working class
and democratic forces throughout the world. (Matei et al. 1972, 301)

Cultul muncii also promulgated particular images of the body
and the physical for worker "consumers": images of active, rugged
work and workers, especially in heavy industry. Leather-aproned
and hard-hatted workers (both men and women at first, but later
only men) were shown engaged in tasks of large-scale production—moving cement or rigging steel, muscles rippling under work
clothes, ruddy faces smudged from their efforts (cf. Hobsbawm
1984; Kideckel 1988).[11] Furthermore, these images were reempha-
sized by the state and workplaces that sponsored excursions to the
countryside or to theatrical, musical, and dance productions. Sport,
as in other socialist societies, was elevated to cult status. Each Jiu
Valley mine sponsored its own soccer teams, as well as competitors
in other athletic activities, like archery and weightlifting. Făgăraş
plants also had associated sports teams, and the soccer team from
the Chemical Combine was regularly one of the best in its division.

Other state socialist policies also privileged industrial laborers, encouraging them to see their interests as linked to those of
other social groups. Though many of these policies had their downsides, from rampant theft of state property to a widespread lack of
consumer goods, workers today mainly invoke positive images of
socialism while ignoring its contradictory realities. Socialist full
employment provided workers with regular incomes. Pensions
and other benefits raised living standards. Enterprise "soft budget
constraints" (Kornai 1980) and labor bargaining (Sabel and Stark
1982) gave workers—both skilled and unskilled—some influence
on managers. Meanwhile, even the socialist economy of shortage
narrowed the distance between social strata, forcing workers into
protracted, if somewhat imbalanced, "second economy" exchange
relationships with people across the range of Romanian social strata
(Sampson 1987). There were modest labor, pay, and "lifestyle" differences between workers and all but the highest level of factory
directors or officials. In the workplace, class distance was moder-
ated by close relationships between workers and supervisors who
were also frequently neighbors, relatives, or schoolmates. Workers
and supervisors lived in the same apartment blocks, shopped at the
same stores, vacationed at the same resorts (though at different lev-

els of accommodation), and attended each others' weddings, baptisms, and funerals. The Făgăraş Communist Party secretary in the mid-1970s, for example, one of the highest-ranking party officials in the region, lived in a small, two-bedroom, moderately furnished apartment.

Though socialism in the Jiu Valley differentiated miners from other social groups, it also met the physical needs of the mining population and their families. Active coal miners always formed a somewhat distinct subculture in Valley communities. However, their distinctiveness became more marked with the vast expansion of the mining industry after World War II. This expansion was first spurred by the USSR to ensure that Romania would pay war reparations, among other reasons. The Soviets forced the formation of jointly controlled mining enterprises, so-called Sovroms, and their cadres took command of the regional political economy to enforce order and maintain production. Romania's socialist government continued to expand mining after the Soviets withdrew at the end of the 1950s. The region's semihard coal (*huilă*) was ideal for power generation and steel production, and thus essential to socialist economic expansion and political legitimation. The expansion of mining, however, also intensified the region's mono-industrial character and further masculinized its labor force, contradicting socialist policy at the time, which was to encourage women to enter the work force. Some Valley women were hired at the three coal preparation facilities, the Viscoza synthetic fiber plant in Lupeni, and the machine tool plant in Petroşani. However, women made up only about 20 percent of the local work force until the end of socialism.

Late socialism radically transformed the mining population, cementing miners' differentiation and their sense of entitlement to certain labor and living standards. This transformation began when 35,000 miners struck the mines in early August 1977 (Matinal 1997). This was not the first strike by Romanian coal miners in response to socialist erosions in working lives (Gorun 2004), though it was the most extensive, publicized, and threatening. The strike was prompted when the Romanian state, in a frenzied attempt to pay off its international debts, demanded increased production and reduced costs from mining. Work regulations were tightened, and the state planned to increase the retirement age and eliminate pension subsidies for the injured (Velica and Schreter 1993, 188–89). Ion and Dragoş Velica (2002, 77) describe the "miserable conditions" prompting the Jiu Valley strike:

> The miners . . . were beginning to feel the typical shortages of the socialist
> regime on their skins, especially those relating to public food supplies and
> to medical assistance. On August 1, 1977, they were threatened by a new
> wrong: a pension law to deprive them of rights they had already earned.

The unified and angry miners refused to negotiate with anyone but Ceauşescu. He was forced to come to the Valley, and ultimately acceded to all the miners' demands. However, mining was
soon afterward transformed. After the strike fervor cooled down,
strike leaders were removed from their jobs, with many taken away
by the Securitate (Matinal 1997, 8). Then, to further dilute miners' political power and ensure uninterrupted coal production, the
regime flooded the Valley with new workers, especially from poor
regions like Moldavia. Recruiters were sent to that region, and officials were allotted quotas of mine workers to be found. Rural people
and surplus industrial workers were promised large salaries if they
moved to the Valley. Military units were also sent to the mines, and
some criminals sentenced to hard labor there.

This influx had vast implications for mining and regional social relations. Production first suffered as the population fluctuated
wildly, since many left as they were unfit for the rigors of mining.
Others were often unskilled, thus wreaking havoc on a system depending on trust between co-workers (Kideckel et al. 2000, 144–
45). However, to retain workers and ensure political quiescence,
the state mining directorate increased salaries and eased labor and
promotion standards. Prior to 1977, for example, it took five years of
rigorous training for an unqualified worker to become a full-fledged
miner. After that year, workers advanced in half the time. Mining
became one of the most inefficient of all socialist sectors, costing
sixteen dollars of investment for every one dollar of production
(World Bank 2004, 6).

Social change in mining was even greater than that in production. Prior to 1977 the region's miners were well integrated into regional social and political networks. However, the strike separated
the mining population from other regional groups, depriving the
miners of political support other than that of their own union leaders. Social rifts developed between the new miners and the non-
mining population, who blame the decline in Jiu Valley life on the
low-brow culture of these immigrants. Unlike earlier Valley immigrants, those who arrived after 1977 came with their families.
Male and female roles became more sharply separated after the
strike, as new apartment complexes were built whose male resi-

Figure 2.2. Nicolae Ceausescu addresses striking miners, Lupeni, Romania, August 1977. Photograph by Petre Liciu.

dents nearly all worked in the mines and whose wives nearly all remained at home. Moldavian cultural habits also intensified in the Jiu Valley political economy. A desire for large families coincided with Ceauşescuite pronatalism and high salaries. Pronatalism was a harsh sentence on Romanian women (Baban and David 1997; David and Baban 1996; Kligman 1998). However, Jiu Valley mining culture emphasized female fecundity as twin to male productivity. Nuclear families with seven, eight, or nine members supported by a single miner salary and state subsidies were not uncommon.

Thus, by 1989 the miners had become a compromised, dependent group, lacking credibility in their own region and wholly misunderstood throughout the rest of Romania. Their revolutionary qualities and resistant agency, as expressed in the 1977 strike, were decimated by changes in demography, in production, and in Jiu Valley society and politics. Consequently, when the revolution broke out, instead of serving as the vanguard of a new social system, they were confused and threatened by the antisocialist events. One former mine union leader suggested,

> We [the miners] haven't been the same since the revolution. At that time the entire country looked to us for some kind of action, but when the train

of revolution left the station, the miners were not on it. We've been looking back ever since.

In contrast to the Jiu Valley miners' extremes of change and protracted political struggles, Făgăraş workers developed more continuously through the socialist period and remained more integrated into regional life and social networks. Still, like their Jiu Valley counterparts, Făgăraş workers were economically reasonably well off but politically compromised. Much of the region's political intensity was spent immediately after World War II in an unsuccessful guerilla resistance (Ogoreanu 1995) and smothered by the brutality of the socialist prison set up in the town's medieval fortress. Throughout the socialist years, local workers and peasants exhibited only smatterings of resistance to socialist domination. Făgăraşeni were particularly pacified by industrial expansion and the relative economic well-being it induced.

Growth in regional cities and factories and perceptions of worker agency were mutually reinforcing. Agricultural collectivization in the villages freed labor for industry. Many people moved into the city, while the increasing ease of transportation between village and city, home and factory, allowed many others to remain in the villages. Peasants became workers, workers became foremen, foremen became directors, and directors became high party officials. Wherever they lived, however, workers in the Făgăraş region had ready access to rural occupations and resources. Făgăraşeni were also particularly oriented to change and upward mobility by means of migration and education, practices largely deemphasized in Jiu Valley miner culture. People in the region had a long tradition of labor-related emigration, which continued throughout socialist years, although fewer migrants went to other countries. Young people from the region sought higher education in considerable numbers. Făgăraş workers and peasant-workers organized themselves into multigenerational "stem" households so that all household members could earn income in one of the sectors open to them: factory work, collective and use-plot farming, small-scale commerce, part-time local service work. This "strategy"[12] generally demanded that men and women make equal economic contributions and that people attend to their personal networks to ensure access to scarce resources. However, this strategy imploded when late socialism generated endemic competition between workers, fostering jealousy and individualism.

Thus, on the eve of revolution Făgărașeni were overworked and politically cowed, though for different reasons than were Jiu Valley miners. They did not react, in fact, in November 1987 when thirty thousand workers from the Red Star tractor factory in Brașov, the county capital, went on a rampage and burned county government and Communist Party headquarters. However, as the system's final spasm began with protests and violence in Timișoara, Sibiu, and finally Bucharest in December 1989, Făgărașeni also raised their heads and regained their political vigor. During the revolution, the region's workers put down their tools en masse, deposed both factory administrators and the region's political leadership, quickly formed a number of independent unions and political parties, and consecrated their actions by praying in the main town square. Interviews in the region hard on the heels of the revolution revealed great optimism about the future. People looked forward to possibilities of economic advancement, to meaningful hard work, and to personal and family success and growth. Unlike the miners, they looked to the future. However, like the miners, they soon learned that their own labor was of questionable relevance to their new society.

Talking Socialism, Thinking Postsocialism

Worker lives in both regions during socialism were thus highly ambiguous. However, in narrativizing the socialist past, even workers who were children fifteen years ago emphasize social integration and the certainty of life. Thus, in the subtext of their narratives, working people are concerned less with accurate history than with how they have been brought low in society today: how they have gone from "workers" to "others." Discussing socialism, workers emphasize its predictability, the general ease with which people satisfied their material needs, and the respect and high-ranked position accorded to workers. These narratives, however, are concerned more with the uncertainties of the present, the perceived lack in the midst of an expanding market, and society's general disrespect for industrial labor and laborers today. Thus, despite the great variation in their socialist histories and experiences, both these working populations reveal present fear and alienation in their narratives of socialism. One thirty-five-year-old Făgăraș worker expressed a common sentiment:

During socialism your job was assured. When you finished school you would apply and within a week you'd be hired. You could live on your pay. You could buy furniture for your house. Then it was much less expensive to live. People today say that "the communists did bad things." Well, maybe they did, but they certainly did good things for young people. Also, they didn't allow divisions to be created between the poor and rich. If you happened to get too much, they would ask you "hey, where did you get all that stuff?" But on wages today you can't live from one day to the next. Now we have come to where we have to purchase second-hand clothing, and in the time of Ceauşescu there wasn't even such a thing. Everyone could buy new clothing of good quality.

Narratives of socialism are never solely about socialism, but typically juxtapose to it the physical threat of the contemporary world. Discussion of socialist security invariably morph into contrasts with today, especially with regard to health, diet, and the role of the state in providing subsidized housing, vacations, and health care. In their emphasis on certainty, the meeting of physical needs, and respect, workers even ignore socialist state control over other aspects of physical lives, such as pronatalism, the limited availability of food, and controls over time and physical exertion (Verdery 1996). By elevating socialism's treatment of their physicality, contemporary worker narratives favorably contrast the hard bio-power of socialism with the soft surveillance of the market, thus amplifying both the agency they had then and the frustrations of today. A Lupeni miner, contrasting socialism with today, paired sport and stress:

Things are so bad in mining that people are very stressed. This situation dates to even before the labor buy-outs, but has become much worse since. It is not just that people work harder, but they are uncertain of the future. I played for the Lupeni [football] team during the time of Ceauşescu. Then the miners supported the team. There was a holiday atmosphere at the games. But now no one goes to the games anymore. Families have problems because of living conditions and costs. People have nothing to do, so they stand around and get in trouble. There are no pills you can take for our condition. What we need is rest and to get away from this stress so that we can get healthy.

Comparing past and present medical care is another common narrative trope. Every factory or mine clinic, people say, was supplied with the best available technology. Workers had regular check-ups and medical leave was dispensed fairly liberally. An older worker at the Făgăraş UPRUC factory compared the physical conditions of work in Ceauşescu's time with those of today:

Then in the large factory halls they would make, like, kind of a green-house. They'd cover things with plastic to make it warm, without needing to use any heat source, nothing. During Ceauşescu's time we used to take baths in the dressing area and come down to dry off in the work hall. It was warmer there. So, now I ask myself, how was it that they could heat things then and now they can't? Was it because people were afraid of a single man? A whole country afraid of a single man? Could this have been the cause? No, I tell myself. It is because our so-called democracy does not perform as it is should.

Another common theme is the former practice of eating and drinking well with friends and relations, activities that signal the good life to Romanians. A woman chemical operator at Nitramonia said,

I remember how it used to be before 1990. We would all come to work dressed well. Then we would look at someone and say, "Look at how beautifully she is dressed," and so on, or "Look at the style that that person has." But now we are how we are. Not only can we no longer admire others, we have nothing ourselves.

Similarly, although large numbers of people lived in small spaces under socialism, when miners and their wives reflect on socialist life they exclaim how well they lived then. They display expensive appliances and housewares and say, "Everything we have here was bought when Ceauşescu was in power."

That people retain these memories, despite the ambiguities of socialist life and the grief of the last decade of Ceauşescu's rule, indicates their strong perceptions of disenfranchisement. However, it is questionable whether their bodies and lives are threatened more today than during socialism. In late socialism, the draconian policies of the crumbling regime made the body a zone of contention. Raw materials, energy, and tools were rationed at work (see Haraszti 1978 for an analogous case), as were bread, milk, sugar, flour, and cooking oil at home. Labor was increased and leaves restricted. Rationing of electricity and heat in workers' apartments threatened their health, as did the state-promulgated "scientific diet," low on protein, heavy on starches. Nonetheless, Jiu Valley miners and Făgăraş workers escaped the worst effects of these policies. Miners were favored right up to the Revolution, and Făgăraş workers always had rural resources to fall back on. Despite this, however, both region's working populations had many grievances, unfulfilled dreams, and physical struggles throughout socialism.

In the last years of his life Ceauşescu even planned to forbid city dwellers to prepare their own food. In Bucharest, state construction companies began building large dining halls where entire neighborhoods, thousands of people at a time, were to take meals. These massive structures, blocks square, topped by large semispherical glass domes, and nicknamed "circles of hunger" (*cercuri foamei*), are still visible today. A few are just as they were in December 1989, and thus a reminder of socialist threats to the body. Others, however, symbolize the changing nature of postsocialist Romania, having been refurbished into expensive shopping areas. The "Bucharest Mall" is owned by interests from the Arab Middle East and houses some of the most fashionable shops in the city, well out of range of most of the city's factory-working population.

The most direct attack on worker physicality was certainly pronatalism (Kligman 1998; see also Şerbanescu et al. 1995 for a discussion of pronatalist echoes in contemporary Romanian demography). Kligman documents the multidimensional effects of pronatalism on Romanian families. The physical, psychological, and social horrors it spawned were legion: the deaths of young and middle-aged women due to botched, self-induced abortions; malnutrition in families unable to feed their growing numbers; the abandonment of unwanted children in impoverished state orphanages; mistrust among friends and neighbors and between husbands and wives; the transformation of sexuality into a life-threatening force; and the alienation of men and women both, but especially women, from their own bodies. Furthermore, pronatalist policy was paired with intensive state propaganda that pushed women from workplace to home and restricted their incomes and independence. Still, as foul as its results were, the most disturbing thing about pronatalism is the degree to which it is dismissed by male and female workers today. The wife of an unemployed miner in Petrila, speaking of life during Ceauşescu's last years (when pronatalism was at its zenith), said,

> Those times even allowed us women to remain in our homes [i.e., without employment] and to take care of the children and household. I had all kinds of activities then. Cleaning, shopping, cooking, visiting. Life was full and beautiful.

Postsocialist Political Economy: Workers' Perspectives

That workers speak so glowingly of socialism despite its checkered realities forces us to consider how the conditions of postsocialism contribute to this selective amnesia and how actual experience is translated into embodied understanding. Reviewing postsocialist phenomena through workers' eyes, we see that change is less the problem than is its rapidity and nontransparency, and that differentiation is less the problem than is the extreme and widening gap between workers and others and the corrupt practices that cause this gap. Workers in both regions strongly support democratization and privatization. However, though supportive, most know such practices are structured to disadvantage them, no matter the steps they may take. Many solutions that workers see to their predicament are themselves highly problematic. These interpretations of the past, and their embodiment as senses of distance and danger, develop from a confluence of factors pressuring working people from all sides.

The changing conditions to which workers respond are vast and multidimensional and affect every aspect of life, from economy and social structure to family life. One study of the costs of restructuring in the Jiu Valley (Boboc 2000, 5), listed nine potential deleterious effects: 1) aggravation of unemployment; 2) falling living standards; 3) depopulation; 4) growth in criminality and social conflict; 5) increase in the number of welfare recipients; 6) amplification of corruption; 7) increase in school truancy and illiteracy; 8) expansion of alcoholism; and 9) degradation of housing. Though all these conditions have, unfortunately, come to pass, they are seen by workers and miners to reflect postsocialist realities that are especially shaped by changed relations of labor and ownership. It is these, then, that particularly animate workers and penetrate their consciousnesses.

Privatization

Privatization is one issue often on workers' minds. Sentiments about privatization are intense, as the process sits at the intersection of competing meanings of citizenship and belonging in postsocialist society; in a socialist collectivity labor is a socially inflected process, while the individualized worker produces for wages, to support individual consumption. Workers are trapped, and their feelings reflect that. Though they accept the validity of privatization, they demand that their past labor in building an enterprise, the identity they developed, and their physical essences and needs be recognized. But this is a decidedly socialist outlook, which doesn't jibe with the reconfigured meanings of postsocialism. The privatization of the person that Elizabeth Dunn defines (2004, 80–82) also implies declining respect for labor collectivities and relationships, and their replacement by commodified labor relationships. Workers come to understand that their value and the value of others now depend on their choices and practices as consumers, not on their contribution to the production of value (Berdahl 2005; also see Lukose 2005, 507 for a comparative Indian context). Though they see the benefits of this new consumer ethic and hope for access to the expanded marketplace, they are uncertain about the worth of the process and its associated identities. As Jennifer Patico (2005) shows for Russian teachers, those who see themselves as producers, whether of goods or citizens, are suspicious of those who drive Mercedes Benzes. Consumption still takes a back seat to fraying collectivities.

Privatization confuses Romanian workers not only by its changes of meaning but also because of the uncertainty of the economic changeover it brings; they do not know where they stand from moment to moment. Romania's path to privatization has been a herky-jerky one, in which corruption has produced great inequalities. Endemic left-right political competition has made privatization a policy football since 1990. Much of the country's left elite adopted a go-slow approach, while right and right-center governments were merely bungling. Hence in Romania economic conversion was spearheaded by global forces as much as by internal interests. International financial institutions required that Romania meet privatization targets for access to loans. Still, the uncertain investment environment, the overly bureaucratized state apparatus, competition from other postsocialist states, and—above all—corruption limit foreign direct investment from Western and other investors, contribute to distortions in the privatization process, and make workers fear for their position in that process.

Workers fear that the privatization of their own factory or mine will mean the loss of their identity and the meaning it brings. However, most deemphasize such fears, as they consider privatization ultimately necessary to put their enterprise on a firm footing and hopefully save their jobs. But, though they support it, most believe the process is typically corrupt and designed to deal them out of the system. Privatization thus is less a transformation of meaning than it is a threat to livelihood. Workers fear, with some justification, that privatization is ultimately intended to either precipitously eliminate jobs, close their workplace outright, or in the best case bring in an unremitting work regime. In either case, as workers see it, their salvation will also be their undoing. The union president at Viromet expressed the typical concerns of his colleagues:

> People believe it will be better to be owned by a patron even though patrons don't always do what they say. Still, it is their only alternative, so we try to explain what privatization means. There are a lot of rumors, too, in the process of privatization, like liquidation of the factory. This scares workers. We will not talk about such things until we know whether they are facts or not. Our union is not against private owners, but we are also not afraid of them. At many other private factories, like Virolite [a neighboring factory, recently privatized], there is no union because people are afraid.

An UPRUC worker echoed him on work conditions:

> Privatization is not the answer because the salaries are smaller and the demand for work is much larger. When foreigners come, as they did in the enameling sections, they give us a Romanian salary and we still cannot afford to buy the things we need. The owners, after all, try to get rich as quickly as possible, and they will therefore not give good salaries. I have spoken to some of the workers in the enamel sections. Their salaries are lousy.

Workers' fears are not unfounded, since they are often kept in the dark about the process and decisions are made without their unions being appropriately consulted. The union leader at UPRUC said that privatization

> is one of the major causes of bad relations between unions and administration. The factory management lies to us and doesn't give us data about what will happen in the future. Investors come and the administration never lets us in on the negotiations; then they say that the investors are not serious. We believe they really don't want to privatize or will do so only when it's advantageous for them.

Meanwhile, another UPRUC worker also spoke of his factory's contentious privatization process, relating it to both corruption and unemployment:

> Now they are dividing the factory into six societies and the rumors are they are doing this to be able to fire people. These guys want us out, either by privatization or by the labor contract buy-outs. When they kick us out you'll see who will remain working at the plant; those guys who have some kind of influence or relationship, like the guy whose uncle is a big director of the state methane gas corporation.

The other type of privatization to which workers refer is the general process affecting the economy at large. Most workers equate this with the end of large-scale production enterprises and the spread of small commercial and service outlets. They see little good in it for people like themselves. This is first because the workers who end up employed in such places are readily cheated, as an Aninoasa electrician pointed out:

> Privatization especially doesn't work. You get hired for two to three months for the trial period and then they let you go without paying you what you deserve. All there is here in the Jiu Valley are small enterprises like bars and food stores. Why don't they build a dairy or something productive that we can use in the Valley?

Second, workers believe the process is stacked against those who try to form businesses with savings or severance pay. Făgăraş workers have ideas for investments but are deprived of lump-sum severance pay. Jiu Valley miners also shy away from opening businesses. Some, like a former union leader at the Petrila Mine, open businesses that soon close due to theft and corruption or more usually due to lack of customers. One unemployed Dâlja miner expressed the common view:

> There was no way that I could have developed a business since all the costs of that are too high. I heard that some guys got together to open businesses, but I don't have enough trust in others to do that.

But many do have such hopes. They want to start chicken hatcheries, mushroom farms, transport companies, bars and discotheques, TV repair shops, and other small stores and service businesses. A few even manage to do so. However, most attempts fail for one reason or another: the bureaucratic maze and high costs of start-up, lack of local disposable incomes, theft by colleagues, distrust between partners, and even outright mafia-like appropriation of successful start-ups by local power barons. Those who manage to overcome these obstacles face jealousy and disparagement from their former friends and colleagues. They labor unremittingly, with few social or leisure activities. Unending fiscal demands from the state mean they must constantly "borrow from Peter to pay Paul" to keep their businesses afloat. A Lonea miner summed up the worker's view of privatization even as he praised socialism when he said that "privatization means that some people now have the right to steal legally. But under Ceauşescu that never would have happened."

Unemployment, the Black Market, and Falling Living Standards

Workers' narratives link privatization to unemployment. Socialism had guaranteed workers jobs, and their loss is a loss of honor and of membership in a collective endeavor defined by both the workplace and one's colleagues. Official unemployment figures are actually far from bleak, but tell only part of the story. The official unemployment rate among Romania's labor force of 6.5 million grew from 9 to 12 percent between 1996 and 1998 (Allison and Ringold 1996, 58; Earle and Pauna 1996, 1998, 205). State ordinances encouraging workers to quit by offering them large amounts of severance pay (called *disponibilizare,* or labor contract buy-outs) also contribute to these rates.[13] I discuss the buy-outs in detail in the following chapter because of their massive effect on the meaning of work and work relations. Since the buy-outs began, official unemployment has declined slightly: to 10 percent by late 1999 (Comisia Naţională pentru Statistică 1999), to 8.4 percent by the end of 2001 and to around 6 percent in 2005.

This trend is salutary, but unemployment is more problematic than statistics suggest, both as an objective phenomenon and as a meaningful one. Objectively, many of the so-called employed are actually barely working. For example, workers in state industries essential for national defense are termed "technically unemployed" (*şomer tehnic*), and receive up to 75 percent of their salaries to remain on call. Other "employed" people, like workers at the Făgăraş UPRUC plant, are less fortunate. They are furloughed without pay when factory orders decline and are called back if orders increase. Subsistence farmers, those who declare themselves self-employed, and even itinerant Roma craftworkers are also considered employed for statistical purposes. Statistics also do not count as unemployed those who have never worked, like recent college graduates, or those who have been out of work for more than twenty-seven months and are therefore ineligible for state assistance.[14] Further, unemployment statistics are in the aggregate and do not show the massive unemployment in mono-industrial regions such as the Jiu Valley and Făgăraş, with its heavy concentration of chemical plants.

Statistics also do not document greater unemployment among certain groups. The unemployed are found in all age groups and both genders, and among both skilled and unskilled workers alike. However, the vast majority are manual laborers, most with a high school or trade school education. These individuals were the backbone of the socialist economy and the focus of the "cult of labor" and thus feel the loss of employment especially keenly. Women workers are also more affected than men (Bacon and Pol 1994; Cornia 1994; Earle and Oprescu 1995; Watson 1993). The image of both active and unemployed East-Central European workers is masculine: the worker in hard hat and leather apron or the aggressive striker on a picket line. However, these images ignore gendered realities even as they intensify the competition for jobs between women and men that began in the first days after the revolution (Codin and Zecheriu 1992). Women workers were generally among the first dismissed and the last rehired. Though women make up roughly 45 percent of Romania's work force (Comisia Naţională pentru Statistică 1996, 152; 2002), they are nearly 50 percent of the unemployed, are twice as likely to be unemployed as men (Earle and Pauna 1996, 831), and are unemployed for long periods more often than the typical male union member (cf. Bacon and Pol 1994, 55–56; Rompres 1998).

Unemployment also facilitates abusive hiring practices, which further discredit the worker as person. On the surface the process seems reasonable and transparent. Employers place requests at local employment offices or post notices (*afişuri*) on shop doors and windows. Information spreads by word of mouth among family and friends. But workers complain that job-seekers must offer large sums of money to those making hiring decisions to even be allowed to apply, and that employers ensure rapid turnover to take advantage of the lower wages they can pay in the six-month probationary period (*perioadă de probă*). Toward the end of the period, employers accuse workers of various infractions (theft is the most common) in order to fire them. Those taking their colleagues' places know a similar fate awaits them in a few months.

These trends in the Romanian labor market have naturally resulted in the development of a large black market in labor (*la negru*). Such a black market is not uncommon in postsocialist societies, but is especially widespread in Romania. Black work is generally viewed as a necessary evil by both workers and state officials, as it allows some income in the midst of privation. Most workers, especially the unemployed, also admit their black work, but in the same breath typically mention slights and grievances they have suffered.

The head of the national office of labor protection (Oficiu Protecţia Muncii) told me in 1999,

> Black market labor is better than none at all and we [i.e., Romania] do not have the necessary resources to control it effectively, in any case. Besides, it is very costly for employers to hire workers legally, so they are also predisposed to hire illegally, despite the fines if they are caught.[15]

People in both regions often mention black work abuses, but still indicate they take these jobs when offered, since they have no other choice. In black work, men are hired for unskilled and manual labor while women, especially younger ones, are sought in commercial and service occupations. Typically people are hired and fired at will, and even physically abused and manipulated by their employers. Some women, once hired, are pressed for sexual favors and threatened if they resist. Other abuses are also common. Black workers never know how long they will work. Many are promised long stints, but let go after a few months. Workers in *la negru* are forced to perform work they were not hired for, including personal services. And though black pay occasionally approximates or even exceeds that of legally contracted labor, unscrupulous employers often pay black workers less than agreed, as these workers have no recourse for redress. Workers thus lose trebly in black work. Unemployment is increased as some people work multiple jobs, wages are generally depressed throughout the economy, and workers' spirits are challenged by the abuses of the system and the knowledge that they must accept them (Birtalan 1999, 8).

Even those who are employed seek black work, because of the surging cost of living. Annual inflation rates have varied from 50 to 200 percent over the last decade, with an average of 58.69 percent between 1990 and 1999 (McMahon 2000). The rate decreased to 26.4 percent in 2001 (Romania National Institute of Statistics 2002) and to about 9 percent in 2004. Luxury goods, of course, are vastly expensive, but basic amenities like food and housing are equally so. A few years ago an average urban family spent 81 percent of its monthly budget on food alone (Ştefan 1999, 6). Steady, inescapable inflation erodes worker senses of the possible, forces households to scramble to make ends meet, and restricts worker social ties and relationships. It encumbers the unemployed, who usually refuse to take minimum-wage, make-work jobs since they feel, correctly, that this will put them further behind the economic curve.

Declining standards of living and longer working hours hinder family, friendship, and collegiality, thus further undermining workers' confidence and sense of belonging. These factors contribute to increased household dissolution, divorce and abandonment, and extensive emigration. Though workers still express sentiments of collectivity and mutual support, the lack of money makes it difficult for them to actually help one another. Socializing outside the workplace, common in the past, has disastrously declined, as has participation in the ritualized aspects of social life, like weddings and baptisms. Worker physical and emotional health also suffers. Increased rates of depression, suicide, heart disease, and stroke, and general increases in morbidity and mortality, characterize worker communities in postsocialist times. They are a logical outcome of othering, impaired agency, and the transformations in labor.

The middle classes, too, are affected by these conditions. Middle-class jobs are generally secure, and a range of new employment opportunities are provided by the new globalized economy. However, the middle classes also struggle with inflation amid rising standards of consumption, and they are concerned for their children's future. State functionaries and service workers, such as government clerks, teachers, and health care workers, are hard pressed to survive on salaries alone and often seek additional black-market employment. Middle-class people certainly understand that corruption fueled the rise of the owning and political classes. However, given their own struggles to stay afloat, they are less sympathetic to labor's plight. They are particularly kept off-balance by the discourse of otherness that has developed about workers in Romanian society. As Daniel Barbu (2004, 243) suggests, speaking of the relations between workers and the Romanian middle class, "to be a worker in Romania today is a social condition totally lacking in prestige and political significance, though this prestige and advantage have not been conferred on any others." A middle-class Braşov County physician's comment was not atypical: "Many workers are to blame for their problems. Those who aren't lazy have what they need. There are jobs if one wants to work. As we say in Romania, 'Whoever looks will find.'"

Labor's Waning Symbolic Capital

The distance from others that workers sense is real and develops in tandem with the decline in the visibility of industrial laborers, and the respect accorded to them, in society generally. Labor's loss of symbolic capital thus disadvantages them in pressing their claims with successive Romanian governments. In postsocialist Romania the list of those deemed responsible for society's economic problems and contentious politics is a long one, including corrupt politicians, rapacious businesspeople, and allegedly anti-Romanian foreign agencies like the IMF and World Bank. Though workers are largely victims of the economic downturn, because of their militancy they are still held partially responsible for it by businesspeople, government officials, and professionals of every stripe.[16]

This critique is multifaceted. First, many claim that labor violence demonizes Romania and creates a poor investment climate. Nonworkers also say the Romanian economy is held back by workers' questionable work ethic, lack of productivity, and general dishonesty, all learned during "the time of Ceauşescu." Worker demands for subsidies and job security also set back reforms necessary for "entry into Europe." Even unemployed workers are not spared. They are accused of collecting benefits while working "under the table," or leaving employers in the lurch by working long enough to qualify for the dole and then quitting. Others are said to refuse both training for new positions and relocation to regions where jobs are available. Still others, especially miners, are accused of quitting work when the government offered large severance packages, and then demanding their jobs back after spending their severance. This critique is connected to that of large-scale industry, especially the socialist variety. In socialist times, Romania emphasized comprehensive, geographically disbursed industrial development. This was partially a response to Soviet attempts to relegate Romania to agricultural production in COMECON, the East Bloc trade organization (Constantinescu 1973). Today many people, workers included, suggest that Romania's comparative economic advantage lies precisely in agriculture and tourism and that industry generally, especially socialist-type industrial overdevelopment, is antithetical to both.[17] However, this critique is only one small step from the denigration and distancing of workers.

Both print and broadcast media play a large role in "othering" industrial workers. The media today define a world in which workers feel ill-prepared to participate and unwanted, in any case. Workers have largely disappeared from daily discourse on television and in newspaper articles. Media stories speak of unemployment, the black market, and the country's economic problems, but analyses are often sensationalized or macro-level, omitting the faces of those affected. When depicted, workers are shown in problematic and compromised situations: for example as both cause and victims of industrial accidents. Newspapers offer steady doses of legal infractions, theft, family abuse and abandonment, and the poor living conditions from which such malefactors arise. All these images suggest that somehow workers' lives are to be avoided. Exacerbating the critique, absence, or skewed images of industrial workers, Romanian media, like those in other postsocialist venues, promote new kinds of employment and related material culture. Newspaper and television advertisements portray middle-class professionals engaged in "clean" activities and using high-tech products like cell phones, computers, and cable TV, with little connection to the "working classes."

Consumption, not labor, is the new watchword of the Romanian media. Thus it is not an accident that worker concerns are also disregarded in other symbolic realms. For example, their issues and interests are ignored in Romanian higher education, and they are deprived of their voice in academic circles. Students today seek training in business, foreign languages, and law but avoid technical subjects related to the industrial workplace, like engineering. Similarly social researchers pay little attention to the world of the worker. I know of no surveys of workers' opinions about the predicament of Romanian society or the physical and psychological pressures under which they and their households operate.

Owing to the identification of Romanian newspapers and broadcast outlets with one political wing or another, media analyses of strikes, job actions, and union leaders' meetings with government officials are often hyperbolized. Worker actions are discussed in ways that support the paper's or station's political allies and deride the opposition. All this reportage is political, however, whether labor actions are supported or opposed. The media thus contribute to labor's othering by deemphasizing the economic realities of workers' lives, caricaturing labor actions, and overemphasizing the differences between workers and others in Romanian society. Such "othering" discourses were especially prevalent in coverage of the so-called *mineriade*, the actual and threatened incursions into Bucharest by Jiu Valley miners in January and February 1990, June 1990, September 1991, and January and February 1999 (Cesereanu 2003; Vasi 2004).

The *mineriade* were shaped by diverse layers of meaning, motivation, and individual and group psychology. I analyze them in greater detail in chapter 4. Suffice it to say here that each march had both political and economic referents, though the first four were ostensibly political and the last two prompted more by economic issues (Gledhill 2005). Nonetheless, despite labor's complex relationship to the marches, media emphasis on their political aspects embellished the social threat the marches implied. Miners' living conditions and perceptions were secondary, if considered at all (Cesereanu 2003, 219–20), no matter whether the analysis derived from the left-wing press (such as *Adevărul* and *Azi*), the critical-reformist press (such as *Revista 22* and *Sfera Politicii*), or more classically liberal or right organs (such as *România Liberă* and *Viitorul*). This discourse is best expressed in an article published after the last marches in the critical weekly *Revista*:

> Today there exist newspapers and newspapers, political parties and political parties, dissidents and dissidents, privatizers and privatizers, and there also exist . . . miners and miners. In June 1990, when they beat us the miners were bad, but when they stoned the Romanian government they were good. Now no one applauds . . . Now we see the real miners [*mineri mineri*].[18] Miners used to go to work, crawl on their stomachs, in the dark, through water. Now there are miners who never enter the mine, but only put on their lamps to march toward Bucharest or give TV interviews. The miners from [the strike of] 1977 we laud in the "Black Book of Communism," but miners today . . . have removed us from Europe. Tens of thousands of [subsidized] dollars for each miner is a demand that prevents any negotiation and enervates the country. Whoever demands this is a bad miner. Now, whether good or bad, all miners believe they deserve dollars, that mine debts should be excused, that they did well when they came to Bucharest to reestablish calm . . . But for what should we thank them: their leaders, roads and buildings, twenty salaries [i.e., lump-sum severance packages], professional retraining opportunities, government access, their claims to represent the essence of Romanian culture, protections they receive, tax reductions, special trains, family associations, mines taken care of, excused debt, their control of Berceanu [former Ministry of Industry]? The miners have become all bad. (Perjovschi 1999, 1–3)

This bill of particulars spells out all the alleged advantages of mining and miners' alleged abuses of those advantages. However, like similar analyses, it contributes to the mutual distancing of society from labor and labor from society. First, the commentary elides discussion of what miners saw as provocations (mine closures, broken promises, lack of economic alternatives). Second, labor is held chiefly responsible for Romanian economic problems. Third, and most critically, the analysis essentializes miners (and by implication other workers) as homogenous, even mocking differences between them. In reality, miners responded in multiple ways to the *mineriade*. Some participated with alacrity. Some feared union reprisal or loss of pay, and were coerced into participating. Others refused to participate at all.[19] These choices reflected family circumstances, age and seniority, the mine in which each worked, and a range of other factors. Most miners did participate in most of the marches and saw the situation entirely differently than did media interlocutors. They explained their actions as attempts to salvage a dying way of life and protect their families after eight years of broken promises by corrupt politicians. They blamed the failure of their marches on slanted media presentation prompted by fears that the miners' message would spread to all Romania's hard-pressed workers. In a group interview at the Lonea mine in August 1999, one miner said (and his colleagues agreed),

> People in Bucharest weren't afraid. We went there peacefully in 1990, but they shot at us. We feel 60 percent of Romanians are for us, including all other workers, but the press turns the people against us. Adevărul[20] is like a foreign newspaper. The press was in our midst at Costeşti.[21] They know the truth, but when the stories come out on TV it is completely different. Why should we even bother to pay our taxes for TV when they lie like this?

Intimations of the Future

Not all workers succumb to postsocialist pressure. In fact, worker agency takes many forms. Some resist through labor actions (though these are becoming less frequent), many others leave the country for good, and still others join the new society aborning or actively work to launch their children in that society. This is resistance by accommodation. They save penuriously and work tirelessly to escape the mine or factory and establish toeholds in local commerce. Everyday forms of resistance are also common. Jiu Valley miners still drink together after their shifts and grouse tirelessly and collectively about work. Făgăraş workers share food and offer occasional loans to workmates. However, in postsocialism, all strategies require a heroic and persisting struggle to be effective. This is not easy, especially when workers are simultaneously trying to secure sufficient resources for a minimal existence. The Herculean efforts demanded by resistance, even by "resistance by accommodation," themselves result in focalization, transvaluation, and denial of much else in workers' lives.

Those who overcome postsocialist obstacles now do so less as laborers acting in concert than as isolated individuals, undaunted by adversity. Such individuals would "get by" whatever conditions they faced. In Romania, most of the two regions' workers, employed or not, face their situation with resignation, increased isolation, unrealistic nostalgia, and an obscured vision of the future. The resistance or successful accommodation of others has little larger effect. Such efforts neither reshape postsocialist society in workers' interest nor spread to any significant degree among the working population. Most people who speak of confronting postsocialist society do so in discursive modes that emphasize *plângere* (complaint) instead of *descurcare* (getting by). Intensely focused (focalized) on their disadvantages in privatization, on their falling living standards, and on their lack of credibility in society, workers typically offer a resigned shrug and point out dozens of reasons why they will not overcome the obstacles they face. Others slake their anger with system-reviling rhetoric that caricatures but does not enlighten. Even where workers parry postsocialist pressures, their resistance fails to galvanize large-scale, effective response. Starting and running a business means a full-time commitment for the rest of one's life. Union work is greeted with suspicion by one's colleagues. Emigration deprives worker communities of their most ambitious people in the most productive time of their lives. Meanwhile, those who leave the country often postpone marriage and childbearing or forego them entirely. Even the capital remitted by émigré workers has ambiguous effects. Though they enable many to survive and provide others the amenities to make life somewhat comfortable (television, clothes, medicines, vacations for one's children, a household appliance or two), foreign remittances fuel inflation, wasteful consumption, and petty corruption.

Thus, Romania's workers see the future as generally problematic, and believe that they are largely unable to shape that future. This dreary outlook is shared by all age groups, both sexes, diverse ethnicities, the employed and the unemployed, miners and chemical workers, and people at every level of education. Workers' futures are rendered even more troubling by what they perceive as threats to the continuity of their communities and workplaces and to their actual lives and health. For example, Vasile Șoflău and Raluca Nahorniac interviewed a forty-five-year-old Nitramonia lathe operator and his wife, who spoke of how the labor bureaucracy spells their death:

SHE: There are many bosses.

HE: Yes. Bureaucracy is very large.

SHE: They foolishly threw many people out of work, but brought in more bosses as they did so.

HE: Have you been to our factory section to see what goes on there?

SHE: Everyone steps on each other's toes.

HE: You should go, just out of curiosity to see how many of them there are and how many should be retired, who take the place of deserving young people. This is exactly the same situation in the Romanian parliament, where there are people of seventy-five and eighty years of age who stay there and read the paper instead of accomplishing something for the country. I have nothing against this, but they should put correct laws into effect. If the country would respect the law as it should, those guys would not be allowed to stay there. I guarantee it. But they don't make the correct laws, because if they did, then all those malingerers would be thrown out. Like I say, I have nothing against them, but others have to have the chance for a future and they prevent it. [. . .]Youth in Romania have no future at all because, like I said, our laws prevent it. Many kids today don't even go to school. They don't do many things that they should be doing. If they finish school, they still end up stuck at home. If they go to university—and I have a university education—they end up stuck at home, because there is nowhere for them to go. What will my son do? There is no possibility for his future here.

SHE: I can't assist him because I lost my job.

HE: He wants to leave the country, but first he has to do his stint in the army. He says to me, "Daddy, there is nothing for me in this country. All I do every day is sit around. I get up in the morning and I sit around. If I'm lucky, I get out to buy a loaf of bread, because I have nothing else to do." I wish I could give him some money to help him leave, but we haven't enough for ourselves and a loan costs too much. If you ask for one million lei and they write one million on the contract, you end up with less than half of that because of all the extra charges.

The same attitudes are apparent among Jiu Valley miners. If anything, they are more pessimistic than most of Romania's other workers, given the increasingly uncertain future of Romania's mining industry. An unemployed miner, formerly at the Lupeni Mine, generalized his situation and suggested,

Everyone in mining is psychologically destroyed. Everyone is very stressed. And things are getting worse. Because of an absence of materials and investment, miners will be hit even harder in the future. You can try to adapt . . . but it will be very hard to do so. I actually took the buy-out because I understood how dangerous it is. I have often thought that mining has no future. Not because there isn't coal. There is, and it is of good quality. Our problem is this new method that they started because of a lack of money. If they don't invest in the mines, they will not be able to maintain workplaces.

And so they sit, arrested in their dreams, certain of the irrelevance and futility of any effort they may make, and conjuring a past that never was to serve as a source of value and meaning that allows them, albeit anachronistically, to envision a different future. Thus, in a little over a decade's time, Romania's once secure and even proud workers have been reduced to a marginal mass whose conditions barely figure in the plans of the state and in the minds of its increasingly distant political and business leaders. Their only hope, the main source of their identity and the spur of whatever action they may manage to take, is their labor and its increasingly uncertain rewards. But this is a contradiction in which they are viciously trapped. It is their labor that has brought them to the impasse in which they find themselves and which continues to erode their sense of possibility.

3   Postsocialist Labor Pains

Fear, Distance, and Narrative in
the Workplace

> Work means to use your body, to use your
> head, to realize something.
> **—NS, unemployed Făgăraş worker**

> Jiu Valley miners don't fear death [in the
> mines]. They fear life [outside the mines].
> **—Alin Rus**

Labor and Embodiment

Under socialism, labor was an essential source of identity, linking individual, community, and society. Such linkages provided the security of protective relationships but also enabled state surveillance and control. Despite such surveillance, the security of labor meant that people could count on getting by, some even living relatively well. Today, however, labor no longer ensures life's necessities, though it still enables, in a different way and for a different purpose, control and coercion. Additionally, in Făgăraş and the Jiu Valley, as across much of the postsocialist world, labor today is often a major source and context of tension, anger, jealousy, frustration, confusion, competition, and stress.

These dysfunctions are both structural and meaningful. Structurally, whether in privatized or state firms, postsocialist labor and workplaces are separated from the other social and institutional relationships to which they were formerly tied. Human relations in labor and the workplace lose their multidimensional character, and labor loses its symbolic presence and importance, as social linkages vanish. Much changes as "the sum of the relationship between employer and employee [becomes] . . . contained [only] in the exchange of labor for wage" (Dunn 2004, 128). Community projects organized by work collectives are abandoned. People no longer take vacations. Subsidies for food and housing, and benefits such as health care, are cut back, often disappearing altogether. Strangers move in next door, and the trade schools down the street are shuttered. Such decontextualization changes human subjectivities, perceptions, and practices. Valorization through consumption, so widely observed in postsocialist society (Berdahl 2005; Mandel and Humphrey 2002; Patico 2005), explicitly encourages people to think and act as individuals. International investors, industrial restructurers, and democratization specialists laud this transformation, and there is much to be said for liberating the individual to enter the open market. The flip side of this change, however, is that it removes such liberated individuals from the embrace of various collectivities. People are no longer guaranteed access to a secure, if minimal, range of commodities. As individual units of production, they themselves become more vulnerable to selection and replacement, and their time and effort are increasingly supervised (while their health and welfare are less so).

The replacement of one set of conditioning relationships in labor by another thus defines the essence of postsocialism. For workers, this replacement is the key context in which new understandings of the world are embodied. Furthermore, these understandings are elaborated throughout society in different behavioral contexts and symbolic domains (i.e., they are transvalued), and in each of these domains they are considered central (i.e., they are focalized). Individuation is modeled in media and advertising, encouraged in education and health care, and especially elaborated in housing. The significance and meaningfulness of this transformation is also shaped by the specific process of change, how it is remembered by those who experienced it, and how it is heard tell of by those too young to define it themselves. In the uncertain push-pull of Romanian privatization, amid rapid and intensive social and economic differentiation and perceptions of workers' "fall from (societal) grace," the process itself becomes daunting, threatening, and rife with dissension within and between the groups involved, as workers' narratives of privatization attest.

There are clear links between the transformed principles of postsocialist labor, embodied sentiment, and bodily practice (Cockerham 1999; Stone 2000; Watson 1995; Weidner 1998) Recent studies (see especially Cornia and Paniccia 2000) even suggest a direct link between changing postsocialist labor and declining health. Satisfying labor is often recognized as "meaning-making," thus alleviating pain (Good 1992, 50). Conversely, people who closely identify with work, workplace, and work colleagues will feel their pain grow and their strength ebb when they find themselves in restructured or deteriorating workplaces, tense relationships, and insecure employment. Workers' bodies, long a site of surveillance in the Romanian state (Bucur 2002), and especially in socialism, are now largely ignored. Perhaps all these phenomena explain the proliferation of images of Nicolae Ceauşescu in factories and other public places.[1]

Changed Meanings of Bodies in Postsocialist Labor

Romanians believe their bodies are malleable, but within limits shaped by experience. Once a body is molded for a particular kind of work, that mold is difficult to break. The body's form does not change in response to work practices, as Lamarckian evolution, the genetics of Trofim Lysenko, or old physical anthropological arguments suggested (Brues 1959). Instead, training or preparation limits perception and action, just as wagon wheels naturally follow ruts in well-used roads. Romanians subscribe to the idea that "you can't teach an old dog new tricks," or, as they say, "What you know in youth, so too in old age."[2] This was brought home to me one day when I asked a former Lupeni miner on a hunger strike why he wouldn't accept another job. He was incredulous I thought that possible. "How," he asked, pantomiming to make his point, "after twenty years of moving with pick and shovel, could I carry a tray as a waiter?" Once habituated to certain work routines, bodies are pleasured by their repetition, and workers accept, or are inured to, any associated dangers. In Făgăraş, workers often justify their refusal to wear protective equipment by saying they are accustomed to the noises and smells. One retired worker from the Viromet plant said he so missed the smell of methane, he returned to the factory whenever he could. Miners also engage in acts of physical bravado that become bolder with age. They are careless of danger as they show off their strength, skill, and masculinity to younger colleagues.

Postsocialism challenges all this. Workers' physical and character pathways are disrupted in different ways. Economic restructuring, privatization, and unemployment destroy links and habits.

New jobs and technologies require retraining even as labor is deemphasized as the source of physical and social identity. Connections between labor and character, and between the body, labor, and society, are eliminated. In privatized labor, to use Dunn's (2004, 82) analysis, individuals are forced to take greater responsibility for their physical and economic difficulties. In Western market societies, long inured to capitalist individualism, this responsibility is a positive quality. But among workers in the Jiu Valley and Făgăraş, whatever their age or sex, such responsibility signals not empowerment but the absolute end of the security, collectivity, and sense of belonging they felt in socialist society.

Body and Agency in Postsocialist Mines

Miners' perceptions of labor, body, and agency today are shaped by the rigors of mining and filtered through the experience of restructured workplaces and their perceptions of themselves as outcast from society. Jiu Valley miners work in conditions reminiscent of the miserable British mines described by George Orwell in *The Road to Wigan Pier* (1937; see also Smith 1996). Despite these conditions (and their past activism), miners under socialism felt respected by society and as secure in their lives and persons as the dangers of mining allowed. Facing these dangers even added to their sense of self, enabling them to see their work, their bodies, and their efforts for the future as strong and effective. These self-perceptions were reinforced by their intense group identity. As many observers note, underground work and the possibility of sudden death frequently catalyzes unified social relations (Freese 2003; Knapp and Pigott 1997; Nash 1979; Tintori 2002). To overcome the mine's dangers, individuals subordinate themselves to the group. Their code of honor commits them to each other while in the underground (*subteren*), whatever their personal beliefs or affinities. As an Aninoasa miner said,

> Underground no one is Moldavian, Oltenian, or even Gypsy.[3] We all take care of each other and help each other. If someone is caught in a cave-in you don't stop to think where he is from. You try to save him. If we only called for help for people we knew and liked, then we would all be in danger.

Miners are committed to one another's safety, which is why "good luck" (*noroc bun*) is the universal greeting to all entering and leaving the mine. A miner's workmates (*ortaci*) thus become the most important people in his life. When miners are asked with whom they prefer to spend free time, their wives or their *ortaci*, they typically choose the latter. This preference is demonstrated in their after-shift drinking; nearly every day until the recent labor contract buy-outs, work teams gathered at local bars to buy rounds and celebrate living through another day by recapitulating events in the mines.

Miners are also united because they are objectified by others. In June Nash's classic case study (1979), entire communities of Bolivian tin miners organized to oppose mine owners, both private owners and the state. In a postsocialist case, Stephen Crowley (1997) contrasts politically "cold" Russian steel mill workers with the near-revolutionary actions of "hot" Ukrainian coal miners, whose unity and labor action, Crowley suggests, jump-started the anti-Soviet revolution in the early 1990s. Jiu Valley miners are assumed to be equally homogenous and unified. Their activism is fabled, from the strike of 1929 to the socialist cult of labor, the massive walkout of 1977, and the recent *mineriade.* These actions are typically interpreted by mass media as evidence of miners' social similarity, group-think, and near-universal support of their former leader, Miron Cozma (Anon. 1999b; Cook 1999; Lloyd 1999; Vasi 2004). But such interpretations are far from accurate, especially in postsocialism.

Postsocialism erodes miners' unity, sense of belonging, agency, and physical integrity. Miners were always somewhat differentiated by divisions of labor. However, group relations have fragmented since 1989, under the impact of falling pay, high unemployment, difficult working conditions, emigration, and ill feelings produced by past *mineriade* (especially the last), and this fragmentation has caused stress and physical decline and impaired the miners' agency. Despite dangerous labor, communal drinking, *cultul muncii,* and media slurs, miners' working conditions no longer produce a shared understanding. Miners today are distanced not only from society but from each other, their households, and even themselves. Social distancing, in turn, intensifies their perceptions of suffering. Over time, this distancing and suffering has produced a small, weak, and unthreatening mining population that lacks the power to shape its own destiny.

Work in the Underground

The changing conditions of postsocialist labor in the mine sit at the base of embodied understanding and the possibilities of agency.

Figure 3.1. A drink before the shift. Photograph by the author.

Generally, work in the mines remains much as it has been over the last thirty years. In the 1977 strike, miners gained a workday of six hours spent at the work site itself. However, each day miners spend an additional four to six hours traveling from home to mine and back, dressing and undressing, receiving and returning equipment, meeting in the mine hall (*sala de punctaj*) to receive orders from brigade leaders at the start of the day, traveling on the underground trains (*cărucioare*) or on foot from mine entrance to coalface and back, and showering after the shift. Work conditions differ from mine to mine depending on the quality of the coal, the nature of the terrain, the size of the mine, the location of the coal seams, arrangements for transporting and sorting coal, and so on. Coal quality decreases and ease of extraction increases as one moves from east to west across the Valley (from Lonea to the ecologically disastrous Câmpu lui Neag pit mine, now closed). East Valley coal in mines like Petrila and Lonea is harder, with less water and ash content. However, these mines' terrain is steeper, and their seams are deeper (Baron 1998). Geology influences, though it doesn't determine, the degree to which labor is manual or mechanized. West Valley mines

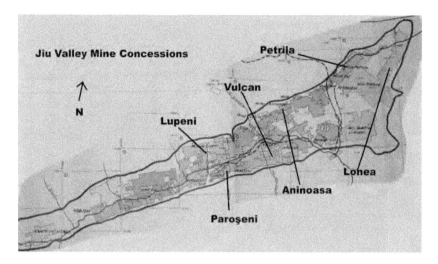

Map 2. Jiu Valley mine concessions.

like Paroşeni are the most mechanized. However, in the main, the process of extracting the semihard, coking coal (*huilă*)[4] looks much as it did in the nineteenth-century heyday of the *minerit*.

Those working underground are divided into brigades of up to forty people, often named by combining the name of the brigade's leader with the depth of the horizon at which it works. Thus, in the Lonea Mine, "Sultan 312" works 312 meters above sea level, while "Bobirnac 350" works 38 meters higher still. Brigades are also distinguished by the work they do; coalface miners (*mineri la front*) are marked off from auxiliaries that carry out ancillary work, such as signalmen, electricians, mechanics, and explosives experts (*artificieri*). There are also "preparation" groups (*mineri de pregătire*), which ready new galleries for exploitation, and "investment" groups (*mineri de investiţie*), which start new projects, such as digging mine shafts (*puţuri*) or bringing in new tools. Significantly, with the closure of four mines, the threatened closure of seven others, and cutbacks in *minerit* activities, the number of investment and preparation groups has declined. Brigades are distributed among four six-hour shifts (*schimburi*) each day. Miners use the term *şut* to distinguish actual time in the mine, entry to exit, from their formal six-hour shift. Brigades rotate weekly from shift four (midnight to 6 A.M.) to three (6 P.M. to midnight), to two (noon to six P.M.) to one (6 A.M. to noon), so that all miners eventually work each shift. Each shift has a special meaning. Shift three is thought best, since there is daylight during nonworking hours so that miners can attend to other matters. Shift one is worst, since miners must wake very early in the morning. On Monday mornings those on shift one are likeliest to be hung over. Furthermore, during shift one more TESA personnel ("technicians, engineers, service workers, and administrators"), are present to oversee miners' activities.

Coalface teams (*mineri la front*) comprise miners, assistant miners, wagon-tenders, and unqualified workers. Qualified miners are spoken of as *mineri mineri,* true miners, a term that separates them from auxiliaries and less qualified miners. All working at the coalface follow the lead of the qualified miner (although in recent years outsiders have criticized qualified miners as poorly prepared). Miners' lives, as well as their pay, depend on his knowledge of how to support the mine ceiling and extract the coal.

Auxiliaries live and work in a separate world from the coalface miners. Fewer demands are made on their bodies and their time. They have their own dressing areas (*vestiari*), and often drink among themselves after their shifts. They also have more formal education than the coalface miners. Beginning in the 1970s, during socialist industrial expansion, Momârlani began to work in the mines close to their rural homes.[5] However, Momârlani mainly have surface, auxiliary, or administrative jobs, which they secure by gifts of brandy and produce to mine bosses.

Most Valley mine galleries and tunnels are obstructed by used and broken equipment and support beams that protrude wickedly from ceilings and walls. In a few mines, like Aninoasa, galleries have been cleared of most debris. Aninoasa administrators were proud that miners can stand upright in nearly all galleries, though the contracts for removing and selling scrap are often corruptly awarded.[6] Outside the main galleries, walking in the mines is universally treacherous. Pools of water, some quite deep, dot the mine floors and are the subject of folktales and superstitions. Picks and shovels accidentally dropped allegedly disappear into bottomless holes, and some miners are said to be able to cross deep pools without getting wet—a sure sign of divine protection. Mine horizons at different depths are connected by narrow vertical tunnels (*suitori*) with jerrybuilt ladders, whose three-meter segments are offset rather than articulated to force miners to climb them carefully. Falling from a *suitor* ladder means certain impalement on the equipment piled at its base. Main tunnels and galleries at different depths are connected by slippery wooden inclines (*planuri înclinate*), where miners will hold on to live electric cables to pull themselves up or keep from falling.

Coalface conditions vary from mine to mine. Some larger mines, like Lupeni, require extensive aeration, which keeps a stiff breeze blowing through the mine. Miners wear wool caps under their helmets to protect against the draft, but complain of frequent earaches. Most work zones (*abataje*) are cool and damp, but some side galleries are as hot as 38–43 degrees Centigrade (105–15 degrees Fahrenheit). Here miners work in their underwear, or more often naked but for helmet, boots, and lamp belt. In such heat men can work for no more than fifteen minutes before being relieved. I visited one such work site, a kind of vision of hell, during a tour of the Aninoasa mine. Stopping to talk to the miners there, I quickly became the object of a tug-of-war between the work team and the engineer who accompanied me. The engineer said we should leave, since the heat was bad for one's heart. But the miners demanded that I crawl with them toward the end of the gallery to see how they worked. They pulled me in opposite directions. Shaking off the engineer, I undressed to my waist and crawled with the team's wagon-tender another five meters or so and jumped off a small ledge into an inferno. The heat was appalling. Every breath burned my throat, nose, and lungs. Those digging coal stopped working when they saw us, and we gathered in mid-gallery near an aeration pipe that blew a stiff current of cooler, clean air. The thermometer near the pipe hovered around 44 degrees Centigrade, and the miners claimed the temperature was probably five degrees hotter at the coalface. Standing naked and seminaked as our boots filled with sweat, we talked and passed around a two-liter plastic bottle of tepid water. The miners asked about conditions in American mines, contrasting them with the brutality of their own labor. When I asked what concerned them most, they complained about machinery and tools but mostly that people didn't understand the way they worked and lived. They showed me broken tools and flaunted their nakedness, as if to justify demands for higher salaries and secure jobs. "This is how we always work," one said. "How can we be blamed for Romania's problems?"

Food and water are constant concerns. Pipes in the mines provide water, but it is often unpotable. Most miners bring something to eat and drink during their six-hour shifts. Those on shift two can eat at the mine cafeteria before entering the mine; others receive a packet of food (*supliment*) from the cafeteria consisting of a bit of bread, pork fatback (*slănină*), or some sausage. The miners hang these packets in plastic bags from nails in the rafters, so the rats don't make off with them. Meals are taken whenever there is time, for example when equipment has broken down. One or two miners will generally eat while others work. Food is shared if not everyone has enough, and bits of food are even tossed to the rats. Miners consider them friends, since they warn of fires, methane concentrations, and other threats. But postsocialism distances even these friends. Miners believe that rats are now less prevalent and thus less likely to warn of danger.

Postsocialism's Effect on Mine Labor

Change in postsocialist labor intensifies perceptions of danger and contributes to miners' sense of distance from, and loss of control over, their dangerous work environment. Mine exploitation has been cut back precipitously, because the buy-outs have reduced the number of workers. This has had equivocal affects. Positively, many dangerous work horizons and peripheral mine shafts were closed, and the accident rate consequently decreased. In some mines, like Lupeni, distances between galleries and operating shafts were greatly reduced, so miners can reach work areas more quickly. Still, with fewer people working, those remaining often must do the work of two, making their *şut* both more taxing and more dangerous. Mine administrators must shift miners between brigades more often, to adjust to labor shortages, economize coal extraction, or balance production and budget. Different types of miners are paid at different rates. Every coalface team must include at least one qualified miner, who can deal with the vicissitudes of coal extraction. But except for complex tasks like digging a *suitor* or deciding what support structures are needed while advancing through or undermining a coal seam, almost any miner can handle most tasks. Thus, to lower extraction costs, administrators prefer teams comprising as few qualified (and thus better paid) miners as possible. For miners, the inverse is true. The more qualified miners at a work site, the safer everyone is. Thus miners complain that the shifting of workers between teams and brigades reduces their solidarity, production, and pay. However, administrators make these decisions with an eye to the bottom line. As one mine engineer said, "Friendship is friendship, but work is work."[7]

Reductions in mine budgets have also forced changes in mining techniques and frequent disregard for safety regulations. These changes also make miners feel that they are less respected in society and more physically threatened in postsocialism. Paradoxically, coal extraction is increasingly labor-intensive despite the decrease in the number of miners. For example, the Lupeni Mine recently closed its last fully mechanized extraction operation, replacing it with the older, cheaper, but more dangerous practice of undermining. In the former, coal is extracted by digging straight into a seam as the gallery is extended horizontally. In the latter, a seam is dug into from below, and coal falls directly onto a transporter belt (Popa et al. 1993). Miners complain about this shift in technique and point out that undermining is harder and more dangerous. Still, administrators justify the practice as economically more efficient, thus allowing the mine to remain open and preserving miners' jobs.

Similarly, administrators and miners disagree about who is to blame for lax attention to workplace safety. Miners accuse administrators of forcing them to work in unsafe conditions and of cutting corners even more than "in the time of Ceauşescu." One Lonea miner echoed many from other mines when he said,

> The shift boss [*şef de schimb*] is responsible for checking the concentration of methane every other hour. If it is beyond 1 percent, then we are supposed to leave the gallery. But sometimes administrators make us work at triple the concentration . . . There are many, many norms that are not respected. For example, they pulverize untreated coal,[8] stairs and other walkways are flimsy, and you have to descend for meters holding on to live cables.

Simultaneously, administrators accuse miners of neglecting safety to earn as much money as they can or to show off their fearlessness to colleagues. In fact, some miners admit they ignore all but the most serious threats to their safety, but see this recklessness as forced on them by others. As a former Lonea miner said,

> No one works nowadays without trampling labor protection norms. According to the rules, in the transport section I am supposed to have one man in front of me and one behind me. But now all work is done with only two-man teams. One is always missing right from the start. Administrators tell you that you don't have the right to go certain places or lift certain objects. But if you respect all the rules you won't earn anything.

Such perceptual dissonance is a product of labor's new embodied conditions. Frequent tool shortages and equipment malfunctions spur miners' fear of poverty, forcing them to feel they must break the rules to maintain production. Tools are the miners' lifeblood and extensions of their bodies and power. However, at every mine we visited miners complained that tools have become both shoddier and harder to obtain since the end of socialism. Shoddy technology also results from corruption, as when salvage companies paint old mine machinery and then resell it to the mines (with the collusion of mine administrators) as new equipment. Work brigades argue over the quality of tools and over access to them, which increases the felt distance between them. To make their point, miners always showed us repaired and re-repaired wrenches, hammers, shovels, and other tools, often ones that they had brought from home to replace nonexistent or broken tools at the mines.

Privatization also worsens the services the mines provide their work force. As postsocialist services decline, miners' bodies and understandings are further pressured. For example, the Romanian National Coal Company (CNH) now outsources all its ancillary activities to a private firm, S.C. Sermin S.A. Miners unanimously complain about the quality of Sermin services, which they illustrate by their filthy showers and dressing areas (*vestiari*). At Aninoasa, miners had received no soap for about three months in fall 1999, where each had previously received a large cake every month. Though Sermin is supposed to provide security in the dressing rooms, miners claim their clothes and belongings are stolen much more frequently today than in the past. Especially troubling are declining food services. Miners say that food at mine cafeterias is worse than before, and they receive less; it "is food fit for sick people, not for hardworking miners." Miners are incensed about this, and blame it on corruption. It is well known that Sermin purchases poor-quality food and related products at inflated prices from local firms, some run by relatives of mine and union officials. Additionally, mine stores offering low-cost, decent-quality commodities have all but disappeared.

One Lupeni miner summed up the situation:

> Look at how sick we are. We are forced to work extra because of lack of materials. The company wants coal but won't give us what is needed to do the job and keep us healthy.

Women's Work

Postsocialism particularly changes labor demands on women, leaving them in a precarious position and at the mercy of massive layoffs.

Women's labor circumstances tend to be ignored in the postsocialist workplace (Weiner 2005). But as well as degrading the position of working women, postsocialism affects the lives of women who do not work, depending instead on the precarious jobs of their husbands. Previously most women in Jiu Valley mining families were expected not to work, but to stay home and care for their families. Many still would prefer not to work, but now see it as necessary to supplement their husband's mine salary, or replace it if it was lost in a contract buy-out. However, few jobs are available for Valley women. Some work in mine offices or for Sermin in laundries, dressing rooms, kitchens, and the like. Many of the women who work for Sermin are widows of miners killed in accidents and explosions, who received their jobs to help them raise their children. Other women work at the three Valley coal preparation facilities or at the various stores and service providers in Jiu Valley towns. Many of these work illegally on the black market, or are legally hired by store owners at less than minimum wage for an initial "probationary period," to be fired for some contrived reason before its end. Many women also take make-work jobs offered by town governments or, along with their menfolk, attend job training courses offered by local branches of the National Agency for Professional Organization and Formation (ANOFP). Until recently, however, they were denied access to these jobs and courses. According to terms set by the World Bank and the Romanian government, they were first offered to people with work histories, thus barring many women at the outset. This restriction was eliminated in 2001.

Though the range of jobs seems large, most have drawbacks. For example, women who work in mining service sectors, who were previously CNH employees with access to the benefits accompanying state employment, are now formally employed by Sermin, the private mine services company spun off by the CNH. When their employment status changed they lost vacation time, salary subsidies, and subsides for heat, housing, and electrical service. They also became non-unionized, and have little power to improve their circumstances. One woman, employed in the Vulcan mine laundry, petitioned the secretary of labor for a change in her and her colleagues' status when he visited the Valley in summer 2002. According to her, he curtly dismissed her when she handed him the petition. At the time I interviewed her she feared for her job, as she felt the Sermin administration would punish her insubordination. Fortunately, however, she was not fired.

Women working at the Valley coal preparation facilities face particularly difficult conditions. During socialism, the labor force here was almost exclusively female, though most miners' wives avoided such work if they could. According to Jack Friedman (personal communication), who did fieldwork in Lupeni in 1998–99, about two-thirds of the six hundred people working at the Lupeni coal preparation facility (*preparaţie*) were women, most of whom were assigned the less desirable late afternoon or night shifts. Work at the *preparaţie,* most of which was manual labor requiring minimal skill, was disparaged by men and women both. Pay was lower than at the mines, but the work was just as dirty and back-breaking. A staff social investigator at the Petroşani General Hospital spoke to us at length about women working at these jobs. The day we met he was evaluating the case of a woman at the Uricani facility who accidentally started up the coal transport band, causing a near-fatality and a colleague's loss of two fingers. This woman was particularly abject. Her husband, a miner, took the buy-out and left with their daughter for his home village in Moldavia. The woman was also mentally impaired after a head injury in a previous fall. The investigator consequently ruled her not culpable for the accident, because of diminished capacity related to her psychological impairment and social disorientation. Though she was an extreme case, he spoke of her as an archetype of the "low-cultured" (*scăzute*) women from similarly wretched Moldavian mining families:

> When a woman is incapable or alcoholic, as many are, the whole family is of low culture. As we say in Romania, "When parents eat bad apples, children feel it in their teeth."

Most black workers in the Jiu Valley are also women. Like such workers throughout Romania, they work long hours for low pay in problematic conditions. However, because of the extensive Valley unemployment and the steeply rising cost of living, more women seek these jobs than can be hired. Maria B., wife of an Aninoasa Mine electrician, took black work at a Petroşani bakery to supplement her husband's wages when their son started second grade. As she said,

> School is so expensive now. We have to buy the notebooks that used to be free, donate to the school fund, buy clothes so our child will look nice and not be made fun of by other children and parents. We also wanted to save the money I earned to buy a computer.

Nonetheless, Maria abruptly quit.

> I worked nonstop and at all kinds of odd hours for a salary of 225,000 lei per month, less than half the minimum wage. Also, because I was from Aninoasa and the owner and the other girls were from Petroşani, I was made to do all the hardest work and had to keep watch over the supplies and money that came into the bakery. I finally quit after two years because the owner accused me when some money went missing. It was just as well, because when I was working my husband and I would fight a lot. I would come home nervous from my work and start fights with him, because he was the only one around. We know many couples in the same situation. Still, as I am out of work, there is no way to save for the computer. The only way we will have money is if we win at Bingo.

Maria subsequently had a chance at a legitimate job (i.e., one with a formal labor contract) as a waitress in Vulcan. However, she passed the opportunity on to her elder sister, a widow with young children whose husband had died in a mine accident a few years before.

As Maria's story suggests, what work is available is often offered first to women in needy family situations. Other working women, especially those whose husbands are also employed, are severely criticized by their colleagues and others. They are said to prevent others from having even a minimal chance to support their families. The wife of a Lupeni miner who continues to work at the Lupeni Mine offices said,

> At work I always have problems. They tell me, "Your husband works at the mine, so you should stay home." I don't know what worth this discussion has. It mainly creates problems between my colleagues and me. [They say] I am greedier because I work at the mine. I certainly don't agree with this, because I was hired here even before my husband.

Such are the conditions of working women in the Jiu Valley. As during socialism, most Valley women do not work. Now, however, a wife's unemployment is no longer a mark of status for a mining family, but just another difficulty with which the family must contend. In fact, the burden of keeping a household together and marshalling its increasingly scarce resources falls particularly heavily on Valley women. They are the ones who must strategize, budget, pick up odd jobs, accept make-work or minimum-wage employment, and otherwise keep the wolf from the door. Many Valley women succeed in this, though their success is equivocal. Some families profit greatly by the skill and success of a skilled and resourceful woman worker. However, as working women often demand greater influence within their families, their husbands are increasingly troubled, or even embittered. It is little wonder that, as a Petroşani physician suggested, "the rate of mental illness in [Valley] families has grown in the last years, and women are particularly susceptible."

Postsocialist Change in Miners' Work Relations

Although the honor code of the underground is strictly maintained, miners' social relationships in postsocialism are increasingly problematic. In particular, mine workers are increasingly differentiated, even the normally unified *mineri la front.* One factor promoting this is backlash from the *mineriade.* The January 1999 strafing and gassing of the miners polarized miners' opinions of the union (the League of Miners' Unions of the Jiu Valley, the LSMVJ, or, as Romanians call it, the Liga) and its leader, Miron Cozma. Coalface workers, *mineri la front,* are especially likely to feel differently from auxiliaries. The former were the backbone of the protests, strongly support Cozma, and readily admit having participated in *mineriade.* Most auxiliaries, however, claim they did not participate and that the marches were mistaken.

Along with reverberations from the *mineriade,* general economic decline and the labor buy-outs have increased social and political distance between miner groups. Though working conditions and pay were never issues between miners and auxiliaries before, the new uncertainty of mine jobs and the rising cost of living bring these front and center. Miners now contrast their working conditions with those of auxiliaries and claim that every miner "carries" at least three auxiliaries on his back. Meanwhile, auxiliaries regularly decry their lower salaries compared to miners'. They acknowledge the harder physical labor of *mineri la front,* but say they face equally dangerous conditions and are paid only one-third to one-half as much. A Lonea machinist said, "If miners make their quota, they get paid more than their salary, but we don't. Our salaries are only adjusted downward when the quota is not made." An Aninoasa electrician discussed the relationship between auxiliaries and miners in physical terms:

> Auxiliaries are less favored than coalface miners. They get paid based on their brigade's production, but we are paid based on the whole mine's production. That's why there are tensions between the auxiliary and the miner. They always get more than us and in the last salary negotiations came out much better than us. I don't disagree their job is harder than ours, and I also know this is the way it has always been. But our work is

also difficult and dangerous. Still, we get along OK with the miners. They need us and we need them. We only go to the bar with them occasionally, but we don't have any problems with them. Our jobs are related to each other, like men to women, and coal is our child, our money, our bread. Still, we are different from them. Our dressing area is more pleasant and better cared for than theirs, which is completely filthy. No one takes care of them since the labor buy-outs. We clean our own, but the miners don't bother with theirs.

He then commented on the increased distance between miners to-day:

I started work at the mines on my stepfather's advice, and mining was a good profession when I began in the early 1980s. Many free things were offered to miners then. Though it was hard to become accustomed to work underground, people were friendlier then, and there were a lot of older miners who would help you and teach you things to make your work easier. Now people are colder and all look after their own needs first, especially because of the lack of tools and frequent breakdown of equipment.

Postsocialist mine work is thus increasingly problematic and fraught with tension, disagreement, difference, and uncertainty. The physical demands on miners increase, and the contexts in which work is done make it seem harder and more threatening. Miners feel more alienated and less in control of their lives than before. Even alienation is more problematic in the present. Previously, miners felt alienated as a group, and they counted on colleagues for support and commiseration. Increasingly, however, alienation is individualistic. Colleagues are less trusted, less available, allegedly less dependable at the coalface. Such increased individualism bodes ill especially for miner agency and practice. And while employed miners feel increasingly distanced, those without work feel triply so, and their circumstances influence all of Jiu Valley life and culture in ominous ways.

Buy-Outs: The Stress and Distance of Unemployment

Of all the changes in Jiu Valley labor, none has been more significant than the worker contract buy-outs of 1997 and 1998, carried out under the terms of Ordinance 22 (Romania Government 1997b),[9] and termed in Romanian "disponibilization" (*disponibilizare*). In these buy-outs workers allowed their labor contracts to be terminated in return for a large amount of severance pay (depending on seniority, from twelve to twenty months' salary) in addition to regular unemployment compensation. Buy-outs were also offered to other workers, including those in Făgăraş and Oraşul Victoria. However, for Jiu Valley mining, labor, social relations, physicality, and agency, the buy-outs have had multiple, breathtaking, and destructive effects.[10]

Everything about the buy-outs has been fraught with uncertainty, differentiation, and intergroup recrimination. They triggered a massive reorganization of mine production. The way they were carried out deepened suspicion between miners and the Romanian government, between miners and mine administrators, and between those remaining at work and those let go. The buy-outs divided those with and without work, often former workmates, conceptually, socially, and economically. Because they were so divisive and produced so much stress, they are the quintessential postsocialist policy.

Distrust is first generated by uncertainty about why workers/miners allowed themselves to be bought out in the first place: whether they chose it or were forced or tricked. In interviews in 1999 and 2000, most of those quitting the mines (except for Momârlani) said they were either forced out or tricked into participating. They spoke of the severance pay as bait (*momeală*) and the buy-out as a trap (*capcană*) into which they fell. Many said they were lied to and promised other work or a chance to return to the mines after a brief period of unemployment.

> The idea circulated that anyone with more than three charges of slacking off, or those who drank, would be kicked out . . . I heard a rumor about a list with the names of unmotivated workers scheduled to be let go . . . and people were constantly checking you out. Later this list changed. I don't know why, but the new list also had some good guys [i.e., hard workers] on it.

The chief engineer at one of the mines verified some administrative differentiation of workers, though he denied any trickery:

> Everyone had access to the same information and left of their own accord. Still, there was a bit of selection. We took aside good workers and asked them to reconsider, if we knew they were thinking of participating. But we didn't do anything to discourage bad workers from leaving.

Unlike this man and those who accepted a buy-out, many active miners and most mine administrators and non-miners suggest that those bought out were motivated by greed or a desire to return to their region of origin. They point out that many went on spend-ing sprees with their severance pay and that many did, in fact, leave for Moldavia or elsewhere. However, the truth is more complicated. Some less capable workers took the buy-out because they thought they would be fired anyway. Some Momârlani returned full-time to their rural estates. Some miners lusted for quick riches, but others wanted to start businesses or emigrate. But although motivations and outcomes differed, the social costs of the buy-outs affected the whole region.

Whatever people's motivations were for accepting the buy-out, the unemployment of thousands of people in the space of two years had startling effects. First, the buy-outs undermined what re-mained of miners' traditional solidarity and group identity. Those bought out suddenly found themselves cut off from fellow workers on whom they had depended for years. One former Lonea miner said,

> As a bought-out person, I am no longer one of the fellows. Your fellows were like your wife. We would share everything and we would always re-ciprocate. Now you are alone; it's like you don't have a family.

Another former miner said,

> As soon as they started the buy-outs I signed up to transfer from the trans-port section to an actual brigade . . . and did as soon as I could. I didn't even wait for them to give me permission. But you know what it means to move to another location . . . it's like you've lost a part of your life.

Many miners felt great shame (*ruşine*) at having lost their work-related identity, especially as many who opted for the buy-out had come from rural communities where labor is accorded special sig-nificance. When they returned to those communities they were stigmatized because they no longer had work. One said of a good friend,

> After he left the mine, he went back to Moldova, but there they set the dogs on him. Then his father told him, "You should have stayed at the mine until the director put a lock on the door of the place."

The wife of an unemployed miner said,

> [My husband] hasn't gone back to his village since he was bought out. You'd think he wasn't even their [his parents'] child any longer. We go back to my parents' place often, but my parents don't know he's left his work.

The large severance packages also had multiple effects. In the first months after the buy-outs many of those terminated did go on spending sprees and bought luxury foods, clothing, and household appliances. Non-miners criticized them, seeing their extravagance as evidence of their backward culture. Meanwhile, bought-out miners with money to burn toasted their former *ortaci*. A Lupeni Mine safety instructor said,

> There were many "millionaires" then, and they all gathered in the bars buying rounds for each other. You could go into a bar without any money in your pocket and come out hours later completely drunk.

But it is not true that the buy-outs gave miners extraordinary amounts of unearned money that they squandered foolishly. Severance pay packages often barely exceeded lost wages, since they did not include the various pay supplements (*sporuri*) that often doubled a miner's monthly salary.[11] Many spent most of their money satisfying daily needs, but others spent considerable funds on chronic health problems left unattended for years. Furthermore, conspicuous consumption had characterized the mining community for three decades, fueled by the media and images of the modern; the miners' spending was not anomalous.

The buy-out was an unmitigated economic disaster. The lawmakers supporting it suggested unrealistically that miners could use the lump-sum pay to start small businesses or seek jobs in other regions (Mariana Basuc, personal communication). However, bureaucratic and fiscal obstacles to opening businesses were as large then as now, and miners' social relations, tight in the underground, were shot through with postsocialist suspicion in the light of day. Thus, most fledgling businesses went quickly bankrupt because of lack of markets or mistrust between partners. Emigration to other regions was also not a viable option. Bought-out miners were publicly offered homes and jobs in other regions by officials, but these often were far fewer than promised and sometimes nonexistent. Miners who returned to their natal regions without such support were seen as interlopers by siblings and parents, whose own resources and inheritances were threatened by their newly needy relatives. Furthermore, miners actually had less wealth than at first appeared, because apartment values plummeted with so many people leaving the Valley at once. Bought-out miners also had few ways to generate other income. Rural jobs are limited, as Momârlani largely satisfy their own needs. State-supported make-work or part-time jobs in private businesses offer minimal salaries and uncertain conditions, which the formerly highly paid miners find insulting or not worth the effort, and they considered new job-training programs irrelevant. Thus, most of those bought out now survive by working in food stores for in-kind pay, doing occasional odd jobs like house painting, emigrating, or collecting and selling wild food. A Lupeni miner said that his bought-out former colleagues have "taken the place of wild forest animals."

Most bought-out miners and their families are now in a spiral of postsocialist decline. Their severance pay is gone and unemployment compensation ended in December 1999. Job prospects are poor to nil. And former colleagues offer little but feigned sympathy because their lives, too, are troubled; they have come to feel the bought-out brought their problems on themselves. The unemployed have few means to respond to their circumstances other than dreams and outbursts. Some enthusiastically invest in the Amway Corporation's consumer products pyramid sales scheme. Many spend thousands of lei daily on EuroBingo or other games of chance. Some are even wistful about the Caritas failed investment scheme (Verdery 1996). Their frustrations are intensified by their persisting belief that they deserve a salary large enough to let them support their families on one income. They believe this because of the high salaries they previously received, their lack of other income, and politicians' promises to preserve the *minerit* and expand opportunities for unemployed miners. The buy-outs have also problematic effects on Valley family life and on people's physical and emotional health and perceptions. Nor are these effects uniquely caused by the conditions of the Jiu Valley; they are also readily apparent in the Făgăraş zone, where the circumstances of postsocialist labor differ, but workers have similar perceptions of their wrongs.

Labor Transformations in the Făgăraş Region

Like Jiu Valley miners, Făgăraş chemical workers fear the end of their industrial way of life and embody these fears in stress, alienation, and detachment. But while the miners respond with collective anger, Făgăraş workers react to the crisis of postsocialism more as individuals. There are fewer collective actions, like hunger strikes, as each worker household seeks to make its own way in the postsocialist remains of the economy. People cobble together resources to keep their heads above water. They used a similar strategy in socialism, when individuals and households competed for

Figure 3.2. A shuttered UPRUC section.
Photograph by the author.

limited resources. Now such strategizing is impelled by the uncertainties of chemical manufacture and the basic conditions of postsocialism; unemployment, steep rises in the cost of living, and the
like.

Like those in the Jiu Valley, Făgăraş workers are confused and
threatened by the state's withdrawal of support for their primary
industry. However, unlike their miner counterparts, many Făgăraş
workers wish the state sector would disappear even more quickly.
Since the end of socialism they have generally looked forward to
the privatization of the socialist factories. However, the process has
been irregular and unpredictable, which has only exacerbated post-

socialist uncertainties and tensions. Since 1989 all the region's large state-run factories have steadily decreased production and shed labor, and the labor contract buy-outs, begun here in 1998, were only the latest way of removing workers from their jobs. As they had other economic possibilities, Făgăraş workers first vied for bought-out status and severance. However, as the private economy sputtered, workers changed their minds and competed to retain their jobs. Factory support services like clinics, shops, cafeterias, and sport teams were also cut back or eliminated. Many workers see the shuttered factories, the lack of new hires, and the end of training programs at regional vocational schools as harbingers of the end of their self-image as forward-looking, cultured, hard-working, and industrious. Though most Făgăraş worker families figure out some way to survive, fear of the future, especially for their children, grinds them down.

The Făgăraş chemical industry began in the interwar period, with the Nitramonia Chemical Works being founded in 1922 (Herseni et al. 1972). The region and its city had long been a center of small-scale chemical manufacture, with numerous related cottage industries like tanning and lime production (Bărbat 1938). Furthermore, the navigability of the Olt River and the strategic location of the city, between Braşov and Sibiu and commanding the entrance to Carpathian passes, also facilitated industrial development. Chemical manufacture expanded greatly during and after World War II. Given impetus by the German military, a chemical plant was developed near Ucea village, and after the war it was expanded into the Victoria Chemical Works. The temporary worker settlements around the plant became the new socialist city of Oraşul Victoria. Nitramonia was also nationalized with the advent of socialism and renamed the Făgăraş Chemical Combine (Combinatul Chimic Făgăraş). The UPRUC factory was built in the mid-1950s to manufacture fittings for the chemical industry. The region's factories reached their zeniths in the 1980s; Viromet employed 4258 people in 1982, Nitramonia over 8000 in 1989, and the UPRUC factory 4991 in 1978, though this figure had dropped to 4746 by 1989.

Făgăraş and Oraşul Victoria were classic socialist company towns. Most local people worked in their factories or depended for income on the pay of those who did. The factories organized local life and provided amenities to workers. The factory Communist Party leadership had oversight of local government, and the integration of factory and local Communist Party institutions kept people in line politically, threatening them with demotion or loss of pay and benefits. The factories built apartment complexes and operated special stores and clinics for workers streaming in from surrounding villages and other Romanian regions. Sports teams, schools, literary circles, and the like either were directly connected to the factories or received most of their support from them. The Făgăraş Chemical Combine was especially well provisioned. Its chief patron was Elena Ceauşescu, wife of the dictator, who trained there for her doctorate in polymer chemistry. The FCC work force received high salaries and significant amenities. Victoria, too, was treated preferentially, having been conceived as a model socialist community; it had even been built without churches. The Victoria factory was located in a park-like setting on the edge of town and so thoroughly dominated local life that even today town residents repeat the adage that "The city is the factory and the factory the city."

Since 1989, Făgăraş factories have seen steady declines in their production, work force, and economic significance. Even at the revolution their technologies were outmoded, their work forces bloated, and their markets restricted. Two rounds of buy-outs reduced the number of employees at the Victoria Chemical Works, now renamed Viromet, from 4210 in 1989 to 2398 in 1998. At the Făgăraş Chemical Combine, renamed Nitramonia after the revolution, the number of workers fell to 2113 by 1999.[12] The UPRUC work force declined to 4746 in 1989, and by 1999 only 1070 employees remained. These numbers reveal only part of the local economic decline. Not only has the work force been reduced, but those remaining are working fewer hours. Though Viromet and Nitramonia maintain three shifts to ensure the continuity of various production processes, the number of workers per shift is greatly reduced. Seven Nitramonia production sections now run at about 20 percent of their 1989 capacity. Nitramonia and Viromet also furlough workers. As their production is defense-related, workers there may be listed as "technically unemployed" (*şomer tehnic*), receiving three-fourths salary to remain at home, available for immediate recall. UPRUC workers are less fortunate. No section operates more than one shift, and workers are also often furloughed as the plant has insufficient orders to keep even one shift fully employed. The Nitramonia and UPRUC factories exude an atmosphere of silence and decay. Production sections that formerly employed hundreds or thousands now sit empty, with locked doors and broken windows. Factory grounds are dotted with twisted piles of scrap and deep potholes, the marks of local scavenging. The precipitous rise and steep fall of Făgăraş chemical production and the gritty postindustrial backdrop only add to workers' burden.

The End of Community inside the Shop

The deterioration of factory relationships further troubles the bodies and souls of Făgăraş chemical workers, just as it does those of Jiu Valley miners. Group identification was similarly strong in Făgăraş factories, although this strength was due more to the length of time that people worked together than to any particular danger or uniqueness of the work. Workers identified with their collective, felt intimately connected to its members, and—though less often in the last years of socialism—incorporated factory colleagues into their personal lives. Furthermore, Făgăraş workers' domestic and social relationships were integrated into the fabric of factory life, while among the miners domestic life and industrial production were separated into distinct social and symbolic realms. In the Făgăraş region before the revolution, husbands and wives, brothers and sisters, friends and neighbors were appointed to work together as a matter of policy, though this has become less common with postsocialist unemployment. The past domesticity of Făgăraş factories is evidenced by aging remains of personal decorations at workstations. An older UPRUC worker had a blackboard on which he had glued paper scraps bearing English words and phrases, with which he could practice his English before a visit from American relatives. Another nearby workspace was decorated with pictures of automobiles. Other decorations are due more to the difficulties of postsocialism. These include soft-core pornography and political posters which, in 1999 and 2000, mainly depicted ultra-nationalist presidential candidate Corneliu Vadim Tudor.

Women were also regularly employed in Făgăraş factories during socialism,[13] though their jobs, which included chemical operator, quartermaster, and supply captain, were often cleaner and less physically demanding than men's. Whatever their tasks, the importance of women's employment cannot be underestimated. It changed them from household dependents to active agents and key decision-makers, and it also tended to improve male-female relations outside the factory. One woman worker said,

> We have pretty good relations at work and talk easily with both our men and women colleagues. We have men on our shift and we are all pack-

ers. We fill up sacks and they take them and put them in the trucks. We talk amongst ourselves about everything; what we're cooking, what work we're doing, how we're feeling.

Făgăraş workers were also more integrated with other groups in the city and in nearby villages. Whereas Momârlani remain distinct from their miner colleagues in the Jiu Valley, chemical workers maintain relationships throughout the rural hinterlands of the Făgăraş region. Many still reside in villages and come to work daily on buses that have served the region since the 1950s. Others are first-generation arrivals from the villages and maintain close relations with village relatives. Still others, long-time urban residents or arrivals from other regions, develop relationships with village-dwelling colleagues. One unemployed Făgăraş worker depended on such relationships to tide him over during his unemployment:

> Sometimes I work for friends. Last year I harvested potatoes with a guy I know who has land in Ludişor [a local village], but I didn't go this year because I was sick. I've known this guy for ten years, since we worked together at the potato chip factory. The first time I helped him was one spring when we put in a water pipe on his property. We ate together, worked together, drank together. It was a wonderful atmosphere. Now he always asks me to help him with his potato harvest, and I almost always go.

The homogeneity of the factory working population, especially the lack of young workers, affects the factory environment and perceptions of work. During socialism local industrial high schools and professional schools fed a steady stream of young trainees into the plants. Older workers who trained them felt that they represented continuity. Today, however, workers bemoan the lack of new hires, which represents the erosion of the chemical industry and thus a threat to their own history and agency. Reflecting on their dying industry, Făgăraş workers feel themselves declining and dying as well. A male Nitramonia worker said,

> There are no longer young people in our factory. There is no longer a school for lathe operators, welders, mechanics. In 1973 when I was in high school our section had four hundred machinists. Now we are about sixty, including maintenance workers. We were the last cohort but one to finish at the professional school; now no one goes there. If people don't go to school and if they aren't apprenticed at work, how will they know anything? How will they survive? Today young people only know things theoretically, because they don't have practical educations. Today we have no future. Youth don't go to school and we can no longer assure them jobs.

A female Nitramonia worker in the quality control section also complained about the loss of many young workers in the labor contract buy-outs:

> In our section many young people left. Youth have left for foreign countries. Some got jobs with private firms and many have gone back to their villages. It is sad to see our section today—without life, without a future.

Workers' sense of physical decline is intensified by factory politics. Every time a new party takes control of the government, factory directors and other top administrators are replaced by a new set of cronies, who then appoint their own people to positions of responsibility and protect their relatives' jobs. Such change unbalances worker relationships and adds to the tension between union representatives and managers. For one thing, new political appointees regularly favor one group of employees over others. A female UPRUC warehouse worker told how a new factory director, a former work team leader (*şef de secţia*),

> gave his former section orders that came in, and then said our section should be closed as it had no orders. So he . . . closed our entire section, though he sent some of us he knew to his former section to work. I knew as early as 1992 that he would close our section, because he started to constantly inventory all our tools.

Since 1989 the directorships of Nitramonia and UPRUC have changed on average every three years. UPRUC, meanwhile, has been in constant turmoil since 1994 because of its convoluted privatization, still going on a decade later (Vrânceanu 2004). Only Viromet management has remained largely consistent. Labor actions there in early postsocialism forced replacement of the factory's director, but he was reinstated in 1992 and has remained in that post since. Comparing Viromet's and Nitramonia's experiences, he said,

> As we Romanians say, "The person hallows the place" ["Omul sfinţeşte locul"], and [at Viromet] people are particularly conscientious. Nitramonia's biggest problem is the frequency of change in leadership. Workers work according to the quality of management, and frequent changes mean that management is poor or unable to convince workers of the rightness of its strategy. Part of Nitramonia's problem is that its administrators still act as if the old system were in place, and haven't adapted. In the old system, they were the center and had the best technology, higher salaries, and the most personnel. So now they have had to let more people go, have more administrative staff to contend with, have older technology, and also a lot of investments were never finished.

Despite his words, all is not well at Viromet either. The factory greenhouses are abandoned, their glass broken or scavenged. Workers complain of nepotism as vociferously as at UPRUC or Nitramonia. The numbers of operating sections and operating hours have declined steadily. And though the factory is on a list of the sixty-four best state-owned enterprises seeking foreign investors (Anonymous 1999a), its privatization is still incomplete and workers fear for their jobs.

Despite these changes, factory life seems largely similar to what it was in socialism. However, by scratching the surface a bit one continually uncovers evidence of loss and uncertainty. For example, though chemical production is little changed since 1989, factories' product lines have decreased precipitously in both amount and variety as markets for their fertilizers, fungicides, and pesticides, previously bought by state and collective farms that are now defunct, have crashed. Other sections, like those that repair aging and outmoded machinery, are overburdened, especially because their labor force has shrunk by a third since the end of socialism. Workers remain comfortable with their workmates, but even this is equivocal. People are comfortable because they have worked together for as long as twenty years, but they know that no new workers have been hired for close to a decade. Furthermore, an aging work force is a tired work force; whatever benefit comes from their long-established, detailed knowledge of production processes is canceled out by their unfamiliarity with new techniques.

With declining production and increasing unemployment, even factory work schedules have changed. One Nitramonia worker described the changing shift structure and its implications:

> We call our work pattern "1-2-3." We work in a "continual flux" and 1-2-3 describes the hours and shifts that we work. This program exists for most of the sections in the Combinat. We work shift 1, 7 A.M. to 3 P.M., for two days, say Monday and Tuesday. Then we work 3 P.M. to 11 P.M. for two days, Wednesday and Thursday. Then we work three days from 11 P.M. to 7 A.M., Friday, Saturday, and Sunday. Then we have two days free, Monday and Tuesday, then we start the cycle again. It used to be regular like this, but now sometimes most of a shift is canceled, and that confuses both people and their schedules. Also, today most service sectors only work the first shift, though they used to work all the shifts. There is now an "intervention team" from the service sectors for off-hours emergencies. In case they have to go to the factory, they get supplementary pay. Factory bosses are usually only there during the first shift; that's why it's better to work on the second or third shifts. All work is better done when the bosses aren't around.

And so factory life continues, with uncertainty the only certainty. People go to work daily, never knowing if that day will be their last. They attend union meetings despite knowing perfectly well that the unions cannot help them keep their jobs. Work teams still gather in their sections to eat lunch. Now, though, the packets that many bring from home are spare, their diet a constant reminder of the decline in their lives and work. One afternoon, when I asked what they were eating, a worker in the Nitramonia repair section showed me the bit of bread and jam in his lunch bag, and with a wan and sardonic look called it "the only sweet thing in my working life today."

Unemployment and the Labor Black Market

While Jiu Valley miners suffer under vast, unremitting unemployment, the situation of Făgăraş workers is somewhat more equivocal. Unemployment in that region has been longer-lasting, less destructive in some ways and more in others. This difference is due both to the variability of the regional economy and to specific features of regional unemployment. Unemployment in Făgăraş factories appeared soon after the revolution and has steadily increased throughout the postsocialist years. As in the Jiu Valley, Făgăraş unemployment not only creates a sense of loss and emptiness, but also widens fissures between men and women, between rural- and urban-dwelling workers, and between locals and those from other Romanian areas. Workers living in the city say those from the villages were allowed to keep their jobs longer, while village-dwellers say they were let go first since they had other resources on which to depend. Workers who emigrated from other regions say they were discriminated against by local bosses, while those native to the region say that immigrants were allowed to keep their jobs since they had no other options. Women with employed husbands were often the first to be unemployed. In a region where traditionally everyone worked at some kind of gainful task, women's large-scale unemployment quickly forced them into the labor black market while eroding their home and family life. One UPRUC warehouse worker, thinking of her own circumstances, described how unemployment eroded social relationships across the board:

> After the revolution people were first united against the directors, but soon began to criticize each other. The Moldavians[14] said that since we had resources in our village households, we should voluntarily quit work. Some men criticized us women, and men and women both criticized me because my husband and I both had jobs.

Figure 3.3.Făgăraş workers at lunch.
Photograph by the author.

Still, despite their concern about loss of jobs, Făgăraşeni re-
acted to the labor contract buy-outs differently from residents of
the Jiu Valley. When the buy-outs were first offered, in 1998 and
1999, Făgăraş workers competed with each other to take part. Many
were almost of an age to be pensioned off in any case, while others
assumed that they would soon be unemployed regardless, and so
wanted to leave with the extra pay. To preserve factory workplaces,
both labor union leaders and factory administrators had to implore
(and sometimes even force) workers to remain. The competition for
buy-outs created anger and jealousy among some Făgăraş workers,
whereas in the Jiu Valley it was competition for the remaining jobs
that did so. But the Făgăraşeni's initial enthusiasm did not last long,
as unemployment increased and emigration became more expensive. Buy-outs are now seen as a threat and workers avoid them by
any means possible, including using bribes and connections. In the
midst of the Viromet buy-out in 2000 I interviewed a machinist
with over twenty years' seniority whose section was soon to close.
Some of his co-workers were able to sign on in other sections but he,
without the connections they had, was to lose his job in a month.
He broke down and wept as he described his situation, made more

dire since his wife, a school secretary in a nearby village, was also about to lose her job in a reorganization.

Like their Jiu Valley counterparts, Făgăraş workers say they were deliberately misinformed about the buy-out's terms and conditions. In a reaction to the miners' extravagance, state regulations have been changed to discourage lump-sum payments. Nonetheless, workers who can demonstrate plans for investment and who have filed a business plan are still eligible for lump-sum severance. However, they were never told about this possibility. Many who had hoped to invest therefore could not. Some had planned to buy tractors to hire out in the villages, while others thought of getting cars or small trucks to use as taxis or to bring agricultural produce from village to city. There were few reports of excessive luxury purchases, as there were in the Jiu Valley.

Some Făgăraş workers have managed to avoid the worst consequences of regional economic change by being classified as "technically unemployed" (*şomer tehnic*). This status, given to workers in occupations deemed to be in the national interest (such as defense production), keeps people on the work rolls and gives them a minimum income even if they are furloughed from their positions. Workers in the Viromet methanol section were employed for three months and received unemployment for nine, but those in the nitrocellulose section worked for only one and a half months and received unemployment for the other ten and a half months of the year. People in both factories were typically rotated into and out of *şomer tehnic* status, so that most were able to maintain their formal employment status until they were forced to accept buy-outs.

Făgăraşeni's fear of unemployment is heightened by the greater extent of privatization in the local economy. Though virtually all workers I spoke with favor more extensive privatization (unlike Jiu Valley miners, who support a continued state role in their industry), their fear of privatization is palpable. Privatization puts downward pressure on wages, limits the possibility of union representation, and generates constant rumors of people being let go for the slightest infraction of workplace regulations. A woman recently pensioned from Nitramonia told a story (which I could not confirm):

> A woman co-worker hung up her work tunic and forgot that she left her house key in the pocket. The key fell into some chemicals, and the section head accused her of sabotage. So they punished her by decreasing her pay grade, and after two months they fired her.

Privatization is seen as two-edged because it is often paired with the labor black market. Unlike Jiu Valley miners and their families, Făgărașeni work extensively in the black market and have come to fear and decry it, even as households are dependent on such work for their survival. Women are particularly involved in *la negru*. Their long history of labor outside the household, the cultural impetus for economic improvement, and the greater range of occupations in the region creates pressure on women to work, whatever the pay or circumstances. One former employee of the UPRUC factory, who now works *la negru* selling food, cigarettes, and sundries in a kiosk on one of the town's main streets, said,

> Even if I make 400,000[15] lei a month, that still helps us to do a little extra for the family. It pays for the telephone or the school field trip for one of the kids. It helps make life a little better, even though my work schedule means that I have to be away from home all the time, even when the children come home from school.

Such work, then, is both emotionally and physically costly to women and their families. People working *la negru* never know what hours they will work each week and frequently work odd hours, especially on Saturdays, Sundays, nights and holidays. Though the husband of the woman quoted above tries to take up the slack in the house (unlike most Romanian men, he prepares many meals for his children), he also says that the unpredictability of his wife's work makes them both lose sleep, worry over the children, and even fall ill more often.

Făgărașeni also often work in part-time agricultural labor (*la sapa* or *la coasă*, hoeing or haying), the rural equivalent to *la negru* as it is unregulated and often subject to abuse. Almost all such workers are young to middle-aged men. Though the mayor of Făgăraș exhorts unemployed urban workers to look for possibilities in the villages, only the most desperate do so. Still, even these jobs are on the decline. Agriculture is increasingly mechanized and farmers in need of day labor prefer to hire migrants from Maramureș County in the north, who work harder and more cheaply than locals. Since farmers fear for their own survival, let alone their profits, they prevent day laborers from gleaning the harvested fields, a common practice "in the time of Ceaușescu."

All in all, then, unemployment has contributed to a vast emptying of energy from the region. Though Făgărașeni pride themselves on their industriousness, many people now aimlessly wander the streets worrying about their jobs, their families, and their futures. The region is most energetic in the summer, when young migrants return from Italy and ply the streets of towns and villages in their late-model cars. Unlike Jiu Valley miners, people in Făgăraş mainly bear their fears and frustrations in privacy and silence. They internalize what the miners have in the past expressed publicly. Their angst, however, is just as palpable, their uncertainty just as gnawing. It is even possible to argue that the unemployed have it easy. It is those who continue to work who are truly overburdened. As well as constantly fearing for their jobs, workers are overworked, work in tense and stressful environments, are disrespected by their supervisors, and receive ever-diminishing wages and benefits. Where once labor was the center of their lives and the linchpin of their identities, today it is the basis of a deep personal and psychological confusion that directly translates into their perceptions of themselves and others and, above all, into their physical essences and approaches to the postsocialist world.

The Body and Agency in Postsocialist Labor

Just as workers' lives and labor have become superfluous in Romanian society, postsocialist workers' bodies are now a source of estrangement and alienation for workers, both men and women, active and unemployed. During socialism state ritual celebrated worker physical power, while state oversight ensured that workers responded appropriately—physically, reproductively, and politically—to state policy and labor mobilization. Thus, though the body was contested as a matter of policy, the security and celebration of labor enabled working people to be at least moderately comfortable, proud, and confident in their physical capacity. Their bodies and their labor together allowed them to feel a sense of purpose and agency and to envision and work for better lives for themselves and their children. Certainly worker agency, purpose, and sense of the future had different inflections in socialism. Many workers, like the Jiu Valley miners who took as their slogan "We give coal to the country," genuinely sought to contribute to socialist development. However, many developed strategies to avoid socialist physical demands, including work, or to manipulate state restrictions to personal and familial advantage. Other people both supported socialism and shirked their duty. But whatever their opinion of socialism, people engaged their bodies.

Today, partly as a result of their precarious employment and their belief that society cares nothing for them, workers often feel physically emptied and expendable. Such alienation manifests in nearly opposite forms of perception and behavior in the two regions. Jiu Valley miners' certainty that their bodies are doomed drives their overwhelming concern for their health and safety. Miners are almost paranoically aware of their physical selves. Though they were always menaced by the dangers of the underground, miners typically saw their bodies as means of protection and self-actualization. However, today's labor regime has turned their bodies against them. Instead of protecting, the body endangers. The surveillance of an overarching state was formerly felt to have both positive and negative effects, but the body's decline is now perceived to be hastened by the absence of state assistance. Făgărăşeni also translate uncertain labor, precarious employment, and the loss of cultural continuity into problematic physical perceptions. In Făgăraş, however, the body and the person have become distinct and separate entities, not so much enemies as strangers; the body is not angrily attended to, but denied and ignored.

Though the workers' bodily identities, perceptions, and practices differ, these different forms of embodiment appear to result from the postsocialist uncertainty and context of social differentiation in which both groups of workers now live. Though miners feel overworked while chemical workers fear their lack of work, they express these perceptions in similar idiomatic ways. Both readily contrast their circumstances today with the socialist past, when work was plentiful, pay reasonable, and personal relations manifested a semblance of egalitarianism. Their common physical distress also spurs their perceptions of threats in the workplace. In Făgăraş workers complain about unremitting cold in winter, poor lighting, dangerous levels of toxicity, and lack of concern for occupational safety and health. In the *minerit* everything is a source of bodily concern: procedures workers are forced to follow, the toxicity of the mines due to administrative inaction, dangerous and broken equipment.

But more than labor's physical dangers, workers' fear of unemployment in the next round of buy-outs or mine closures puts stress on their bodies, health, and well-being. The doctor at the Lupeni clinic, who avers great respect for his miner patients even as he criticizes their health practices, notes, "People are more scared of dying at an early age than ever before. Still, there are fewer requests for medical leaves, because of their economic difficulties."

Romanian culture has taught people that labor is more than work. An occupation (*servici*) was thought to nourish the body and the spirit. Still, as troubled as workers are about their physical declines, those without employment (or state assistance) fear even for their lives. Their number is steadily increasing in the competitive class circumstances of postsocialism, and they express their fear in jealousy of and bitterness toward others who manage to eke out a living. The Lupeni hunger strikers put it succinctly when they complained that some received extra nourishment while they were left with nothing:

> Compared to us, even pensioners live well, because they suck from two tits.[16] The places they send us for jobs are phantom firms [*firme fantome*]. We here are all kinds of workers . . . drivers, miners, cooks, bookkeepers . . . and all these services are needed. Why can't we gain access to some of them? The only reason they tell us about these jobs and publicize how the other hunger strikers in Vulcan [a neighboring mining town] were able to get jobs is to draw our attention away from our protest, so that we will go to these places, and then we will disappear when we die of hunger.

Thus labor, or the lack thereof, in postsocialist times is demoralizing and dangerous, and leads to untimely death: of oneself, one's colleagues, one's family members. Death and sadness stalk the postsocialist workplace. Coal miners, of course, learned to live with death every day. However, in the postsocialist mine death is doubly painful, as it comes in the course of a job that confers little respect. As one Lupeni miner said, "They [the government] hope we will all disappear. Whether we do it by taking the buy-outs or dying in the mine makes no difference to them, just so long as we disappear." A worker at the UPRUC plant spoke even more sharply about the constant presence of death in postsocialist life and labor:

> One of my work buddies died at forty-three and one of the foremen was forty-one. He died of prostate cancer . . . The director of marketing at UPRUC, who was thirty-six, died two years ago. Another neighbor died at fifty-one of cancer, and then there was the eighteen-year-old kid who fell from a train. Such unexpected death is the worst for the family, because you have to get together the necessary money in just a day or two. If someone is sick for a long time, then you can slowly get the money for the expenses that will follow. We think about and talk about death all the time at work. It can't help but affect our work. When someone dies at sixty or seventy, you think he had a full life, but someone dying in their thirties or forties is a great tragedy.

With death ever-present, workers feel they have little opportunity to respond effectively. Both the Jiu Valley and Făgăraş regions are famed for their history of worker resistance to political and economic oppression. However, as discussed in the following chapter, today there is little they can do to keep the shadow of decline from their door.

4   The Postsocialist Body Politic

> The body is bound up, in accordance with complex reciprocal relations, with its economic use; it is largely as a force of production that the body is invested with relations of power and domination; but, on the other hand, its constitution as labor power is possible only if it is caught up in a system of subjection . . . ; the body becomes a useful force only if it is both a productive body and a subjected body.
>
> **—Michel Foucault, The Body of the Condemned**

> Every day we tighten our belts. I don't mind that others have more than me. But ministers eat with two mouths.
>
> **—TN, Nitramonia mechanic**

Bodily Metaphors and Political Perceptions

The individuation of postsocialist labor and threatened and differentiated consumption sit at the core of workers' perceptions of society's declining respect for them and their increased fears for themselves, their families, and their futures. Dissonance between workers' perceptions and those of society at large particularly frames their political perceptions, practices, and possibilities. Miners and factory workers both saw their labor as critical to society in the socialist past, and both see it discredited and unrewarded today. Both believe that their work ought to earn them respect, expressed in both a secure living wage and a significant political voice. But in society at large workers, miners especially, are considered overpaid, pampered anachronisms whose demands, expressed in strikes and

marches, hold Romania back. Workers feel they are acting to redress wrongs faced by all working people in postsocialism. But the
general public believes that their political activities frighten investors, waste resources, and support those with poor work ethics and
poorer senses of social responsibility, and this belief is reflected in
the mass media.

Unlike Romania, some places in the postsocialist world confer
both economic rewards and political respect on those who undergo
physical suffering as a result of socialist labor and society. In post-
Chernobyl Ukraine, defined by Adriana Petryna (2002) as a "risk
society," workers and others stake claims on resources by docu-
menting their pain in the wake of that disaster. Those who suffered
violence at the hands of the East German and Czech security forces
have also been accorded special recognition and recompense in
those societies' attempts to reestablish the rule of law (Borneman
1997). However, in Romania, the inverse seems to hold true. According to workers, the harder they worked to build socialism and
the more they suffered in its dismantling, the more they are rejected
and alienated in postsocialism.

To Romanian workers declines in consumption, political disenfranchisement, and physical decline go hand-in-hand. As Romanians say, "Politics passes through the stomach" ("Politică trece
prin stomacul"). Thus workers continually invoke bodily images
and metaphors to define national politics and their alienation from
those politics. They typically contrast engorged politicians with
starving workers. An Aninoasa miner bemoaned the political straits
into which Romania had fallen by paraphrasing a German proverb:
"A good leader leaves office much thinner than when he came in.
But all our leaders, no matter their political party, are fat when they
leave office." Meanwhile a Făgăraş worker from the Nitramonia
plant spoke of political leaders who "eat expensive meals in fine restaurants," contrasting them with his and his family's meager diet.

Even international and global political issues are related to consumption and interpreted in bodily terms. Thus workers (and others) often place much of the blame for Romania's problematic economy, and hence their own declining standard of living, on demands
placed on the country by the World Bank, the IMF, and other international financial institutions. One issue that still rankled as late as
2002, though it had long left the front pages, was the World Bank's
requirement that Romania close the Timişoara County Pig Raising
Complex (COMTIM) so that another might be built down the road

in Kecskemeti, Hungary. The requirement enraged Făgăraş and Jiu Valley workers—especially the latter, since they had to purchase pork instead of raising their own pigs as many Făgăraşeni did. They directly related the pig complex's closing to their own bodies and health, arguing that COMTIM was one of the most productive pork complexes in Europe, and that its closure meant even less pork in their diets (even though COMTIM production was largely destined for export), thus threatening their health and well-being.

The intersection of international politics and physical meaning was impressed on me in a bittersweet way in the first years after the fall of socialism. Returning to Făgăraş in the mid-1990s, I was informed that my former host in Hârseni village, Valeriu, had just passed away and that his wake was still going on. So I left the city for the village to pay my respects. When I arrived at the home I saw my former host laid out in his coffin in the receiving room (my bedroom some twenty years before). His sister and other relatives were arrayed around the coffin keening and mourning, but his widow was nowhere to be seen. I asked where she was and was told she was in back, in the kitchen. So I left the coffin and moved to the back of the house. When I came to the kitchen door I saw Cornelia bent over a table with her two children, wearing widow's black and crying profusely into her handkerchief. She looked up, recognized me, and mournfully addressed me. "Oh, Mr. David," she said in one breath, "why did my Valer have to die? He was such a good man. He suffered so his last years. He was in so much pain. And why won't they let Romania into NATO?"

Though they suffer from their losses, workers perceive their postsocialist suffering and physical decline as giving them some degree of moral and political rectitude. Conversely, they consider many of those whose consumption has increased lavishly in postsocialism to be morally putrid, despite their apparent health and well-being. A Lonea miner expressed this view of political leadership when he said,

> It is difficult to maintain a healthy life in Romania now. We [miners] are pushed down, but others do not gain. Those who succeed only use others, but do not use their own selves. They also become weak, especially in spirit, because they do not take individual responsibility. Character must come from inside the person, but those in control are like mannequins who are only pretty on the outside but hollow or dirty within.

The belief that elites are morally degenerate intensifies the threat workers feel to their own lives and the impossibility of improving them. Workers (especially Jiu Valley miners) still see leaders as paternal figures (Borneman 2004; Kideckel 2004c) and expect from them the same solicitousness and material support that parents offer children. They look to leaders to protect their jobs and incomes. When this protection does not materialize, leaders are glossed as failed parents and workers as abandoned, mistreated children. Thus a woman office worker at the Lupeni Mine said that "these people [the Constantinescu government] are only concerned about their own needs, so we Romanians, their children, suffer and die of hunger."

In worker discourses, socio-economic prosperity per se is not the source of moral corruption and physical decrepitude. Rather, corruption depends on what one does with wealth and power, how one consumes their outsized bounty. Many of the postsocialist wealthy became rich in incredibly short periods of time after the Revolution, either by initial occupational advantages, through corruption, or both. However, no matter the source of wealth, workers respect those who give back to the community and disparage those who don't. In the Jiu Valley, for example, people contrast two men who became wealthy after the Revolution. B is a former state property inspector who used his position corruptly to accumulate a wide range of property, including restaurants at the base and top of the chairlift at Părâng Mountain, a popular recreation spot often visited in the past by miners and their families. People were incensed when B cut off public access to the chairlift for two weeks one summer to ferry workers and supplies for the construction of his restaurant at the top of the mountain. He is often the focus of Valley gossip. People note his crabbed stature and say he is bent over by corruption.

In contrast to B, P is a former forestry agent who became rich by selling timber. In some ways P is also morally culpable. Valley people decry the destruction of upland forests, and much of P's logging is of questionable legality. But P used his fortune to erect a cross in the center of his town. He donates money to civic projects, gives food to poor Valley children, and also donates beer and food for the miners' December celebration of Sfîntă Varvara (Saint Barbara), their patron saint.

Workers' perception of the physicality of class difference reaffirms their suffering at the hands of exploitative others, who gorge on and deplete their bodily powers. A Lupeni Mine rescue worker and his wife graphically illustrated this as they talked about everything from economic conditions to health to comparisons of socialist and postsocialist politics:

HE: I work so hard in the underground and I have no food to give to my children. We are virtually down to our last chicken. Others work in suits and ties and earn much more than me. Who wouldn't want to be able to work in a suit, instead of in a filthy miner's tunic [*salopeta*]?

SHE: Yes. And when the tunic rips the wife has to sew it. And they are so dirty that you have to wash them many times in order to get rid of the smell of sweat and the smell of the underground.

HE: There are some guys who don't wash their tunics, and these are the most miserable people you can imagine: people who don't live an orderly life. Others who don't wash their tunic think, "Why should I wash it today, because it is just going to get dirty tomorrow?"

SHE: Washing is the most important thing, because you catch illnesses from the unwashed. Filthy clothes give your husband skin diseases.

HE: Now when I come out of the underground, they generally give us laundry soap to wash with, when they give us soap at all. The mine is supposed to give you two towels and one kilogram of soap a month. But there is so little soap that we have to bring it from home and also take our work clothes home to be cleaned. And the soap they give you smells so bad, and it even causes you to break out in boils all over your skin. Still, as bad as it is, I am happy that I have work. Many others don't. Why, I ask, was it possible for Ceauşescu to provide places for people to work while these guys in power just send people out into the streets? Give us secure work that lets us live decently. I'm not asking to live like a *boier* [large landowner]. No one likes to go down three to four hundred meters every day into the earth. When Ceauşescu came to see the mines, so that he wouldn't get dirty, they gave him special coveralls and they took him to a workplace that wasn't disturbed, and there were security agents mixed in with the workers. But at least he went into the mine. When Iliescu came, well, he only stayed in the mine courtyard.

Politics and Production

Especially in the context of political change and new hierarchies and practices of postsocialist production, workers feel distanced, disenfranchised, and physically threatened. Tensions and mutual suspicions between workers and their superiors are artifacts of the transformation of ownership and the ensuing unemployment, corruption, and uncertainty (Dunn 2004). Workers also believe that this transformation makes it less likely that mines and factories will remain open, that workers will earn reasonable wages, and that they will be able to maintain their standard of living. Privatization and restructuring affected worker politics because organizational changes in factories and mines eliminated many midlevel administrators who had mediated between workers and upper-level managers. Furthermore, factory and mine administrators are replaced every time there is a change in national government, which also increases the political tensions between them and workers. Managers at every level hire their friends and fire their enemies, and often explicitly threaten workers (Bolger 1998).

In the Făgăraş region, workers complain that political appointees on the shop floor are overbearing, incapable, unproductive, and ubiquitous. They say these new bosses order them to follow incorrect production procedures, show constant favoritism in apportioning work assignments, and ignore the ideas and needs of workers. A Nitramonia foreman (*maistru*) reflected on his downgrading and on the quality of his new bosses:

> In the past we *maistrii* used to have influence [*un cuvânt despus*] over the workers. Now we have been moved aside because there are so many bosses [*şefi*]. All work is better done when the bosses aren't around. When we are treated more nicely, we work with more intensity [*spor*] and commitment [*drag,* literally "love"]. But when we are pushed, we do what we want. The new bosses like to give instructions, but some don't know what they're talking about and give stupid [*prost*] instructions. You really have to look out for these guys. Still, since some bosses also took the buy-out and left for Italy, their overall quality has improved. Still, there are too many of them. Nowadays there is about one for every three workers. We should try to change this, since they have large salaries and this decreases the pay for the rest of us.

In contrast, foremen in Jiu Valley mining still play important roles during all phases of mine production, help maintain production levels and miners' wages, and thus garner great respect from miners, whom they supervise and whose safety and pay depend on the foreman's abilities. In the mines foremen are recognized by their yellow helmets, which set them apart from black-helmeted miners and white-helmeted engineers and supervisory personnel. They are ubiquitous in the galleries during each shift and lead by example and fearlessness.

However, miners' relationships with other administrative and supervisory personnel, the so-called TESA (technicians, engineers, service workers, and administrators), have particularly deteriorated because of miner strikes and walk-outs, mine closures, the labor contract buy-outs, and above all the *mineriade.* Miner-TESA relations vary from mine to mine and depend on the extent to which administrators participate in local community activities, how often they visit work areas (contradictorily, miners decry TESA personnel for visiting both too rarely and too often), and how much attention they pay to safety regulations and practices, among other factors. Since the fall of socialism, miner-TESA relations have been uncertain but generally problematic. In early postsocialism, roughly 1989–95, miners often walked out to protest local mine administrations, forcing the company to shift administrators from one mine to the next. Though anti-TESA strikes have subsided, miners' respect for TESA personnel is still fragile, and the TESA personnel know it. Many mine engineers fear for their safety if they enter the underground alone. Though local labor actions have decreased, miners still believe that mine administrators are corrupt, that they ignore work rules, and that their incompetence and lack of commitment are responsible for declining coal contracts and thus for threats to miners' livelihoods.

The Decline of Labor Unity and Activism

Workers' loss of faith in their unions and the great strains in labor unity that this loss indicates are a more significant cause of their sense of alienation and endangerment than are their troubled relations with their superiors. Romania's once-powerful unions appear increasingly ineffective and uninterested in labor's actual lot. Until recently Romanian workers were the most militant and organized in all of Central and Eastern Europe (Kideckel 2001), and through the first decade of postsocialism labor actions were ubiquitous. Localized walkouts, nationwide general strikes, and threatened invasions of cities and towns, exemplified by the *mineriade* of the Jiu Valley miners, dominated the news. Furthermore, worker concerns received great attention in national politics. The National Labor Agreement (Contracte Colective de Munca), which defined broad worker rights and appropriate work conditions, was originally drawn up in 1992 and was revised in 1999 to raise minimum wage rates and expand health and unemployment coverage (Romania Government 1992, 1999a).

Nonetheless, postsocialism quickly overtook the unions, whose ability to improve labor conditions is now questionable, as is their leaders' commitment to the workers' cause (Kideckel 2001; Rodina 1994). National strikes are still occasionally called and marches threatened; in December 2005 all Romania's public school teachers, from prekindergarten through university level, went on strike, as did Bucharest transit workers, and mineral miners from northern Romania threatened to march. But these strikes were met with

great derision and a sense that labor's national demands are removed from the actual conditions of daily life. Some even say that
unions fight not for labor so much as for the privileges and renown
of union leaders, while a mine engineer in the Jiu Valley percep-
tively suggested that "labor unions in Romania don't strike for better pay, but for better legislation." And in this the unions have had
some success; Romania's new labor law, no. 53/2003, became effective on March 1, 2003. According to a business-friendly legal digest,
the law stipulates that

> Every element of the Labor Law applies to every employer in Romania no
> matter how many employees it has. The Law requires that every employer
> enter into individual written labor agreements with every employee for an
> unlimited duration of employment . . . [Exceptions are] only permitted in
> certain specified cases, such as for persons performing seasonal activities.
> Even where there is a collective bargaining agreement, it only represents
> the general framework . . . applicable to . . . individual labor agreements
> . . . [Thus] a torrent of perplexing legal requirements . . . have added an ar-
> ray of unorthodox protections for workers. These protections are, in many
> cases, so burdensome that employers will curtail new hiring . . . the pro-
> tections will stifle productivity because workers are virtually guaranteed a
> job for life . . . In its efforts to help the worker, the Romanian government
> has . . . actually damaged the very people they sought to help. Less people
> will be hired, less jobs will be created, less business opportunities will co-
> alesce, and fewer investments will be made. (Rubin Meyer Doru and Tran-
> dafir 2003, 2–5)

Indeed, if experience is any guide, this explicitly prolabor legislation
will remain largely ineffective. Workers will be dismissed for causes
that may or may not be legitimate, and the law will be evaded in
other ways as well. Hearings on illegal dismissals will take so many
years and cost so much to resolve that workers will not press their
claims. And, if worse comes to worst, black market hiring will render the law irrelevant.

Unions remain responsible for ensuring that labor laws are enforced on local populations, but recent years have seen the disappearance of local activism. Until the late 1990s local walkouts and
strikes were common, especially in the Jiu Valley, though somewhat less so in Făgăraş. However, they have declined significantly of
late. Făgăraş emigration has dampened labor's spirit and intensified
competition between those remaining, who increasingly believe
that walkouts get them nowhere. Meanwhile Jiu Valley miners are
a fearful, frustrated lot in the wake of the contract buy-outs, mine

closings, military and police action against miners during the last *mineriada,* the arrest and imprisonment of miners' union president Miron Cozma, and the rise of a compromised, uninterested union leadership. Miners increasingly feel distanced from their unions and from their leaders (Kideckel 2000a). An Aninoasa mechanic expressed this disaffection:

> There hasn't been a union meeting [to deal with a substantive issue] since 1990. We are only called when they have elections. We were called to a meeting once in 1996. They gave us food to eat and also drinks. They called us in order so that we could vote for Cozma for senator. The Liga is especially at fault. They should be more attentive to the miners' needs. As far as the Liga leaders are concerned, I only have black feelings about them. They just want to fill their own pockets. To buy villas and have foreign cars. Our leaders just have a lot of desires. They are people who serve much as Ceauşescu did, that is, for life. Constantin Iliescu is our union president. He is a friend of Cozma. He was my colleague, just like me. But now he's at least three times as rich as I am. If we try to change this, it will have no effect. If anything, I even put my job at risk by doing so.

The decline of sentiments of belonging is especially seen in the sharp decline in community-wide walkouts, in which workers in one plant struck in support of striking colleagues in another. In Făgăraş, for example, three strikes by UPRUC workers in the mid-1990s supporting more rapid privatization were virtually ignored by their Nitramonia counterparts. The lack of labor unity in Făgăraş derives in part from the different ownership structures of the two major factories, Nitramonia and UPRUC. Nitramonia, though suffering from a misguided attempt at privatization (Şelaru 2004), is still state-owned and its union leaders, though mouthing support for privatization, sought and received state subsidies for the plant and the union. On the other hand, as UPRUC was rapidly privatizing (a process it completed in summer 2004), union leaders there tried to intensify that process by pressuring administrators to consider more offers. Thus, the formerly close relationship between labor leaders at Nitramonia and UPRUC is now quite tense. At a public meeting of the Făgăraş Council of Union Leaders, the two groups made mildly derogatory remarks about each other, though they phrased them humorously. The leader of the main UPRUC union accused his Nitramonia counterparts of kowtowing to the Nitramonia administration, and implied that they personally benefited from the factory's failure to privatize. Nitramonia leaders, meanwhile, accused the UPRUC union leader of erratic, dangerous, and buffoon-like behavior in his attempt to goad administrators into more rapid privatization.

Disunity has spread to the shop floor as well. The main Nitramonia union was split by personal rivalry between more and less militant union leaders; a group of employees in the special explosives section of the plant defected and affiliated themselves with the League of Jiu Valley Miners. Similarly, interunion rivalry at UPRUC has compounded worker disunity, already spurred by the troubled process of privatization, which had developed into a running battle between management and the head of the main labor union, and by nepotism in the factory directorate. One UPRUC forge worker described the problems in factory political relations:

> People are no longer united the way they really were, like for example Cozma's miners' union.[1] We were a united syndicate, but these mafia types [i.e., the new union leaders] stole that from us. If our syndicate were as united as the miners', or the railway workers' union . . . then we could organize a proper strike with everyone participating and really achieve something. But at our factory, where we only received a 10 percent increase in our salary during the last negotiation [compared to an inflation rate over 50 percent], well, people didn't do anything about that . . . we are too disunited. There are two unions in our factory, but the other one is soon to disappear.[2] In our syndicate, Unification, we have about five hundred or six hundred people, but the other one has only about one hundred. The rest of the people in the factory are not union members.[3] After 1989 they created that other union, Independence. They were mafia types. Anything the director said, that union would approve it. That's the way it was.

To his credit, the UPRUC union leader encouraged organizational democracy and activism[4] during the factory's troubled privatization. However, his support for union militancy has strained workers' already difficult relationship with factory management. And maintaining member activism is a Sisyphean task, given increased migration out of the region, workers' fears that political action will harm their sector's chance of privatization, and the general torpor and apathy that comes with the diverse problems of postsocialism. A union shop steward and twenty-five-year UPRUC employee described his co-workers' waning enthusiasm for political engagement:

> People are basically fed up [with the union] and don't come to meetings any longer. People are divided. Not all are as badly off as others. There are some that make a living from other sources, from relatives outside the fac-

tory. Many have children who have left for other countries. And it's sufficient for them to get sent a hundred dollars a month . . . Others have left
the union because they think the dues are too high. Why should they give
this money when nothing is done with it?

A Viromet chemical operator linked declining labor solidarity, social differentiation, poor health, and stress in a particularly heart-
felt way:

> There have really been no strikes at Viromet. Once we went on a "Japa-
> nese strike," where you wave papers [*banderole pe mînă*], but basically peo-
> ple here are very subdued. A more militant strike wouldn't really do any-
> thing for us . . . what will it change? Still, I support the miners' actions in
> January. Their biggest mistake was not going on to Bucharest. They should
> have also called on other workers . . . to participate. We were ready to go
> too. Cozma should have gone all the way. Our conditions in Făgăraş are
> at the same level as the Jiu Valley, and Cozma was fighting for us all. But
> now workplace relations are changing, since bad times create bad people.
> At the plant we are no longer as united as before. Some people are lucky
> and some are not, and those who are really don't care much about oth-
> ers after they get their luck. Luck is different from "opportunity" (*şansa
> vieţii*). You [get opportunity] through your work, but luck is different. It
> just happens. I also believe in luck, but our family's luck has been pretty
> limited. With all our problems, the lack of things and constant worry cause
> ill health. Part of the problem today is that you are always thinking about
> what you can do, about what you need to do to survive. You are chewed
> up by it [*eşti macinata*]!

Solidarity is also waning among Jiu Valley miners, despite the
near-universal belief in miner solidarity among other workers, aca-
demics, and the general public. In fact, miner disunity is striking,
considering that massed miners are the archetype of postsocialist labor action. But its reasons are clear. First, miners fear losing
their jobs in the wake of mine closings and contract buy-outs and
so restrict their militancy. Miners' widely different responses to the
last two *mineriade* also created considerable bitterness among them.
Many say they were against the last marches and were forced to
participate. Some say the last march was only for Cozma's benefit
and helped neither the miners nor the Valley economy. Others declare they would walk through fire for Cozma. Even so, Cozma is
gone and unlikely to ever return to a position of prominence (Shafir
2001), and the miners' union (Liga) has no respected leaders to take
his place.

Miner fragmentation is especially noticeable during the now-

Figure 4.1. Union meeting at the Lupeni Mine.
Photograph by the author.

rare walkouts. Until recently, when miners from one mine walked out, others through the Valley followed as a matter of course. But as a Lonea miner explained the situation today,

> Us guys at Lonea are more united than at the other mines. In 1994 we led a strike [over working conditions], but when we walked out the guys at Petrila kept working. So when they struck a few years after, we continued to work, too. They asked us why we weren't helping them and we told them, "Where were you when we were striking?" But the real problem is that the union doesn't provide any unity for miners. They are just for themselves.

The relationship between the miners and their union has deteriorated steadily in postsocialism, and with Cozma's arrest has come completely undone. Miners criticize current union leaders as corrupt and uninterested in their problems. Alienated from the union, many are willfully uninformed about Liga affairs, except that they complain about the union's extraction of biweekly dues. Some miners are even uncertain who their leaders are, but maintain that they are corrupt nonetheless. Such views were obvious at a meeting (*apel*) of the Lupeni branch of the Liga, organized by the branch president, Costel Postolache, who was also Cozma's successor as president of the entire Liga. The *apel* was held in the assembly hall where miners receive work orders from brigade leaders before their shifts, and scheduled during the changeover between shifts one (6 A.M. to noon) and two (noon to 6 P.M.). Miners who attended either had just left the mine and were tired, or were on the way in and in no mood to linger. Most were in clean work clothes, so were clearly on shift two. Since there were no miners in street clothes, representatives of shifts three and four weren't in attendance.

Before the *apel*, Postolache told me that such meetings, at which he and the miners discussed important issues, were held regularly, and that miners were quite involved in union affairs. Clearly, this was not the case. Miners I questioned could not recall the last *apel*, and this one had been called only to formally approve changing the dates of a temporary mine closure over the summer, decided in advance by the union leaders. No other issues were discussed. Furthermore, the miners paid virtually no attention to him. Postolache couldn't have looked more different from the miners in his lime-green suit and matching tie as he climbed a stairway and, towering over the miners, called the meeting to order. He spoke so quietly, and there was so much background noise, that he was hard to hear. The miners talked throughout his presentation, and there was no discussion of the changed dates. In a scene reminiscent of Communist Party meetings, all the miners assented in unison when Postolache called the question.

In contrast to this purported discussion, a buzz went up when Postolache informed the miners that my colleagues and I were present, doing research on miner health. He asked them to sit for interviews and respond to questionnaires, but almost immediately miners began to crowd around us to complain about the union, their health, and their inadequate medical treatment. Some mentioned that health insurance costs are deducted from their pay, but then they have to pay again when they actually visit a doctor. Some talked of the poor treatment they receive at the mine clinic. One joked that if you come in with a cut finger, they will amputate your hand. Still others spoke of high health care costs and claimed that medicine at the mine clinic is more expensive than in the hospital. One miner said that the union "talks a lot but does very little," and another that "the only one who helped was Cozma. All of us were with him, but the country cut off our head, so fighting is no use any more."

These responses clearly index the miners' integration of the physical and the political in the context of their felt alienation from union and society. The unity of the physical and political is particularly shown in opinions of Miron Cozma, their arrested leader. Whether or not they supported him in the last two *mineriade* of early 1999, miners still believe he was committed to protecting their physical integrity. Cozma began his career as a subengineer at the Petrila Mine. During and after the revolution he gained and maintained power as much by paternalism and attention to the personal and physical needs of individual miners as by bluster and threat. For example, during his tenure the union provided cash to help out if there was illness in a miner's family. Miners claim that during his tenure they could all afford subsidized annual vacations to Black Sea resorts or health spas. Cozma organized strikes to force the Ministry of Health to make beds available at state sanatoria for lung treatments for Jiu Valley miners. Cozma and the Liga organized picnics in Jiu Valley upland areas and even trips to other parts of the country. Miners claim that these restored body, spirit, and community and that their lack today indicates that current leaders are unconcerned for miners' health and well being.

Though many miners understood the extent of union corruption under Cozma, they still looked the other way. They believed that, using his bluster and connections, he could keep the mines open. They were also satisfied with their pay, increased as it was by union-negotiated add-ons for hard work, night work, dangerous work, and even for being faithful to the union. To many, Cozma could do no wrong. He was "the Morning Star of the Coalfields" (*Luceăfarul Cărbunului*), whom they would follow anywhere. Others, however, were alienated when the union forced many to march to protect Cozma in the last *mineriadă*, in Stoeneşti in early 1999. It was this split in opinion, exacerbated by the police attack on the miners and Cozma's arrest and imprisonment, that opened even larger rifts between miners, which persist to this day.

The decline in miners' solidarity has paralleled the decline in their support for the Liga, itself fueled by the corruption of current union leaders and their relative wealth. A Lupeni miner said,

> You can see how well off they are when you look into the union courtyard. Each of these guys probably have two Cielos[5] and maybe five Dacias.

> While us guys are working and filthy in the underground, the leaders walk around in beautiful suits. The dues we pay go directly into their pockets. Their salaries are at least three times ours. What do these people do with this money? . . . well, when they get into accidents with their cars, they just turn around and buy another.[6]

Events at the 1999 Miners' Day ceremonies at the Lupeni Mine highlighted miners' disrespect for Liga leaders and their alienation from national politics. During the ceremonies each local union leader, mine directors, and some visiting politicians, including then-former president Ion Iliescu, laid wreaths at a shrine in the mine courtyard. The only union leader the miners applauded was Romeo Beja, president of the Paroşeni Mine union and Cozma's disciple.[7] They also cheered for representatives of Corneliu Vadim Tudor's right-wing Greater Romania Party. Delegates from the centrist Alliance for Romania and the Democratic Party, both of which supported industrial restructuring, were met with stony silence. Iliescu, who later gave a pandering speech,[8] was the only national leader present. When I asked some spectators why other politicians didn't show up, two women whose husbands had recently lost their jobs said in unison that "the others know they would be beaten if they came to the Valley."

Workers and Miners in National Politics: The *Mineriade*

Workers' antagonism toward national politics and politicians is thus palpable and linked to the sorry state of mining and industry in both Făgăraş and the Jiu Valley. Their unions may be uninterested and local factory and mine administrators corrupt and incompetent, but workers ultimately consider the failure of their production institutions national in scope. Because of this, they feel even less able to improve their lives; their frustrations are magnified, and their apathy broadened and deepened. Worker and miner engagement with national politics has been in free-fall since the end of socialism, and today the alienation is mutual and complete. In testimony to their frustration and apathy, many people of both regions ignored voting in the last presidential elections. However, those who did mainly supported the extremist Vadim Tudor, despite the miners' long relationship with Ion Iliescu and the Făgăraş workers' conservative, center-right orientation.

Of all developments since the end of socialism, the six *mineriade* of the Jiu Valley miners especially weakened workers' and miners' position in Romanian society, and clouded their self-perceptions in the process. The violence of the marches has had ramifications long after the marches themselves, and they failed to influence Romanian politics or to stem the loss of jobs and the decline in incomes. When Jiu Valley miners and even Făgăraş workers speak of their declining fortunes, the *mineriade* are invariably mentioned. Furthermore, the change in their political fortunes has also reinforced changes in their consciousness. The marches have had indelible effects on workers' bodily self-perceptions and have contributed in an outsized way to their sense of threat and physical distress.

The immediate causes of the marches varied, as did the nature and extent of their violence (Gledhill 2005; Vasi 2004). In the first four marches, in January, February, and June 1990 and September 1991, the miners were called to Bucharest by Ion Iliescu in veiled radio and telephone messages to "defend the revolution." Each of these marches ended in violence, which, the miners say, was provoked by security police in their midst. The June 1990 and September 1991 marches were the most violent. In the former the miners attacked and dispersed an encampment of protestors who had occupied University Square, in the center of Bucharest, for about two months (Abraham 1990; Beck 1991). They also attacked opposition politicians and students. In September they massed in Victory Square and invaded the government buildings there to bring down Prime Minister Petre Roman.

Miners also claim they were manipulated in the last two marches, in January and February 1999. In January they spontaneously marched for economic justice after the buy-outs. In February they marched again, angered by what they felt was government duplicity in the January negotiations between the government of Prime Minister Radu Vasile and the Liga over the future of the mining industry (Dinescu 1999; Croitoru 1999), and to protest the arrest and incarceration of union president Miron Cozma. Many miners say the government engineered the violence of the Costeşti march by allowing it to proceed, knowing it would be viciously repressed, in order to convince the World Bank that it was serious about transforming, or even eliminating, the mining sector.

Notwithstanding received wisdom, the marches had disastrous effects on worker unity. Some analysts see the *mineriade* as examples of miner collectivity, if not homogeneity, and as clear examples of miner agency (Vasi 2004). At first glance, such analyses seem reasonable, given the miners' group spirit, similar dress, and pack-like actions. However, closer examination shows that miners had very different motivations and levels of participation, and were significantly divided over the worth of the marches. Many participated with great spirit and with definite goals in mind: political in the first four marches and economic in the last two. Some enthusiastically committed violent acts to support leaders or ideologies. However, others participated only half-heartedly, and only at the request of local union leaders or to honor commitments to colleagues. Some miners, having never seen Bucharest, went to enlarge their own knowledge of their world. Many refused to go at all.

Thus, on closer examination, the illusion of purposive self-interest in the marches disappears. All the marches except the penultimate one (which was in response to mine closures) served the interests of other individuals and groups and ultimately restricted miners' options, reputations, and capabilities. The miners were used as actors in dramas created and orchestrated by others. Consequently, if there was any agency in the marches, it was a counterfeit one. Additionally, the marches impaired miners' ability to conceive and act on alternatives, whether through protest or self-improvement. Jonathan Spencer (2000, 121) points out that past violence constrains future actions, and the violence of the *mineriade* certainly did so for Jiu Valley miners.

First, the *mineriade* changed the way the miners (and workers) perceive and were perceived and treated by the Romanian state and much of its people. An increasingly critical media demonized and essentialized them as a violent, unthinking mass. Miners criticize television in particular for distorting the motivation and nature of the 1999 *mineriade*. They feel that television alone was responsible for other Romanians fearing the miners' actions and dismissing their protests as self-serving. A Lonea wagon tender echoed the common view when speaking of the January 1999 protest:

> We feel that 60 percent of Romanians are for us, including all other workers, but the problem was that the press turned people against us. *Adevărul*[9] is like a foreign newspaper. The press was in our midst at Costeşti. They know the truth, but when the stories come out on TV it is completely different. Why should we even bother to pay our TV taxes?

In response to what the miners considered their demonization, they distanced themselves from society—as they were simultaneously distanced from it—and were thus left with fewer options and greater suspicion of other social groups. The violence also encouraged discrimination against Valley residents by Romanian governments and both foreign and domestic investors, which also meant that fewer options were available for residents.

Second, the violence of the *mineriade* also spurred the breakdown of miners' social relationships and their relationships with mine officials. Thus, the waning ability of miners to call on each other in time of labor or community conflict further restricted life possibilities. Many strongly criticize those who participated in the violent marches of 1990–91, though many no doubt have a selective memory of their own roles in them. Another Lonea miner said,

> Real miners did not go on these marches. Only the worst people went. Not all who wear a helmet and mine tunic and enter the mine are miners. Of every ten, only one is a real miner. A real miner not only has qualifications as a miner, but also has other training; he takes responsibility for his workmates.

Still another Lonea miner echoed his sentiment:

> I wasn't at any of the Bucharest marches . . . Those who went were chaff. Miners are on a scale. First there are real miners [*mineri mineri*], those who work hard at the coalface, then there are drunks and other flunkies who don't work. In every mine you'll find a drunk, a manipulator, a convict, people who make scandals.

Meanwhile, those who participated in the 1999 marches in Costeşti and Stoeneşti blame their failure on the refusal of other miners to join their ranks. Many refused even though colleagues called them traitors and union representatives threatened to eliminate their union benefits. That auxiliaries avoided participating, while coalface miners turned out in large numbers, also deepened the developing distance between these two groups.

Good relations between mine technical staff and administrators (TESA) and miners are critical if safety and production in the underground are to be maintained and miners' needs for such things as work clothing, leaves of absence, and work verification are to be met, and these relations also suffered as a result of the violence. In the Costeşti *mineriadă* of January 1999, the marching miners chanted "Down with TESA." Commenting on this, a Paroşeni engineer said Cozma and the union purposely fomented the violence and are thus to blame for the problems between miners and TESA personnel:

In the last *mineriadă* Cozma made the greatest mistake possible: he destroyed the system of relationships between TESA and the miners. He
made the miners feel like slaves, and he diminished TESA as knaves and
scoundrels. And this is a man who never worked in the mine . . . he was
just a subengineer.

Third, at the individual level, miners look back on the *mineriade*
with a wide variety of sentiments. However, to whatever extent they
see the *mineriade* as legitimate, their discourses about them evoke
their feelings of distance, frustration, betrayal, and anger, and their
belief in the futility and meaninglessness of political engagement.
Some miners are unrepentant about their involvement and would
march again if called on. One former Petrila miner said,

> We marched on Bucharest because we believed, as the whole country be-
> lieved, that Iliescu got rid of Ceaușescu. So we considered those attacking
> Iliescu as bad. Coposu[10] was an outsider. He lived in Paris. There were
> rumors that he was trying to get rid of Iliescu. We miners said, "How is it
> possible they are trying to get rid of the guy who got rid of Ceaușescu?"
> Eighty-three percent of the population of Romania wanted Iliescu in the
> election, and this was the same as the proportion of miners who voted for
> him.

In contrast to this unrepentant miner, others see their involvement
as a mistake and blame themselves for the problematic direction
in which Romania has developed over the last years. As a Vulcan
miner told Alin Rus,

> I am sorry I participated in the mineriade . . . if at the revolution we won
> certain rights, the *mineriadă* of June 1990 was a leap backward to the old
> system. After the Revolution the security police and informers began to
> disappear and that was good. But after the *mineriadă* they appeared again.
> Now I understand that those who opposed Iliescu were enlightened. (Alin
> Rus, personal communication)

The *mineriade* were also the signal experience for integration of
the physical and the political, first in positive, but ultimately in negative ways. By the end of the marches miners' experiences had come
to shape a habitus of subordination and distance. The early marches
emphasized collectivity in dress, action, and stance. When the first
marches entered Bucharest the miners were dressed in work garb,
complete with helmets and tools. There was a cocksureness in their
gait, because they considered themselves principled heroes fighting for a higher cause. Thus comments about the early marches
offered images of almost ritualistic communitas: the train ride to

Bucharest, collegiality in the capital, the exhilaration of thousands massed in common uniform, even the bonds of violence. A former Petrila miner and union leader linked miners' unity and purpose with their physical qualities and emotional lives:

> Sure, the miners were called to Bucharest then [January 1990]. The "informal telephone" was absolutely working. I was coming from the country, from Christmas celebrations. When I got to the Petroşani train station I saw my buddies in their work clothes. There was a happy and excited atmosphere. Then a call went out that said that the young Romanian democratic revolution was in danger, so more people started to arrive. As people heard on TV about others leaving for Bucharest, they felt they had to go. When people left, they were dressed as miners. Those who came from the city got their outfits at the mine dressing area. We believed we were defending the government. We left with good thoughts [*gînd bun*], not to beat up anyone. I participated in all the early marches and they were all like circuses . . . lots of chanting, fooling around. A lot of us went to have a good time. Some guys went to see the capital, where they had never been. In the march against Roman [September 1991], somebody made sure we had lots of food and drink. It was like a wedding. People chanted, "Hurrah, hurrah, we're going to Bucharest."

Appearance mattered because it distinguished miners from others and set a collective miner identity against non-miners: "us" versus "them." When they attacked protestors in University Square in June 1990, miners say, their appearance set them apart from the objects of their wrath: "intellectuals," students, and the "hooligans, ruffians, and street people." The miners singled out those with blue jeans, beards (though miners are themselves frequently unshaven), and eyeglasses to rough up (Abraham 1990; Beck 1991). Later, when the violence was investigated, they denied responsibility and said that security forces masquerading as miners were to blame. A Lonea miner said about the September 1991 march,

> We miners weren't really the ones at fault. We were pushed from behind. They put security police in with us. Those guys in blue jeans, fighting, were not miners. We were all in our work clothes.

Whatever the truth of these events, their results are obvious. By the last two marches, after years of mine closures, unemployment, rising costs of living, and post-buy-out decline, the miners were politically neutered, marginalized, and fearful for their jobs and futures. They registered these conditions and feelings physically. The 1999 marches were a last-ditch effort to defend their threatened lives, to force the government to keep its promises, and to protest the imprisonment of Miron Cozma. In the first marches the miners dealt out the violence, but in 1999 they were its recipients; blockaded, beaten, and gassed by police (Anon. 1999b; Gheorghe and Huminic 1999). Betrayal and physical abuse were the dominant themes they expressed in interviews about the 1999 marches. Speaking of the January march in Costeşti, a Lupeni Mine team leader and union activist emphasized that the miners marched only after the government has betrayed them:

> We had no alternative but to go to Costeşti. We struck for three weeks in January over the threat to close the mines. We wanted to negotiate, but no one came except for [one senator], who headed an unofficial Senate commission with no power to do anything. We knew what happened with the lies of the contract buy-outs and we thought that would happen to us too. We only planned to rally, and not to march. Cozma asked permission to hold the rally in Petroşani but was denied. After that we lost patience and people began to shout, "To Bucharest, to Bucharest." Then the government made things worse when we were gassed on the way to Tîrgu Jiu . . . As far as Stoeneşti [the February march] is concerned, we didn't go just for Cozma, but because the Costeşti principles weren't applied. Cozia[11] meant a lot to us. We had an agreement and we believed in that agreement.

Thus, the miners of the new millennium are not those of 1977 or even 1989–90. Costeşti and Stoeneşti were the final blows that rendered Jiu Valley miners politically irrelevant in Romanian society and incapable of effective action in and for their own lives. But the significance of the *mineriade* extends beyond the Jiu Valley; the marches mark the transition of Romania's workers from movement to immobility, unity to division, and optimism and forward thinking to doubt and uncertainty. These changed outlooks manifest broadly: in stress and struggle within the family and household, in frustrated gender relations, in declining physical and emotional health and well-being, and in a reduced belief in life's possibilities. The *mineriade* were thus a death knell for workers' power in postsocialist Romania and ended public interest in meeting their needs and supporting their projects. If politics passes through the stomach, the *mineriade* produced the acid that sparked the ulcer in postsocialist Romania's collective body.

Labor, Hunger, and Politics

Workers see their disenfranchisement and loss of respect and options manifested especially in their declining life circumstances;

problematic diet and health, deteriorating housing and clothing, declines in their physical capacity to work. As so many of their concerns are filtered through the body, their attempts at redress also often take corporal form. In one of the last walkouts in Făgăraş, for example, organized to protest the lateness of pay at Nitramonia, workers were given a loaf of bread each day, to symbolize the factory's theft of bread from their mouths (Popescu 2005). Similarly, workers (and others) have used hunger strikes to express postsocialist angst and anger at ill-treatment by the state and its agents. Hunger strikes spread throughout Romania soon after the fall of socialism, staged by those with claims against particular agencies: pensions or passports denied, wrongs at the hands of economic institutions, justice denied in courts of law. In the late 1990s the hunger strike was transformed into a tool through which unemployed workers often demanded jobs.

Hunger strikes were especially prominent in the Jiu Valley after the mine closures and contract buy-outs. The most notable of the dozen or so Valley strikes was in Lupeni in autumn 1999, when over three hundred protestors encamped around the monument to the 1929 strikers. Another occurred in Vulcan in spring and summer 2000, again over unemployment and promised jobs that never appeared. These strikes all had a common structure, combining both the militancy of workers' anger and the torpor of their resignation. Strikes were begun by one or two individuals who, out of their own frustration or quest for recognition, organized their neighbors. The strikers then gathered in places where they could shout their claims to pedestrians and passing motorists. Some strikers adopted extreme tactics. They carried bottles of gasoline and waved them at passers-by, threatening to immolate themselves. Others sat silent and lethargic near their makeshift tents.

Typically, the protestors are first ignored. However, if the protest grows, media coverage becomes more extensive and local authorities ultimately step in. Investigations are then organized and some jobs offered, after which the protests tend to dissipate, even though most people's needs have not been addressed. Meanwhile, many local citizens deride the strikers, especially for the bad publicity they create. Some Lupeni and Vulcan residents claimed that strikers wouldn't accept work even if it were offered, because it wasn't luxurious or well paid. Others claimed that many protestors were not former workers, but lazy people who never worked (read Roma), who hoped to profit from the grievances of the genuinely jobless.

Figure 4.2. Hunger strike in Lupeni, September 1999.
Photograph by the author.

These claims were probably somewhat accurate. However, no matter the ethnicity or motivation of the strikers, workers' embodiment of their fears for their physical health and well-being in postsocialism were clearly evident in the strikers' discourse. During the Lupeni strike, for example, the strikers said that when they took ill they were denied treatment in the local hospital or, if they were treated, test results were fabricated by doctors for political reasons. One man who identified himself as a former miner said,

> The hospital is controlled by adherents of the UDMR [Democratic Union of Magyar Romanians][12] and of the PNŢ [National Peasant Party], so they lie about our blood tests to show we are healthy and not in need of medical intervention. Tests of our glucose levels are changed from "too low" to "just right," because orders come from above telling doctors to rig the tests or lose their own positions. No doctors have even come from the hospital to see us or give us medical tests. One of the reasons that the Jiu Valley is so discriminated against is that it had the lowest percentage of votes for those in power. Now it is the Valley of Tears, a second Auschwitz. Look at this monument [the one honoring the Lupeni strikers of 1929]. It shows how the Peasant Party and the right generally treat us people in the Jiu Valley. They shot our parents and killed them and now they kill us just the same, but do it slowly, through the economy. We have enough coal

in Valley mines to last fifty years, but Emil [Constantinescu] brags to the World Bank, the IMF, and other foreigners that come to the country that his greatest accomplishment is the closing of all the mines in the Valley.

The atomizing, alienating quality of postsocialist workers' experiences, and their perceptions that they are bereft of social supports, are expressed in their claims that virtually all other groups in society, including government, their former unions and union leaders, businesspeople, and others, somehow conspire against them:

All our problems and politics pass through the stomach. We have no clothes to wear, and the only decent set of clothes we keep in our houses is for weddings and funerals. We don't have jobs, because they are given to others. Look at the retired people. They [pensioners] live well because they have both a pension and a job, though we have nothing to nourish us.[13]

Thus the strikers are often backward-looking, longing for the security of socialism in place of the depredations of capitalism. Both of these are typically defined in physical terms: as physical continuity and access to food. One unemployed truck driver, linking Ceauşescu, the current government, and perceptions of famine and death, said,

Ceauşescu brought people closer to God. We miss him. Then we had bread, fatback [*slănină*], meat. Now the word "hope" doesn't even exist anymore. We will shame the Romanian government by crossing the border illegally. The only thing I want is for representatives of the foreign press to be there, so they can interview us about the horrible place Romania is, and then we will show them and embarrass Constantinescu. We believed him when he came here and said that we should economize with our household budgets, but what good did that do us? Look at Constantinescu and you can see what has happened in the country. Before he came into office he was thin, but his face is fat now and shows how he eats from our suffering. If we had enough money we would take him to court and charge him with genocide.

In their anger and frustration, workers often make unrealistic demands. Though the Lupeni strikers mainly demanded well-paying, permanent jobs, they said that these would not be found in Romania, since no one cares and all are corrupt. Thus, they said, they would work anywhere to feed themselves and their children. They would be happy "even to go to Bosnia, Albania, Kosovo, Russia, Bulgaria, Israel, or Iraq so that we might work."[14] A number of the

Lupeni strikers even demanded I provide them telephone numbers for the UN Commission on Human Rights, Amnesty International, or other organizations to whom they could protest their treatment by the Romanian government. They were certain the world needed to know of their problems, but the government prevented that too.

Workers in National and Local Politics

The disappearing worker is as much image, then, as it is reality. Both Jiu Valley miners and Făgăraş chemical workers believe their only political role today is to be manipulated, used, and then betrayed by Romania's politicians. The miners, in particular, bear special enmity for Ion Iliescu, who they say treated them this way, but from whom they thought they deserved special consideration. It was they, after all, who responded to his call to "defend the Revolution" in June 1990 when they marched on Bucharest against intellectuals, opposition politicians, and University Square protestors. They marched again at his behest in September 1991 to bring down the government of Prime Minister Petre Roman, then locked in a power struggle with Iliescu. Throughout the 2000 campaign in which he ran against sitting president Emil Constantinescu, Iliescu often gave unqualified support to miners and the mining industry. However, when he reassumed the presidency, that rhetoric flagged. Though no mines closed, rumors persisted, restructuring continued, and jobs were eliminated. Iliescu and Prime Minister Adrian Nastase, both of the Social Democratic Party (PSD), were constrained by Romania's desire to join NATO and the European Union. But the miners believed that he had used them for his own devices, and they therefore supported Vadim Tudor. In the words of an unemployed miner from the Dâlja Mine:

> The future of the Valley depends on who becomes president. Before, I would have voted for Iliescu, but he's done nothing except talk. The best president for this period of crisis in Romania is Corneliu Vadim Tudor. He'd hang those who deserve it. This is an extreme solution, but it is a solution.

Workers feel themselves powerless and meaningless in local as well as national politics. This is especially true in the Jiu Valley, where the *mineriade* opened great political and cultural distance between mining families and other residents, many of whom criticize the miners so broadly that their attitude can be considered a type of Moldavian "Orientalism" (Said 1975). Given their alienation from and suspicion of other groups, miners rarely participate in Valley civil society, whose NGO sector has grown apace in recent years. In 2003 there were over 165 organizations working to promote economic development, sport, religion, and self-help groups for the unemployed, for pensioners, and for abused women, among others (World Bank 2004). Many of these met only sporadically, if at all, and miners were typically suspicious of these organizations and their leaders. For example, they see the proliferation of organizations for the unemployed as designed less to help them than to provide more people with positions of leadership and control. Some young people from mining families join sport groups. Miners' wives occasionally seek advice from women's groups, but many miners consider this an erosion of their own domestic authority and prevent it.

Făgăraş workers see national politics much as their Jiu Valley confederates do, though workers are seen with somewhat more equanimity in the Făgăraş region. Făgăraş workers and citizens have historically been politically conservative. Before socialism they supported right-of-center National Peasant and Liberal parties, and in the 1996 election they voted mainly for the Democratic Convention and Emil Constantinescu. However, declines in their fortunes prompted changes in their electoral behavior. Like Jiu Valley miners, Făgăraş workers blamed national political leaders for their deteriorating economy and supported Vadim Tudor in the 2000 election. But despite this, and though they express strong support for the miners' marches, they largely assume that voting and marching are futile. Though frustrated like the miners, Făgăraş workers evince little anger and adopt a long-suffering pose. When they do grouse, often about the declining quality of local services, especially health care, their complaints also suggest alienation and an us-versus-them attitude that distances them from local authorities instead of linking them in a way that could help resolve problems.

Like the miners, workers do not participate in the sizable regional NGO sector, both secular and religious, including women's groups, pensioner societies, and cultural foundations. Făgăraş civil society is a product of past local activism and locals' self-image as the heirs of an Austro-Hungarian civic culture and as independent resisters of communism (Ogoreanu 1995). The Făgăraş NGO sector is thus much more integrated into local life and history than its Jiu Valley counterpart, which has been only recently implanted by groups seeking to ameliorate miner unemployment and social problems. Despite this difference, workers, like the Jiu Valley miners, do not participate much in civic activities, and Făgăraş NGO leaders bemoan their inability to reach much of the population. As one civic leader said, workers are "too concerned about where their next meal will come from, or plans to migrate to Italy, to support our work."

Thus, the political alienation of the once-proud Romanian worker is now nearly complete. Workers believe that they have neither national nor local support and can count on none but themselves, and their own capabilities are also on the wane. In this way workers' political stances and perceptions, though not unrealistic, contribute to their own embodied distance from Romanian society and fears for their own and their families' futures. Politics passes not only through their stomachs, but through their souls as well.

During socialism nearly all civic institutions were run by the Party, and worker politics were largely a prop for Party legitimacy and control. Today there are few barriers to political and civic participation, and there is a veritable marketplace of organizations through which to express one's identity and improve one's prospects. However, workers lack both the conditions and perceptions that would let them take advantage of such opportunities. Many have sufficient time to be involved, but believe instead that politicians and governments alone must solve social problems. Meanwhile, the "sufficient time" of the unemployed is dissipated in worry and the struggle to make ends meet. Most workers believe they lack money and other resources to engage their world. Certainly organizational dues are minimal, but actual participation is costly, depending as it does on people's trust, affinity with leaders, and above all expectations of results. And in these workers are sadly lacking. Though these lacks are due largely to their work experience and political conditions, their social and domestic lives reinforce their sense that they are struggling in a world out of balance, wandering disembodied and fearful through the fog of postsocialism.

5   Houses of Stone or of Straw?

Postsocialist Worker Communities

> *Casă de piatră!* [May you have a house of stone!]
> **—Romanian salutation to engaged or newly married couples**

> Whatever else households do, they reproduce the labor power that firms deploy.
> **—Charles Tilly, *Durable Inequality***

Domestic Changes and Postsocialism

Withering workplaces, distanced politics, heightened differentiation, and the decline of the economic, social, and biological oversight of the "zadruga-state" (Verdery 1996, 64) particularly stress worker domestic lives. In the same way that workers are disentangled from state and factory collectives and set on their own path of individuation, postsocialist households are increasingly evaluated according to the extent of their differentiation from others, both in consumption and in the achievements of their younger members. However, evaluations on both these grounds may be positive or negative. Households may succeed in accumulating and consuming goods, and their youth may achieve great things; but they may also be unable to participate in the marketplace of products and services, and their children may fail. Challenged to launch their children or enter the market, postsocialist worker households struggle to develop short-term coping strategies (Dobrescu, Rughiniş, and Zamfir 2000; Stănculescu and Berevoescu 2002). However, these new ways of getting by match neither present expectations nor past (i.e., socialist) achievements, contributing to workers' embodied stress.

Family structures and relationships typically have helped workers get by. However, in this time of large-scale and uncertain economic and social change and the changing possibilities of postsocialist labor, worker families are often ill equipped to cope. Even if they do, they often perceive lack, made more obvious by the contrast between their circumstances and the splash of the postsocialist marketplace, the lavishness of the business and political classes, and the better chances others' children seem to have. To confront the market for both positions and possessions, some families constantly adjust their strategy. They adjust work schedules, diets, and jobs to garner necessary resources or opportunities, but this leaves less time for other responsibilities. Other families encourage younger members to emigrate, so that they can earn foreign income, relieve pressure on those remaining, and achieve something in the only way open to them. Others scavenge, forage, barter, or scratch out a bit of a garden wherever they can, such as on the grounds of the vandalized "Dallas" housing complex[1] in the Jiu Valley town of Vulcan. Some few even succeed, though their social ties are often lost in the process.[2] Many, unable to cope, turn external pressures inward in waves of recrimination, anger, and abuse. As Barbara West's worker informants in Szeged, Hungary, trenchantly suggested, "the family is ruined" (West 2002, 41).

Next to uncertain employment, Romanian workers and miners both say that their struggle to maintain minimum living standards (*strict necesar*) is the greatest source of stress in their lives. The effort required to get by as consumers or members of families in the postsocialist context reinforces workers' perception that their engagement with society is troubled and that they are weak (and growing weaker) and under physical threat. People feel forced to act as they do to avoid the worst effects of postsocialism. Furthermore, many strategies people adopt amount to little: brooms trying to sweep back the postsocialist deluge. All the planning and strategizing takes precious time, energy, mental effort, and money, and affects the mental and physical health and well being of worker families. But whatever the response, large or small, structural or emotional, the transformations in relationships that were once stable and predictable, and in the contexts of these transformations, both feed and are fed by the uncertainty of postsocialism, and they intensify the stresses that lay workers low.

Figure 5.1. Emigration billboard, Petroşani. Photograph by the author.

The Changing Meaning and Shape of the Domestic

Workers first perceive the threat of postsocialism in the workplace, but next it appears in their homes and families, on their dinner tables, and in gatherings with friends. Food and housing are key symbols in Romanian culture, and the home is the face families turn toward the world. The quality of one's physical home, diet, and domestic life generally is thus conflated with the health of the family and household. However, the difficulty of securing food and housing in postsocialism makes them loaded and problematic signifiers. Thus, much as postsocialist labor shifts its emphasis from collective production to individualized consumption and achievement, so too the individual's chief source of identity and valorization shifts from workplace to home. In postsocialist Estonia, for example, domestic consumption of increasing amounts and varieties of Western goods is thought to indicate a return to normalcy (Rausing 2002), while houses are decorated in a faux-Swedish style to attract resources from external donors (Rausing 2004). Thus, in postsocialism, as new styles, values, objects, and careers fill up workers' frames of reference, the gulf between their expectations and the reality faced by their families, friends, and communities grows larger and more troubling.

As many have noted, during socialism there was a fairly clear boundary between public and private spaces, thoughts, and relationships (Milosz 1953; Verdery 1996). The shortages and monotonousness of consumer goods meant that people's homes offered a spare haven, but a haven nonetheless, from the demands of state surveillance and workers' forced political performances. In the socialist Jiu Valley and Făgăraş, workers in the same workplace were often assigned apartments in the same hardscrabble housing complex. Though the apartments were small and had few amenities, their similarity to one another promoted a sense of equality and common identity among their occupants. In the developing postsocialist market economy, however, the home offers no such haven. Paradoxically, the boundary between public and private has been removed, and the home has now become an extension of the public sphere in many ways. Frances Pine (2002), for example, speaks of a "retreat to the household" among Polish postsocialist workers.

Similarly, in Romania, unemployment forces many people to stay home for lengthy, often interminable, periods of time rather than in the regular, repetitive cycle of factory or mine work. Falling living standards, pursuit of resources, emigration, and the like require loved ones to be often away from home, and when they are home, they are often too preoccupied or exhausted to be emotionally present for their families. The outside world also intrudes into worker homes through the hours now spent in front of the television, which bring new kinds of individuals and products, at least virtually, into the home. Television programming and advertisements glorify consumption and achievement that are beyond most people's reach, and people begin to compare themselves with these depictions, finding their homes inadequately furnished, themselves inadequate providers, and their children inadequate successors. People who had earlier expressed pride in their homes and offspring now see them as falling short of expectations and consider this shortfall a clear indicator of their overall decline. In particular, the increased cleanliness made possible by Western products indexes membership in the new social order (Drazin 2002, 104), and workers see their difficulty achieving and maintaining such cleanliness as a clear indication of their failings in postsocialism.

The postsocialist home is also an indicator of the ultimate form of individuation: corruption. In Romania people's wealth is judged by the speed with which they can build a proper home, whether in village, city, or vacation area. People take note of those who build lavish homes in just a few months and speculate about the sources of their money and materials. In the Jiu Valley people often comment on the many chalets, large and small, that appeared almost overnight on Pârâng Mountain, outside Petroşani, and Straja Mountain, overlooking Lupeni. Similar comments are made about the lavish villas that have been built in Făgăraş villages, like Dejani, close to the Carpathians. People imply these new homes are funded by diverted state subsidies to local government or to the mining or chemical industry, or by miners' and workers' union dues. That administrators and union bosses use miner labor to construct their homes is common knowledge in the Valley. Miners feel they must accede to these demands or risk losing their jobs. Nonetheless, in doing so they are left feeling disadvantaged in the postsocialist wealth grab, and alienated to boot.

Despite postsocialist change, Jiu Valley miners and Făgăraş workers and their families treat public and private spaces much as they did in the past. For all its disintegrative effects, postsocialism has yet to erode the Făgăraşeni penchant for order and cleanliness, even in public spaces. Most worker apartments in Făgăraş and Oraşul Victoria were spotless when we visited them, as were public areas outside homes and apartments. These were regularly swept and washed, and neighbors often placed plants on stairs and landings in apartment blocks. There were even occasional acts of collectivity. In autumn 1999, when the Park housing complex in Făgăraş faced both a water shortage and a lack of hot water, residents mobilized their neighborhood association, protested to city authorities, and even talked about sharing water, though they never actually did so.

Most miners' apartments I visited were as clean and well kept as in Făgăraş, although the families living in them were sometimes larger. Even two-room apartments housing seven or eight were fairly orderly. Miners' homes were also often well provisioned with brightly colored faux-Persian carpets, a large display case (*super de sufragerie*) for a collection of porcelain figurines, a color television, a washing machine, and small electrical appliances. However, unlike the interiors of homes, the public areas in and around the apartment complexes were poorly maintained. In some neighborhoods, like Lupeni's ill-named "Rose" and "Tudor Vladimirescu" in Petrila, graffiti covered the walls. Windows and doors were often broken and shards of glass hung menacingly in their frames. Yards were strewn with garbage and stairwells smelled of urine. The most notorious Valley districts were Petroşani's "Airport" and the "Dallas" neighborhood in Vulcan. "Airport" apartments are mainly occupied by Moldavians, who arrived after 1977. When I told Petroşani friends that I was going to interview there, many were dismayed. "Dallas" was similarly demonized. An engineer at the Paroşeni Mine said only the most degraded people (*cei mai scăzuţi*)), people who had arrived after 1977, lived there.

Postsocialism also forces large changes in the use of the home as a site for creating, maintaining, and celebrating wider networks of social relations. In fact, the economic crunch has meant that postsocialist workers' participation in ritual and other celebrations has declined precipitously both in amount and in intensity (Creed 2002). Networks are further atrophied because people repair their own homes, rather than hiring others to do so, which had formerly allowed them the joy of a gathering centered on a domestic project. People even claim they are reluctant to visit or invite others to their homes, because offering hospitality is a real hardship for many. Some people are also ashamed of their housing and its amenities. One UPRUC worker kept a broken television and cassette player in his living room so that others would think he "owned some things in the world."

Given the importance of domestic space in forging and maintaining social relations, workers often cite the decline in the quality of their housing as further evidence that the state cares little for them. In contrast, during socialism, despite the public-private boundary, the workplace and the domestic group were interdependent and mutually supportive. Socialist farms and factories often used family labor: a collective farm might sign an entire family to a contract, and factories often hired family members and put them to work together (Kideckel 1993). Workers' apartments were subsidized and heated by socialist enterprises, which also contributed labor and materials for their maintenance. Today, these codependencies are also on the wane. Workers believe that their housing is deteriorating because the large state enterprises have not kept their end of this bargain. As these enterprises become financially hard pressed and withdraw support or limit the services they provide, workers perceive their workplaces as threats not only to their physical lives while at work but also to the quality of their domestic lives.

The situation in the Jiu Valley is instructive. Most miners live in aging housing, none of which is in good repair. The worst of the lot are "worker colonies" (*colonie*), built at the time the mines were opened, many as early as the 1870s and 1880s. The *colonie* were built next to rail lines so the trains could unload coal and other supplies for residents. When new, the *colonie* were socially effective, multiethnic neighborhoods where residents watched out for each other's children and developed common associations for their daily lives. Today, most are ramshackle, cramped, and ill heated, with poor lighting and brackish water (when it runs at all); many residents are members of marginal populations (read Roma) and the crime rate is high. Visits to the Vulcan settlement in summer 2002 showed the extent of decline. On the surface the *colonie* was lively. Music blared from "boom boxes," and knots of people stood chatting on nearly every street. But beneath this surface were myriad human problems. One day I witnessed a brawl involving a dozen people caused by one resident's dog biting another's child. I visited a home in which three people, including a baby of eighteen months, lived in an eight-by-eight-foot room, without heat or electricity. In another home an unemployed widow with twelve children bared her breast to show me her untreated infection. Throughout the area people lie on sidewalks while family members pick lice from their hair. According to Bela Nagy, an unemployed miner and president of the *colonie*'s Association of the Unemployed, suicide has become common because of peoples' inability to provide for their families.

In autumn 1999 the lack of heat and hot water in large housing complexes in both regions was a major source of tension. Făgăraş apartments, including those in the "Park" neighborhood (the first large complex built under socialism) and the "Pig Market" (Tîrgul Porciilor) area (formerly the site of periodic animal fairs), were without heat as the weather turned colder through October and into November. The problem was that the Nitramonia plant, which provided heat to virtually all the city's large apartment blocks, was operating on a reduced schedule as it couldn't pay its bill to ROMETAN, the state methane monopoly. Families with small children, especially those in corner apartments with greater exposure to the outdoors, particularly suffered. Făgăraş workers were organizing for a general strike when the heat finally was turned on in mid-November.

Similar heating problems in the Jiu Valley were due to the restricted operation of the Paroşeni central heating plant (*termocentral*), complicated by the structure of the local heating network.

Here, in the midst of Romania's major coal-producing region, the problem seemed to be a lack of coal.[3] When the Valley's first apartment complexes were built in 1953, they were heated by coal-burning furnaces in each building. The Paroşeni plant was built in 1970 to heat newer Valley apartment complexes. As the Ceauşescu regime economized on coal in the late 1970s, many of the older apartment buildings were connected to the main heating network. As a result the system was overloaded, leaving all the buildings on the distribution chain with insufficient heat. But since miners received electricity subsidies from their housing associations in exchange for their monthly allotments of coal, Jiu Valley families used space heaters to take the edge off. Făgăraşeni merely froze.

Lack of clean hot water was another concern in both regions, and an especially serious problem with great political significance in the Jiu Valley. Miner flats typically had no hot water at all, and the cold ran only a few hours per day. The lack of hot water in Valley radiators meant that pipes were at risk of bursting, with high attendant costs for cleanup and repair. Furthermore, what did come out of the pipes was dirty, brackish, and heavily mineralized. Every miner family kept the bathtub filled with water to force-flush toilets and for other household needs. The sediment in the tubs showed the problematic water quality. One Aninoasa miner family had running water only from 3 to 7 P.M., but when it rained the town authorities cut off the water entirely, as it was so easily contaminated. The man blamed his son's illness and a local hepatitis outbreak on the water. Since the early 1990s, the family has had to get drinking water from a spring in a nearby village.

As well as being of poor quality, water was expensive, and miners saw its cost as a metaphor for their political disenfranchisement. Though everyone in the Valley complains about water costs, different groups have different explanations. The non-mining population sees the problem as due to poor technology and bad planning. However, miners suggest that the cost of water is set purposefully high because state authorities discriminate against people in the Jiu Valley because of the miners, and setting high water costs is part of the state's plans to force them from the Valley. A mine union steward in Lupeni paired the cost of water with state responses to miners' political activism:

> The cost of water in the Jiu Valley is the highest in the country. We pay 6,000 lei per cubic meter while the rest of the country pays 2,700. With-

out a doubt, since the mineriade, the Valley is discriminated against. How can a liter of [tap] water be more expensive than a liter of mineral water? Those that rob us are protected with lawyers and with friends in high places so there is nothing we can do.

A retiree from the Dâlja Mine spoke of water quality in the context of class differentiation. He was particularly bothered and angered by a conflict with his downhill neighbor, who had sued him because of sewage run-off. His complaints clearly linked social differentiation, failing housing, and failing bodies:

> During socialism we had water filters from England at Petrila and throughout the Valley. Now there are none because those in high places have stolen everything. Look at all the resort homes [*cabane*] on Părâng Mountain. Through honest work you can never earn enough to build a *cabană*. Look at my house. My roof is covered in cardboard. If I didn't have six million lei from the buy-out, my daughter couldn't have had her kidney operation. Look at these shoes [he removed them from a nearby closet]. They are cardboard too. They're supposed to be for my funeral,[4] but they are the only shoes I can even afford now.

Water problems are also often seen as gendered. Both Valley men and women often blame the poorer health of local women on lack of hot water. They said that menstruating women, in particular, needed to be clean and the only way to ensure that was with hot water. Another Dâlja miner said,

> Women in the Jiu Valley are as sick as we men because they have to wash their bodies with cold water. I can get warm in the mine, but my wife has no such possibility in our house.

The relationship of water, politics, and gender was also evident at protests on Miners' Day, August 6, 1999, commemorating the seventieth anniversary of the Lupeni strike, held at the "Lupeni 1929" memorial. People milled about waiting for Ion Iliescu, the then-former president (who would soon run in, and win, the 2000 presidential election). One young man had a large notebook filled with names of people who, he said, had unfairly lost their jobs in the last round of buy-outs. He was in the midst of a group of older women, all of whom pointed at the book and shouted for me to record their remarks. The women yelled about their husbands' loss of jobs, peoples' illnesses, poor living conditions, the cost of water, and the lack of hot water. I asked if they could complain to someone with power to help them. The young man responded,

> When we complain, they [the center-right Democratic Convention] say, "Hey, who did you vote for?" and "Why don't you ask them for hot water?" The [Democratic Convention] are the ones that you have to ask for jobs, too. I don't know how often these people eat each day, but we seem to eat only once a month.

Housing and Sociability

Neighborly sociability had been the saving grace of worker housing in both the Jiu Valley and Făgăraş. However, this is also threatened in postsocialism. During socialism, buildings and housing complexes were apportioned to particular mines or factories, so one's co-workers were frequently one's neighbors. In Făgăraş, for example, UPRUC workers moving into the city from local villages had the right to rent (and after socialism, to purchase) apartments in the "New Field" (Cîmpului Nou) complex. Today, privatization and unemployment have shaken up the housing market and hence the status and relationships of neighbors. Some workers sold their apartments to others. Some emigrated, leaving apartments vacant. Some brought in relatives to live with them because of the need to economize. Whatever the cause, trust and sociability between neighbors has been eroded, and there are fewer people on whom one can rely for assistance if needed.

In the Jiu Valley town of Petrila, the two buildings of the Sadoveanu[5] complex housed workers from the Petrila and Lonea mines. Built in the 1950s, but looking much older, these buildings sit surrounded by broken glass in the middle of a gravel lot. Earlier they housed *nefamilişti,* unmarried miners, but their apartments were now assigned to any in need of housing. Both were being renovated when we visited, and there was dust everywhere. Windows were broken, and the hallways were so dark I had to light a match to see the apartment numbers. Still, the grim living conditions were in some ways compensated for by the relationships among neighbors.

A Lonea wagon-tender (*vagonetar*) lived there with his wife and two sons in two rooms that faced each other across a dark hallway. The wagon-tender, a large barrel-chested man, slept in one room with his teenage son while his wife and eight-year-old boy stayed in the other. They were hoping to exchange apartments with the *nefamilist* whose room adjoined the *vagonetar*'s. If they could get his apartment, they might be able to get permission to knock out the wall and create a two-room space for the entire family. They were excited about the possibility. As in so many other marriages in postsocialism, living conditions contributed to great physical distance between spouses (though they had never thought to put the boys together and share a room themselves). The *vagonetar* thought having work colleagues close by was a benefit of living in mine housing. He and his wife were friendly with a childless couple with whom he worked. Though unrelated, the couples called each other *cuscrii* (in-laws) and during our interview each often answered questions posed to the other. Both said that having work colleagues as neighbors kept each family informed about what happened at the mines.

But notwithstanding the experience of these miners, buy-outs and privatization have wreaked havoc on collegiality in worker housing complexes. The buy-outs built walls between the employed and others. Many families tried to sell their apartments and return to their home regions, but apartment prices plummeted in the rush to sell. Meanwhile, bought-out miners who stayed in the Valley, or returned when unable to take root elsewhere, no longer had the wherewithal or desire to participate in neighborly exchange, which increased the distance between neighbors. Similarly, in Făgăraş, some neighbors who worked together at UPRUC stopped speaking as a result of tensions between the two factory unions and over privatization. One couple, both formerly employed at the UPRUC factory and now with part-time black market jobs, elaborately planned their schedules to make sure one was home when the children returned from school. They didn't trust their neighbors and they said children get in trouble if left alone too long.

As people emigrate and as households scramble to survive, which sometimes means distancing themselves from neighbors (who are sometimes even work colleagues), wider social and ritual relations atrophy. Gerald Creed (2002, 57), in fact, suggests that this decline has in turn led to a lack of anthropological concern about postsocialist ritual. Diminished participation in and increased material poverty of postsocialist ritual especially contrast with the extraordinary elaboration of ritual practice in late socialism (Kligman 1988; Kideckel 1993). Ritual is a particularly trenchant form of consumption, and in late socialism it was a form of household resistance to the state even as it illustrated and increased celebrants' social and symbolic capital. It still does so today; the weddings, baptisms, and funerals of notable persons are ornate and the subject of endless commentary and media attention, just like those of celebrities in the West. The decline of ritual in workers' lives thus provides further evidence of their restricted consumption options and loss of social capital in postsocialism.

The retrenchment of ritual is obvious in many contexts, from visiting practices to changing rites of passage. Informally visiting colleagues in their homes was an especially important way to maintain social relations. During socialism's heyday people offered guests food and drink as soon as they entered a home and continuously throughout a visit. In Făgăraş small shot glasses were filled and refilled to overflowing with local fruit brandy, which was complemented by cinnamon nut bread or other pastries. Though miners' hospitality was not as lavish, visits to workmates, who were also neighbors, still strengthened work group solidarity. Now postsocialist hospitality parallels that of the last years of socialism, when rationing contributed to the fraying of social relations. Though people are compelled to maintain social relationships, they have little money or desire to do so. One UPRUC worker had just returned from a village cemetery some twenty kilometers from his apartment, where he had gone on the Day of the Dead (Ziua Morţilor) with his wife and brother-in-law to tend his father-in-law's grave. Having just spent a large sum for gas, clothing, and flowers, he said,

> We had friends until just a few years ago, but now we mainly stay in our house alone. People can't afford to have friends nowadays. We can't afford vacations either. Before, we went to the Black Sea all the time, but we haven't since 1990. The last wedding we attended was five months ago and we had to save three months for the gift. Last year we were godparents (*naş*) for my wife's cousin, which cost us seven million lei. To be asked to be *naş* is a double-edged sword. If you refuse, it is shameful, and if you don't, you set yourself back monetarily. We were the third family the couple asked and we are hardly even related to them.

An Aninoasa miner also spoke of conflicts over ritual expenses:

> We are invited to a wedding next week by the godparents (*naşi*) and probably won't go, as the gift will cost seven to eight hundred thousand lei, and it will take us many months and loans from CAR[6] to make it up. It is shameful to not go and we have been afraid to tell our *naş* because of what he may say. It is shameful to not go to a wedding because it is God's will that we marry only once in life. So, even if we don't go, we will still give a gift of 100,000 to 200,000 lei. It is particularly hard to attend weddings now [i.e., in autumn], since we must put away food for winter.

Funerals, though, are one ritual that retains its significance among the miners and workers of the Jiu Valley and Făgăraş zones, especially those of workmates. Given the overwhelming concerns about death and cultural continuity that postsocialism produces, the concern for funerary practice is understandable. Furthermore, by helping colleagues pay funeral costs, workers and miners defy the economic and political constraints on their consumption and express what remains of their solidarity and collegiality. Miners' coffins are typically carried to the cemetery on flatbed trucks, led by flag bearers and the local funerary brass band (*fanfara*), and followed by a cortege of family, co-workers, neighbors, and others. Funerals for miners killed in mine accidents are especially elaborate. The coffins of highly respected individuals, like a forty-one-year-old Lupeni Mine foreman killed in a cave-in in autumn 1999, may be carried on the shoulders of colleagues rather than placed in the truck. Miners who die of natural causes or after retirement are unlikely to have large funeral corteges. The funerals of fourteen miners killed in a fire and explosion at the Vulcan Mine on Miner's Day (August 6) in 2001 were especially emotional. Their deaths were particularly traumatic as they occurred on what should have been a holiday; the miners were forced to work by the National Coal Company administration (Kideckel and Rus 2003). Their deaths produced an outpouring of emotion in the region, and some miners even became physically ill after attending their funerals.

Among Făgăraş workers funerals differ little from what they were in socialism. However, when people speak of such ceremonies, they often reinforce their fears about regional continuity by noting that fewer people attend funerals, since so many have emigrated from the region. They also speak of sharing the labor and expense of colleagues' funerals and the importance of maintaining traditional elements of funerals, no matter their cost. These comments indicate workers' preoccupation with consumption in postsocialism, which in turn signals their distancing from the practices that define postsocialist identities. One UPRUC worker was especially eloquent about his and his colleagues' concerns when he linked high mortality in postsocialism with both the importance and the difficulty of maintaining funeral rituals, including consumption, and his and his colleagues' collective efforts to do so:

> People at work are dying all the time . . . About twenty of my colleagues died in the last four to five years . . . When one of our colleagues dies we help in various ways. We dig the grave, we collect money according to what we can afford, but no one says anything if you can't give much, because we all have difficulty. A funeral costs a great deal. You usually invite about two hundred people for a meal of soup, beer, and a second course at a restaurant. There are also expenses for the wake. The cost of a funeral these days is about seven million lei. Though this is very expensive, you shouldn't change the traditions. If you do, people will laugh at you. It is better to bear the financial costs than to have people talk behind your back.

Food: Full Bellies and Hungry Souls

The changing availability and meaning of food and drink also contribute to postsocialist distancing and frustration. Food is not merely
nutrition to Romanians, but signifies happiness and the quality of
both physical and social life. Difficulty obtaining food thus implies
unhappiness and a deteriorating quality of life. The Lonea wagon-
tender contrasted food-getting today with what it was in happier
times:

> For a healthy diet we should eat meat at least twice a week, but now we
> are lucky if we eat meat twice a month, and that is usually chicken. Still,
> we are luckier than most, since my parents live in the countryside and
> we get food by going and helping them. That is where we now take our
> vacations, though before we used to go to the Black Sea every year with
> colleagues and their families.

Romanian culture places a very high value on eating well, and
people strive to do so. Consequently, with some exceptions, most
Romanians, including the miners and workers we studied, eat relatively well and are not malnourished.[7] Still, postsocialist provision-
ing requires more thought and planning than before, and diets have
also changed for the worse. Food is much more expensive (Popescu
1999; Ştefan 1997, 1999).

The difficulty of obtaining food, the appearance of new foods,
and rising standards of consumption skew perceptions of diet and
produce a hunger more of spirit than of body. Miners in particular
decry change in their diets, since they feel what and how much they
eat determines how well they work. They say they need to eat more
meat and more *slănină* (pork fatback), even though their health is
ultimately threatened by their high-fat diets.[8] Miners complain
about both the food at the mine cafeterias and their meals at home.
Cafeteria contracts are often corruptly awarded, and at the mine-
operated stores prices have risen and food quality fallen. In each
mine I visited, store shelves were poorly stocked with products that
were stale and old, as salespeople admitted. Miners' wives also decry both the quantity and quality of the food they can serve their
families.

We surveyed family diets in summer 2002 in both the Jiu Valley
and Făgăraş. Women were asked to keep track of or remember the
composition, source, quality, and quantity of meals served over one

week's time. Households in the Jiu Valley typically missed four to five meals per week, their diet was remarkably unvaried and heavy in starch, and nearly all their food was purchased. Făgărașeni have more varied and ample diets than miner families, since they have better access to food grown in nearby villages or in their own gardens. But Făgăraş families now also miss two to three meals per week. One Nitramonia worker said his family eats meat as often as they did during socialism: regularly at Christmas and Easter and about two to three times per week otherwise. Still, the family eats sparely. The man brings a "brown-bag" lunch to work consisting of *slănină*, a hard-boiled egg, farmers' cheese, and bread. For lunch at school his children bring just bread and butter or bread and jam, with a bit of sausage and some cookies. In the evenings the family generally eats sausage, potatoes, eggs, and sour soup (*ciorbă*). Almost everything but the cookies comes from his parents in a nearby village. He mentioned that his diet compares favorably to many co-workers, who come to work empty-handed or with only a bit of bread and jam. He will often give those fellows food at their lunch break. In Oraşul Victoria, many workers had no garden space at all. Viromet workers had to fight the county government to keep the small plots on which they grow root crops and keep pigs. The county wanted to privatize the land to sell at auction.

Whatever the objective nutritional situation of postsocialist workers, the meaning of food, like that of housing, reflects postsocialist distancing and differentiation. Images of the wealthy dining, drinking, and partying offer stark contrasts with workers' conditions, and workers use descriptions of their food to indicate the low state to which they believe they have fallen. An unemployed Lupeni miner said,

> I have to pay a debt of 7,380,000 lei or I will be thrown out of my home. One way we survive is by collecting wild food. This is the only thing that keeps us alive. When winter comes, there will be no more wild food, so we will have to steal. In the time of Ceauşescu our country could export food. Now all we have is a failed reform in a wealthy country. Look at us compared to Bulgaria. They have nothing next to us, and yet their lives are much better. Those with big stomachs have salaries of fifty to sixty million lei per month. They should try to live like we do, to not eat for three days or to raise their children like we are forced to.

Privatization, international imports, and advertising create new dietary expectations, and when these expectations are frustrated, workers are convinced that they have been singled out for sacrifices that others need not make. The importance of new foods was brought out in interviews with the Lupeni hunger strikers:

> When my five-year-old heard talk about chocolate, she asked what it was, because she had never tasted it. Another guy brought a kiwifruit home, and his kid asked how he was expected to play with that toy. He didn't even know it was fruit.

Men, Women, and Children in Postsocialism

Postsocialism also produces large-scale change in family structures, as families attempt to adapt to and cope with economic uncertainty. However, the scale of these changes varies widely across the postsocialist world (Pine 2002, 97) The greater the economic change and uncertainty, and the fewer the economic opportunities, the greater the extent to which households must adjust structurally. Thus we see such change among Jiu Valley miner households to a much greater extent than in Făgăraş, because of differences in the ways households are economically integrated in the two regions.

Jiu Valley miner households are typically nuclear families. As many miners arrived in the Valley after the 1977 strike, few families have extensive local kin networks. Workers in Făgăraş also typically reside in nuclear family households, but their mainly local origins mean that many have close relatives in nearby villages, on whom they rely for various types of assistance. Regional variations can be illustrated, even if only cursorily, in statistics. In the Jiu Valley, for example, the rate of marriage has decreased, while rates of divorce and family abandonment have greatly increased.[9] Crime, including violent crime and domestic violence, has increased.[10] Prostitution and procuring have appeared for the first time (Judecătorie Petroşani 1999). As an Aninoasa electrician said, there would even be more divorce if it were less costly:

> A divorce costs millions for the lawyer, the arbitrator, and to open the process at the court. That's why people stay together. My sister's divorce took one and a half years, and would have taken longer but managed to end just before summer. In summer nothing gets done at the courts. Also, divorce is one thing, but then you have to pay separately for assistance with dividing the assets.

In the Făgăraş area, households and families seem to be less affected by postsocialist strain. Virtually all statistical indicators here show trends opposite those of the Jiu Valley, though these statistics do not account for the vast numbers of Făgărașeni who have migrated out of the region. The number of divorces in the region barely increased in the first years after socialism's end and steadily declined in the last four years, as did the number of families abandoned by their head.[11] Meanwhile, the marriage rate has remained steady at what it was during the years immediately following the Revolution. Similarly, the frequency of violent crimes has increased only slightly.[12]

These different trends result from the intersection of different regional cultural patterns and economic possibilities, set in the context of different forms of postsocialist change. Whether households prosper, merely survive, or succumb to new postsocialist conditions depends on the extent to which people understand the necessity of change, actively engage with new sources of labor and income and the individuals who control them, and cooperate with others to plan strategies and actions. In other words, the success, bare survival, or downfall of worker and miner households depends on the extent to which they act as agents. However, households in these regions vary in their ability to deal with these challenges.

Some husbands and wives, more often in Făgăraș than in the Jiu Valley, confront postsocialism together and craft even tighter relationships. Conversely, some other couples, more often in the Jiu Valley than in Făgăraș, fail to communicate, and undermine their relationship in the process. Stories are told in the Jiu Valley of working spouses who each accepted a buy-out without telling the other, depriving their families of all their income in one fell swoop. Some husbands take on more work or even domestic responsibilities, like childcare and cleaning, to enable their wives to work outside the home. This is less common in the Jiu Valley, as it was often thought shameful for a miner's wife to get a job. When wives are forced to do so today, the necessity may contribute to household stress, conflict in and out of the home, and other social problems. Comparing the domestic division of labor and the integration of households into regional economies both in past times and today shows these processes more clearly.

Domestic Divisions of Labor in the Jiu Valley

Throughout the history of Jiu Valley mining, the roles of working men, on one hand, and stay-at-home wives and children, on the other, were rigidly separated. This division grew from the region's mono-industrial character, and was supported until recently by high miner salaries. It was strengthened by the influx of Moldavian immigrants after the 1977 strike, as they practiced the same gender role differentiation. Within most Valley households, spouses generally had little to do with each other. He worked in the mine, she in the home. He earned the money, she budgeted and spent it. Even when women worked in mine offices, cloakrooms, or laundries, at lamp and mask stations, in coal preparation facilities (*preparaţie*), or at the few other regional factories, men and women had distinct spheres of activity and sociability.

Relations between Jiu Valley spouses were thus often distanced and tense. Wife-beating and marital rape were not uncommon. Men expected absolute attention when they returned from their shift (after stopping at the bar). They were fed and left alone to eat, and often fell asleep at the table as their families tiptoed around them. Women stayed in the kitchen when a miner entertained workmates at home. Still, despite or because of the distance, men and women became dependent on each other. As a Lupeni Mine labor instructor suggested, each was incomplete without the other:

> Miners know how valuable their wives are. Some miners, of course, are lazy and stupid and don't think clearly about this. But others consider their wife the person who maintains family stability through her strong character. I respect my wife but won't lift a finger to help her. And that's the way that all miners act. It's an appreciation of one's wife, but it is not love. When I'm at work I know that my wife is taking care of the house, the children, cleaning, and so I have a sense of completeness, of serenity. That way I am able to escape my fatigue.

Women echoed these sentiments. Without his mine wages she was lost. Furthermore, though she was totally dependent on her husband, this dependency paradoxically gave her the means to develop her own life, though within limits. As Alin Rus suggests,

> There is a tendency to see [gender] relations in the Jiu Valley in this period [post-1977] as working to the complete detriment of women. However, even women's declarations indicate otherwise. For example, the wife of a miner from Moldavia told me, "We came here from Moldavia . . . from a village. It was very difficult at first . . . but you know how it is in Moldavia, in the village . . . large families, many children, our household was incredibly poor. Certainly it wasn't easy, especially with my husband in the mine, but . . . life here was better than in the country." For women coming from rural areas, urban status was a real plus. Housework . . . was

much easier than in the villages, where women worked in more unfavorable conditions . . . So the majority of women who came to the Jiu Valley saw this as real progress. The fact that they were subordinated to their husbands was not considered an impediment but accepted as their natural condition. (Rus 2002, 3)

Thus, despite large numbers of people living in small spaces, grueling work, and the combination of alienation and dependency, miners and their wives claim today that they lived well in socialism. They display furniture, appliances, and other housewares, stating that "everything we have was bought when Ceauşescu was in power." The wife of a Lupeni Mine work team leader said, "We had many things then and much to do. You could see people at the market every day. I visited often, and when I went out I would make sure to dress nice." But postsocialism changed all that.

Postsocialism first creates a contradiction: Jiu Valley women are more often expected to work in paying occupations, but such work is also seen as a threat to their husbands' waning dominance. Furthermore, the disastrous Valley economy and women's lack of education and work experience limits their employment opportunities, forcing them into poorly paid, exploitative black-market positions. They are often soon fired, or they quit because of the exploitation or because their husbands are not supportive of their work outside the home. Tensions in households where women work and men are unemployed are particularly elevated. In these situations men both judge themselves and are judged by others to be poor providers, and they believe they are less honored by their families. Women workers also suggest they are poorer housekeepers and less respected because of the decline in their families' standards.

Economic change has also influenced relations between Valley parents and children. In the past, boys from mining families followed their fathers into the mines, while girls married at a fairly young age. Today, these options have largely disappeared. Mine jobs are scarce, and health, safety, and wage issues also make them undesirable. Not a single young man with whom I spoke was enthusiastic about mining. Some were not opposed to it, but only if its many problems were resolved. As a bought-out Lonea miner said,

Many children used to want to become miners, probably because people spoke about the mines so often in their families. But now in the Jiu Valley even the mines are not an alternative for our kids. Every job you can find is paid with a miserable salary.

Lack of employment also means that children from mining families now wait longer to marry, seek more education and training, or even attempt to emigrate (though less often than Făgărașeni). Large families are also a thing of the past in the Jiu Valley, as younger miners realize they are ill able to afford them, and women in the Valley no longer gain social value by having many children. Though childlessness is considered a great sadness in Romanian families and Romanian culture generally, some younger miner couples have decided to forego children altogether. They do so, however, as much for existential reasons as for economic ones. A thirty-five-year-old Vulcan electrician said, "I cannot think of bringing a child into this world. There are no possibilities for them and it is wrong to create another just to share our misery."

Domestic Conditions in the Făgăraş Zone

The lower tension in Făgăraş domestic life relates to household labor in the area having always been flexibly assigned, so that the region's various resources could most easily be acquired. In Făgăraş, with few exceptions, men and women see themselves as partners, yoked to each other to secure an income and maintain their standard of living. Men and women also make budgetary decisions together. For example, a recently unemployed Făgăraş woman and her son told me about a lengthy family argument about spending a large sum of money they received from a relative after the 1989 Revolution. The young man and his father wanted to purchase a tractor, and the woman wanted new furniture. Though the men ultimately won out, the debate lasted for over a year. This could not happen in the Jiu Valley, where women make most daily budgetary decisions, but men have final say about "big-ticket" purchases.

The structural circumstances of Făgăraş families also differ from those of Valley folk. As in the Jiu Valley, nuclear families predominate among Făgăraş worker households. However, as many regional workers moved to the city from nearby villages or still commute to the factories from the villages, most workers have extensive kin networks throughout the region. Thus, family relations have a different tenor in Făgăraş regional life. People rely on their networks to help meet their household needs, but also feel greater social pressure to participate in family rituals and occasionally provide labor for relatives' various projects. In the economic pressures of postsocialism, people feel greater pressure to live up to their responsibilities to their social network, greater shame about their occasional inability to do so, and greater anger when others fail to live up to their responsibilities to them.

The extensive emigration of Făgărașeni also has a wide range of both positive and less salutary effects on regional domestic life. Income from work abroad is the chief means by which people in the region can maintain a degree of stability in domestic life. In particular, the stable marriage rate in the region is due precisely to such income. August has thus become the favorite month for marriages, since many young migrant workers, mostly men, come home to marry during their vacations. There were seventeen marriages in one August week in 1999. Most migrants are "guest workers" in Italy, and in the summer almost every other car in town seems to have Italian license plates. Though income from labor abroad facilitates marriage, labor migration also places great pressure on existing marriages, and people consider it responsible for most divorces. They say that migration enables both the migrant worker and the spouse left behind to indulge in adulterous behavior. An UPRUC worker said,

> Many people divorce as a result of going to Italy. Invidious people tell rumors about migrants, like how a man [in Italy] is seeing other women instead of working, or tell the man that his wife is sleeping around behind his back. This happened to my neighbor, who was gone for six months and came back to stories of his unfaithful wife. I know of two other cases of divorce related to Italy: a man with no kids, in Italy for two years, came back and saw his wife at a bar with another man. Another workmate came back unexpectedly because of a stomach ailment and found his wife with others at their home. My wife says that she would kill me if I went with other women while I was away. I also expect my wife to be faithful. If I work so hard to make a home, then my spouse has to be respectful. You don't divorce for banal reasons.

Emigration also promotes competitiveness and individuality, both in individual migrants and generally within the region. Like so many migrants, Făgărașeni in Italy depend on network relations to find employment, housing, and other resources. Different Făgăraș villages even specialize in different kinds of work; Hârseni, the village I lived in in the 1970s, was known for its *garajisti* (garage attendants). Migrants' remittances inflate prices in the region and also contribute to the competition to build lavish housing. Paradoxically, although emigration fuels competition between families, the lives of individual migrants demand extensive sacrifice. Some migrants delay getting married or having children for decades, or give these up entirely, because of their commitment to sacrifice.

Thus Făgăraş families are somewhat more stable than those of the Jiu Valley miners, owing to their greater resource base. However, those sources of stability also contribute to diverse social and emotional problems. Făgăraşeni, in fact, suffer from the same deterioration of male-female relationships that overtakes mining families. Domestic abuse, alcohol abuse, mental illness, and the frustrations of unfulfilled expectations also trouble Făgăraşeni. Unlike miners, however, they have been brought up to keep their problems private. According to Maria Eşan, director of the local Organization for the Protection and Defense of Women,

> No one knows what goes on in our homes. People in Făgăraş are very private and it is shameful to let others know our difficulties. This is part of the problem, since people won't seek treatment. But even if they do, the hospitals aren't set up to help them.[13] Women come into our offices every day, bruised and beaten by their husbands. Men drink more and they are angry and frustrated about their jobs. Many children are left to fend for themselves on the streets, and this is not just the situation with Gypsies, but in Romanian working families as well.

Though Mrs. Eşan spoke anecdotally, diverse evidence supports her claim. For example, there is some indication that poverty, as well as unemployment, has sharply increased in the region. In 1996 the local soup kitchen (*cantina de ajut social*) was serving about 150 people per day, which, according to its director, was 50 percent more than at the end of socialism. The soup kitchen's clientele has also changed. During socialism it was mainly old people without income or family support who availed themselves of its assistance. Now many younger families with children also show up for meals. The number of abandoned children is also on the increase in the region. In 1996, for example, the Făgăraş Children's Home had 112 residents, about 25 percent more than in 1989. These numbers date from the mid-1990s, but, according to informants like Mrs. Eşan, they have continued to increase, especially after the labor buy-outs began in 1999.

Despite increased poverty and its associated problems, Făgăraş regional cultural practices help families persevere in postsocialism. Whereas in the Jiu Valley the burden of childcare fell mainly on women, in Făgăraş families children have always been thought both parents' responsibility. This has averted some of the tensions that have built up in Jiu Valley households as domestic roles have changed. Joint Făgăraş parenting is clearly indicated in Vasile Şoflău's interview with a male Nitramonia worker (MN):

> vs: Should the whole family, both parents, be occupied with their children? What do you think?
>
> MN: The whole family? Of course! If you have a family with many children, well, you just have to care for them. Some people don't do this, but if you have taken the responsibility to create a family, then you have to take care of them as well. Isn't that so? You can't leave your kids or your wife on the road, can you? If you're married and you have children . . . well, that's it. You just can't go to the bar anymore, to get drunk, come home, and beat your kids. That's not correct either.
>
> vs: But aren't there people like this?
>
> MN: Sure. I've seen them on the television. There are those like this. But in all of Făgăraş I do not know of anyone like this, or better, I haven't seen such things with my own eyes.

However, the commitment that parents like him have made to their children is increasingly difficult to keep, both in Făgăraş and in the Jiu Valley, and this difficulty is a source of great frustration to parents. As a Nitramonia foreman said,

> My only hope is my daughter, and she is a good student with excellent grades at university. But where will she find work when she finishes university? There are no jobs for young people, and I don't want her to have to go to Italy to clean children's bottoms after all her years in school. Our sacrifices would be OK if they meant a future for our children, but that is also very uncertain.

Făgăraş workers understand that postsocialist conditions are the source of these difficulties. However, even more often than miners in the Jiu Valley (Friedman 2003), they see their children's limited possibilities as evidence of their own failings. Though workers may narrow their visions of their own futures, they still hope for better for their children. Thus some save penuriously to enable one or more children to emigrate. Others allow their children to remain dependent longer and provide them with small monetary stipends. Still others send younger children to live with relatives in the countryside. Whatever the strategy, children are marrying later and, married or single, remain longer in their parents' homes in both Făgăraş and the Jiu Valley.

Despite their parents' sacrifices, Făgăraş children know that

their parents' failure to successfully engage postsocialist change
has restricted their options. They are frustrated by diminished economic and educational prospects at the same time that globalized
culture and media urge them to question their parents' lives in new
and different ways. In some families, the availability of new, media-
promulgated cultural images and elements creates a sharp divide
between the generations. Such a division is common in modern,
industrial, changeful society, of course, but it is experienced and
perceived more sharply in postsocialism. Children often consider
their parents guilty of complicity with socialism. Older workers perceive their children as much more advantaged than themselves, the
"generation of sacrifice." Parents also feel unable to communicate
with, let alone control, their children. A Nitramonia worker interviewed by Bianca Botea considered young people both wiser and
less educated, more knowledgeable and less prepared, than her own
generation, better skilled but less likely to achieve something with
those skills. But her comments seem to refer as much to herself and
her own frustrations as to the nature and advantages of youth:

> I think they are wiser than we are or were. When we were their age, what
> did we know? They are much more involved with the world. They behave
> differently than we did. They dress differently . . . maybe we did the same
> when we were their age, though I still think they are much freer[14] than
> us. They borrow a great deal from the West. Television has shaped them
> to be different. For example, in the time of Ceauşescu we never heard
> of handicapped people . . . and this is only one word . . . We really didn't
> know about cigarettes, or weekly discotheques, even if they are only on
> Saturdays for just two hours. We didn't know about drinking, or going
> to someone's house and staying out until the morning. We didn't know
> about kissing at fifteen or sixteen. But look at them now, staying out the
> whole night at the discotheque or staying together all night in someone's
> home when the parents are away. We never did anything like that. They
> are not very well educated. When walking past you on the street, they are
> disrespectful.

Embodiment, Agency, and Postsocialist Households

Family life in both regions is thus as uncertain as other aspects of
life in postsocialism and reinforces workers' sense of powerlessness,
formed in labor and cemented in politics. Household transformations are especially threatening as the household was, for a long
time, the sole area that provided comfort and predictability and
was, along with work, a place to exhibit mastery over life. Now,
however, home seems out of control, and this contributes mightily

to the fear and alienation that define worker lives today. In particular, the household is the locale where people daily experience their bodies as out of their control and under threat, as a result of declines in nutrition, loss of sleep over economic worries, fraying marital, generational, and network relationships, and stress-related physical and emotional exhaustion.

Postsocialist pressures contribute to a common set of embodied perceptions even as they shape different senses of body and the physical in the two regions. Because of the separation of men's and women's roles in the Jiu Valley, postsocialism facilitates the development of a fundamental tension between miners and their wives. As men's locus of activity and control shifts from mine to home, women are increasingly encumbered by men's greater presence in spheres formerly under women's own control. Furthermore, the consumption practices by which women previously valorized themselves are severely restricted. At the same time, women are both pressured to earn income from employment and criticized for doing so. This dilemma manifests in both physical and psychological ailments.

Jiu Valley women are generally responsible for their family's public face, and thus expressed great concern that they and their children look presentable when out in public and that their homes be outfitted with the latest gadgets. These concerns meant that they held their families to high standards of consumption, and the severance packets of miners who had accepted a buy-out were often used, if at all possible, to purchase goods intended to mark the household's status: good food, clothing, and household appliances. But the possibility of such purchases is severely restricted today, leaving Valley women with declining senses of self and purpose. Most Valley women, without jobs or money, stay at home inactive and bored. Adding insult to injury, they are also publicly condemned for their inactivity, which many non-miners suggest contributes to the high incidence of adultery and alcoholism. But whether this connection is actual or imagined, the boredom and worries of Valley women are real enough and contribute to increased rates of emotional illness and physical distress.[15]

Jiu Valley women have little to do but sit and worry, or work incessantly for a pittance. For their miner husbands, however, there is no rest whatsoever, either at the mine or at home. In their labor miners feel increasingly subordinated, physically threatened, overworked, and disrespected, and these perceptions are now often recapitulated at home. Thus many miners feel that they have no escape but an early death. They show high rates of depression, alcoholism, spousal abuse, alienation from children, and suicide. In the past, miners took pride in their physical selves. Difficult working conditions were used to show how capable they were of meeting even the most rigorous physical challenges. Today, there is no less pleasant nor more contradictory a sight than a lean, muscular, sinewy miner wringing his hands while complaining of his declining health and his inability to do much about it.

Relations between men and women were always more equal in Făgăraş. However, this too has changed under the pressure of unending labor and declining resources. For both men and women, household life now means worry, regret, and uncertainty. People continually crane their necks to see the next problem that may be heading their way. Many say the world has become a bad place (*lumea rea*). Unlike miners, who persist in expecting high salaries, Făgărașeni suggest they can get by on what they earn through strict budgeting, clever use of existing resources, and the mobilization of social ties. However, they no longer have access to all the small things that made life pleasurable: vacations, gifts for the children, picnics, and lavish weddings and baptisms. The cost of everything must be scrutinized, and every expense represents something else they will have to do without. Life has become drab and sullen and, for many, a labyrinth of silent suffering. An Oraşul Victoria worker couple explained,

> Romanians are like rats. We only learn by experience. When the Revolution came we were happy and optimistic. But now, after we have learned so much about what this thing called democracy is and what it means, well, now we know what to expect from life. All we have seen is corruption and lies. If my mother were running for election, I wouldn't even vote for her, since we no longer know who we can trust. We live in our homes, we go to work, we come back to our homes, and that's that.

Thus, in both the Jiu Valley and Făgăraş regions the instability and drabness of home life are inescapable reminders of the fall from grace workers have suffered in postsocialism. Though family and household are still looked to for succor and comfort, too often they fail to provide them and only contribute to further worry about, and anger at, postsocialist conditions; people are distanced from society and fear for their families, their futures, and their own survival.

6   **Strangers in Their Own Skin**

Workers and Gender in
Postsocialism

> Ultimately gender cannot be adequately un-
> derstood except in relation to other structures
> of social asymmetry.
>
> **—Sherry Ortner, "The Problem of 'Women' as
> an Analytic Category"**

> Us women always got along with the men
> in the factory. But after Ceauşescu fell we
> started to fight to keep our jobs.
>
> **—Worker at the UPRUC-Făgăraş enameling
> section**

Postsocialist Gender Change:
Uncertainty and Predictability

Changes in labor, politics, and family life have profound effects on
workers' gender identities, practices, and possibilities. The uncertainties of postsocialism open up a variety of possibilities for both
men and women. As Susan Gal and Gail Kligman (2000a, 37) suggest, gender change is broad, sweeping, and somewhat unpredictable:

> In East Central Europe, change is simultaneously occurring in the institu-
> tions and routinizations of work, in images of masculinity, femininity, and
> marriage, as well as in narratives about life course and life strategy. The
> resulting patterns of gender relations, we suggest, are not only diverse, but
> hardly resemble the patterns in the past or present with which they are
> customarily equated.

Worker families also manifest various and changing gender possibilities, as they have diverse regional predilections and models from which to choose in the postsocialist marketplace. However, within the broad spectrum of new gendered possibilities, and despite the different experiences of postsocialist workers (including Jiu Valley miners and Făgăraş chemical workers), workers' postsocialist experience converges on a few patterns. In particular, there are erosive pressures on masculine identities and intensified, fragmentizing demands on women (Pine 2002). Together these contradictory pressures generate frustration, and even conflict, in gender and sexual perceptions and interactions. Thus gender change among postsocialist working populations only increases the confusion and stress of life and helps to produce distanced and fearful citizenry. Belonging and getting by in one's gendered skin, in other words, is as profoundly charged and challenged as belonging and getting by in labor and in society, and this challenge has equally serious consequences.

The pressured masculinity and fragmented femininity of postsocialist worker communities that I see differ from what is commonly assumed about postsocialist gender. The received wisdom is that culture, society, and politics are all masculinized, and men privileged over women. Masculinization is fostered by the private economy and grab for resources, among other phenomena. The end of socialism, with its (occasional) policies and rhetoric of gender equity, proportional representation, and subsidized life, also contributes to this, even if a gendered politics is somewhat more possible in postsocialism. Thus, Peggy Watson says,

> Democratization has "opened up a space" within which women can . . . organize . . . [but] at the same time . . . the transition to liberal capitalism offers men the opportunity of putting a greatly increased social distance between themselves and women. (1993, 71)

Gal and Kligman concur:

> Democratization comes more clearly into view if one asks how men and women are differently imagined as citizens, or how "politics" itself is being redefined as a distinctively masculine endeavor. (2000a, 3)

Meanwhile, speaking of Romania, the United Nations Development Program claimed that

> the economic, political, and social transformation that took place in Romania in the 1990s affected women and men differently. And a signifi-

cant differentiation persists in men's and women's level of participation in productive activities, income from labor, health conditions, and mode of participation in public life. (2000, 1)

Though women's circumstances in postsocialism are dismal and men's stock is generally on the rise, the conditions of men and women from worker families suggest a more nuanced picture. First, though the gendered lives of workers and worker families are, *pace* Gal and Kligman, in some way unpredictable, the norm of that unpredictability can, in fact, be ascertained. Because of the marginalization of their labor, their political alienation, and their limited access to the new consumables that valorize gender in the postsocialist environment, the gender identities and practices of worker men and women in diverse postsocialist venues (Pine 2002; Weiner 2005) also suffer.[1]

Certainly, many groups in postsocialism have experienced positive gender change. Within the political, professional, and commercial sectors of postsocialist society men's and women's horizons have broadened (Marody and Giza-Poleszczuk 2000; Nagy 1997), their quality of life has improved, and the possibilities available to their families have multiplied. Women architects, linguists, computer personnel, and social researchers, to name a few, rise through the new class order in their own right (Kovács and Váradi 2000). Other women gain power and wealth through liaisons with powerful men (Patico 2000). Some middle-class women improve their physical desirability, and hence their employability, through exercise and aerobics (Svendsen 1996, 1997). Both men and women are more likely to have meaningful work, and many middle-class women have a greater voice in both the workplace and the home and greater powers of self-determination, including the ability to leave the labor market if they choose (Harsanyi 1994; Lechanu 2003).

Unlike middle-class women with their expanded horizons, however, women in worker families are faced with new challenges arising from the general decline in their living standards, and find it increasingly hard to fulfill the responsibilities of their gender roles. Furthermore, both male and female workers question their capabilities and express confusion about changing sexual essences. Their sexuality is increasingly criticized and found faulty, both by outsiders and by workers themselves. And for both men and women, reconstructing masculine and feminine identities requires difficult negotiations within family and household in the best case, and intensified stress, anomie, and social problems in the worst. Thus, workers in large-scale state capital industries, men and women both (but mainly men), have lost gendered privileges and the possibility of acting on reliable gender truths. The erosion of their labor and wages means their positions within their families are eroded as well. Education personnel, health care workers, and service workers, also both men and women (but in this case mainly women), are increasingly marginalized. All the newly unemployed and underemployed, men and women in relatively equal numbers, fall prey to the exploitation of labor black markets. It is small consolation to a Bulgarian peasant household head (Creed 1999) or a Czech male prostitute (Bunzl 2000) that postsocialism privileges their sex.

This bruising of worker personal identities and sexual selves can be likened to what Sherry Ortner termed "gender damage" (1996, 9). Workers' postsocialist experience strips away the predictable contents and practices of their sexual identities, provides few tools for creating new practices, and leaves people with troubling insecurities about themselves and their significant others. This frustration of gender has significant consequences for the day-to-day lives of men and women as they try to make sense of other changes besetting them. Some, like the unemployed, are especially deprived of time-honored male and female roles, though new gender practices and the discreditation of workers mean that everyone, not just the unemployed, must reevaluate gender roles and relationships.

Such reevaluation is especially visible in domestic life. For the most part, working-class men and women have "traditional" views of male and female family roles, but these are now challenged at every turn. Though women's economic contributions to the family's survival are recognized, particularly in Făgăraş, the mass of postsocialist workers, men and women both, support neither gender equality nor feminist programs as they understand them. Feminism is misunderstood in Romanian society generally (Roman 2001), equated with exaggerated sexuality or forced diminishment of male breadwinners. Workers particularly consider it a threat to the appropriate order of things. Changes in postsocialist gender at the national level, such as uninhibited youthful behavior, media emphasis on female sexuality, and the ubiquity of sexualized images, are also thought symptoms of a world gone mad, and not simply a consequence of a market-oriented society.

Men's and women's perplexity about gender is readily apparent in their interpretations of their physicality. Jiu Valley miners have always been attuned to their physical selves. However, in the more threatened postsocialist work regime they are increasingly concerned about their bodies failing them and preventing them from earning a living. Valley women also see their physical qualities in decline, though mainly because they cannot obtain the clothing, make-up, and other things they consider necessary for a proper feminine appearance. These physical limitations and transformations make trying to take action to address changed life conditions still more difficult and confusing. In other words, for postsocialist workers, gender conceptions, practices, and identities also conspire to restrict agency, or at the very least to confuse people about what is possible for them in postsocialist circumstances (Nicolaescu 1994, 123).

Charged and Distanced Sexuality

Within the breadth and reach of postsocialist society, men and women have different understandings of proper gender divisions of labor, children's sexuality, and beauty and allure. However, one thing common to workers across regions and genders is their general discomfort with today's more eroticized society. Workers in both Făgăraș and the Jiu Valley think that the prevalence of sexualized imagery indicates a decline in society that is mirrored by their own poor treatment. Both groups look askance at new gender images spewing from national and regional media, and decry increases in formal and informal prostitution and the generalized increase in overt sexuality. Even though young miners line up for *porno*[2] at the kiosk on Petroşani's main street and male Făgăraș workers place cheesecake pin-ups on their workstations, miners and workers are generally disturbed by the ubiquity of sexuality and concerned about their children in the sexual onslaught.

Evidence of changing sexuality is everywhere. Prostitutes ply their trade openly along international truck routes. Prostitution is even visible in workers' own towns. Broadcast media show a plethora of sexualized programs and advertising. Pornography is available at almost any newspaper stand in Făgăraș and in Jiu Valley towns. In Petroşani, booksellers and newspaper vendors hang their explicit wares from the metal armature in front of the post office. Elderly women dressed in headscarves and heavy wool stockings sell tabloids whose covers depict full frontal female nudity.

Women working near the Făgăraș factory workstations adorned with soft-core pornographic images said they avoided looking at them. One woman likened the displays to the behavior of children.

She said that the men put them up just because they couldn't before (see Kurti 1991 on the suppression of sexuality by socialist morality), and would soon tire of them. Of course, it has been well over a decade since the first pornographic displays went up, and men said they had no plans to remove them.

Workers are first concerned about the effects of changing sexual mores on their children. One Făgăraş couple, who were struggling hard to maintain their standard of living after the man lost his factory job, abruptly stopped discussing their economic problems to express great dismay at and fear of changing sexuality. She said,

> Today's world is hard to figure out. Boys and girls begin to be sexual far too early . . . in high school, at fourteen or fifteen. Now and then I walk by the Transilvania [a local discotheque] and see girls fourteen, fifteen, who are more naked than dressed. They smoke cigarettes and hang out with hooligans and vagabonds. We really don't have anything against erotic films on TV, and I'll even watch for a while. Mostly, though, when they appear I change to cultural programming. Our daughter knows what we expect. When she sees something erotic on TV she puts her hand over her eyes.

As well as changing sexual mores, the political economic circumstances of postsocialism, and especially its economic challenges and new consumption standards, confront both Jiu Valley miners and Făgăraş workers with new meanings of male and female. In the past, men and women in the Jiu Valley miner communities were highly differentiated and had conservative understandings of masculinity and femininity (Rus 2003, 105). Men were to be strong, stoic, and detached; women servile, responsible, and nurturing. Changes in the Valley have put pressure on this hyper-masculinity and -femininity. Some unemployed miners adopt female domestic roles, while many women try to work, some for the first time. But these inversions affect perception. People fear for their physical health. They acknowledge declining interest in sexual things. Neither men nor women feel they live up to past standards. Men feel threatened at work and as providers. Symbolic emphasis on male control in society and family backfires, leading men to be frustrated by their subordination in labor and their increased difficulty in providing for their growing families in times of rationing and economic decline (Friedman 1999). This frustration dovetails with historical models of Romanian men, who have thought "of themselves as potential martyrs, as fate-wronged people, and as losers, to the effect that in certain limited situations they act as such" (Pecican 1997, 204). Meanwhile, women, as elsewhere (Magyari-Vincze 2004, 38), feel both compelled to work and distraught at doing so. Even those seeking escape from women's burdensome roles through employment are degraded by *la negru*, and all must scramble to make ends meet on declining household budgets.

In Făgăraş, the discontinuities in gender roles arising from economics are somewhat less excessive. Men and women were more integrated in household and regional economies in the past, women were more nearly equal to men (and gender equality was apparent more in deed than in word), and men and women typically saw each other as partners in caring for household and family. Still, though gender roles have changed less here than in the Jiu Valley, the demands of postsocialist labor and economizing still produce a great sense of loss and lack. Among men, this manifests in a sense of failing to live up to the expectations of others, while Făgăraş women are more stoic about their postsocialist lot. Both, however, feel that they lack time and energy and are concerned about their children's futures.

Gender Implications of Changing Consumption

Changes in postsocialist consumption especially affect gendered self-images among Jiu Valley miners, Făgăraş workers, and their families. The presentation of self and of home matter greatly to workers. Their inability to keep up with the vast stylistic changes they see among others and on television reminds them daily of their distance from and discreditation in postsocialist society, and they contrast their lives today with their lives in socialism, however rose-tinted those memories. People speak of their hard-pressed and dingy lives today, and mention in the same breath that during socialism they purchased new clothing and shoes, went to restaurants, attended weddings and baptisms, and took annual vacations to the mountains, the seacoast, or a health spa. Today's restricted consumption indexes, more than does the general drabness of life, the social disrespect and exclusion that haunt workers and make them anxious for themselves, their families, and their futures.

Analyses of changes in consumption in postsocialism rightly and typically focus on what such changes imply for changing social class and/or group identity. However, the meanings of masculinity and femininity also depend on, and are typically expressed in, material consumption. Miners, their wives, and even their children are especially conscious of appearance and document their frustrations as men and women by contrasting their deprivation today to the purchases that were possible in socialism and the self-expression these allowed. Făgărașeni have been generally less concerned about the material expression of identity. However, they too feel that declines in their lives are marked by the growing difficulty of providing extras for their children's education and especially of participating in social events and exchanges. Furthermore, Făgăraș gender-related consumption anxiety is heightened when people compare themselves with migrants returned from Italy. Local men and women both feel disadvantaged when they hold themselves up against their brothers and sisters who return to the region each year driving late-model cars and wearing the latest fashions. Moreover, the mass media typically emphasize Western gender ideals and elide Romanian ones (Nicolaescu 1997, 145).

Changing postsocialist consumption practices and limitations on people's ability to consume are enacted differently by Jiu Valley men and women, because of their differentiation as laborers and consumers. Miners are particularly conservative in their response to changing consumption standards. Fearing for their jobs and angry about declines in their wages compared to others', they disparage the new consumption standards by finding fault with changing feminine standards of beauty. In contrast, Jiu Valley women react to declines in their disposable income by desiring the new styles and practices, which they fear are passing them by. Thus, men and women differ on whether cosmetics are essential for women. Many men feel that cosmetics detract from women's natural beauty, which, according to a Lonea miner, "should come from within." Referring to ads for cosmetics and related items, a Lupeni miner told Bianca Botea,

> I don't have much good to say about them. If a woman is fine, she is fine, and that's all there is to it. You don't have to make yourself up like a Christmas tree. Only those who are not pretty have to have money to make themselves so, or to have money they get involved with other foolishness, like prostitution. Cosmetics are used a lot in that profession. But it is not the clothes that make the person, but the person determines the clothes. Well, it's another thing if a woman needs to get made up because she has to go someplace and doesn't want people to laugh at her. People would make fun of her because they would say that she is not so well prepared [*pregătit*],[3] that is, that she doesn't know how to do things.

In contrast, miners' wives thought cosmetic advertisements attractive and compelling, as suggested in an interview with a Lonea miner and his wife. Though she barely took part in the interview, when the topic turned to beauty and its significance for women in the postsocialist world, she became animated and said,

> [In order to be somebody,] a woman must absolutely be pretty and must dress and present herself nicely. If she is pretty and looks good she will go farther in the world. If a woman has a bad character [*puturoasă*] she still can do things [to improve her appearance], and if she doesn't know how to, then you teach her, like the ads show. You have to arrange her in any way you can.

Unlike women, who feel their postsocialist success depends on dress and cosmetics, Jiu Valley men are still powerfully moved by older images, in their case of strong, unadorned, silent masculinity. Though these are also conjured by Westernized cinema and television, men see their ability to manifest such gendered ideals as limited by their economic conditions. In interviews, informants often paired mentions of masculine desiderata with statements that their circumstances made it difficult for them to attain those qualities. An Aninoasa mechanic described what an ideal man should look like:

> Harrison Ford. He's a real man, but I only see him on TV since that is our only cultural activity. We don't go to movies or plays, because we don't have the money and the town doesn't provide these things anymore.

A Petrila coalface miner similarly suggested that, to be attractive, a man "should be like those who appear in American films. But we don't have the ability to look or be this way."

Compared to their Jiu Valley counterparts, both men and women in Făgăraş are less impressed by style and are much more practically oriented. In fact, people generally look much more rough-hewn in Făgăraş than in the Jiu Valley. Even Făgăraş youth are less fashionable than their Jiu Valley counterparts. More people seem to wear leather jackets in Valley towns than in Făgăraş, where people of all ages are more often dressed in cloth coats, nylon jackets, and homemade sweaters. Young people wear fewer tracksuits, and far fewer men wear earrings. Nonetheless, the practicality of the Făgăraşeni is as much a function of the restricted possibilities of postsocialism as is the style-consciousness of the Jiu Valley residents. To a person, Făgăraşeni would be more stylish if they could. But the basic demands of home and family come before concerns about self-presentation. They restrict their consumption to things "absolutely necessary," as a Nitramonia woman worker told Raluca Nahorniac:

Figure 6.1. A bought-out miner and his son.
Photograph by the author.

When I buy clothes I only get what is absolutely necessary, like clothes for
winter . . . boots, mainly, for me and my daughter. I get what I can, though
I do try for a bit of style. The only reason we don't buy from second-hand
stores, like so many others, is because you never know what kind of illness
you can get from other peoples' clothing. If we need to go out, we want to
dress nice, so we will borrow something from our relatives if necessary.

Another Nitramonia woman worker echoed her:

I wear what I can. We are not pretentious, you know. We wear what we
are able. Still, we have to dress in something minimally adequate. We can't
walk around in tatters or in second-hand clothing for five years straight,
although many do. I don't buy second-hand clothes because I am against
it, because you don't know what might happen wearing such things. You
could get an illness, and I am afraid of that. We are very much worried
about our health.

Later she connected her plain style of dress to postsocialism:

I always dress the same. City clothes are also work clothes because conditions today don't allow us to have two different kinds of clothing to wear
the same day. Before 1990 we might look at someone and say, "look at

how beautifully so-and-so is dressed," or "doesn't so-and-so have nice style?" But now, when we are as we are, we are not permitted to dress so fancily. Anyway, people here don't judge you on how you dress. Everyone is pretty easygoing and nonjudgmental. What really matters today is not your physical appearance, but whether you are able to put food on the table and whether you can pay your debts.

Făgăraş practicality also influences make-up practices. Though make-up is highly desirable to women in the Jiu Valley, in Făgăraş it is almost irrelevant, as one woman worker from the UPRUC factory indicated:

> I've never used mascara or rouge in my life. If some people like that kind of stuff, well, that's OK for them, but it doesn't look good on most women. More important are money matters, family issues. Make-up doesn't make a woman more attractive. Beauty and elegance come from cleanliness. You need not constantly follow fashion, because if you do then you won't be able to bring bread into your house. It's irrelevant how one looks. The most important thing is cleanliness, cleanliness, cleanliness.

Peoples' attitudes about comportment and appearance have changed little since the end of socialism. Their sentiments, however, are now filtered through postsocialist circumstances and thus they consider it difficult both to adopt new styles and to maintain older ones. The resulting frustration does not enable resistance; rather, it is just one more nail in the coffin of worker agency and sense of belonging. Workers' frustrations imply not only that their lives are unfulfilled, but also that little can be done to improve their situations. They starkly highlight the distinction between what exists now and what they have lost since the end of socialism.

This distinction feeds directly into people's perceptions that they cannot live up to the demands of their gender role. As people's desires outstrip their grasp, they are confronted with existential questions such as "What can I be?" and "What shall become of me and mine?" The person of the postsocialist worker, the worker's actual physical state, thus ceases to have a definite corporal existence. The physical person becomes the embodiment of postsocialist uncertainty and the essence of the damaged self. This phenomenon is clear in the way workers watch television and read newspapers. When they interact with these media, all the confusion, uncertainty, and unfulfilled dreams of the postsocialist working life surface, calling into question their self-worth, their future chances, the respect society gives them, and even the essence of their gender.

Media, Gender, and the Frustrations of Democracy

Much of the damaging pressure on workers' gender identities and senses of self relates to the changing postsocialist media. Television is ubiquitous in these regions, and watching television is nearly the sole recreation in workers' cash-poor world. In almost every home we visited the television was on, and it even remained on through our discussions. The habit of keeping the TV on throughout the day, whether or not anyone was watching, began during the Romanian revolution, but it is now standard when people are not at work. However, though they watch TV slavishly, workers, miners, and their partners have decidedly ambiguous views of Romanian media.

They are suspicious and dismissive of television (and of much of the Romanian press) because of the way it depicted worker job actions, and largely blame the media for how workers are perceived in and dismissed by Romanian society. Workers also see TV as the purveyor of many new products and practices, such as housewares and new types of food, which are considered markers of modernity. However, though they desire many of these products, they also find some highly threatening. The images that the media present, television in particular, highlight people and styles that workers would emulate if they could. That they cannot, however, makes the positive images of new media a source of frustration and uncertainty, especially about their physical and sexual selves. Thus, whether desired or detested, such "media dreams" ultimately challenge worker self-images. The products, processes, identities, and relationships that TV beams into their ramshackle apartments contrast with and critique the meaning of their own lives and circumstances.

The manipulation of gender images by media outlets for political purposes has been observed in other postsocialist crisis situations, such as that in the former Yugoslavia. Jasmina Lukić (2000, 398–400) shows that the profusion of media outlets in postsocialism, itself a function of the inflation of the market, requires people to make difficult and ambiguous choices to define their identity in moments of social uncertainty. This ambiguity both reflects and deepens workers' confusion about their own selves and increases their sense of being distanced from society. As new media are harbingers of both modern style and moral dissolution, simultaneously attracting and repelling, they freeze workers' choices and ability to act. Arjun Appadurai (1996, 53–54) considers media-impelled imagination to be a chief source of agency in a globalized world. However, though Romanian workers' imaginations may be fired by watching television, the images they see constantly remind them of all the obstacles they face in trying to realize what they imagine. Every now and then imagination breaks through, as with the Făgăraş union leader who claimed he learned about "Japanese strike techniques" on television. More often, though, workers relate to TV as did the young widow at the Nitramonia dispensary, who summed up the frustrated pleasure, sadness, and unlikelihood of action in front of the postsocialist television:

> We have a television, but it's broken. It is Russian-made and has been broken for two or three months. That's too bad, because I like television. When I'm home, watching television is pretty much all that I do. I like films, televised news magazines, news reporting. I like the ads, too. They open people's eyes, but they still really are just for people with money. I really like all kinds of films, but the main ones I like are sex, adventure, and "shoot-'em-up" kinds of films. Now I mainly watch TV at my girlfriend's. She is divorced and I watch at her place. Our kids are the same age, so they play and we watch TV. But that is all we do.

Despite TV's importance in their nonworking lives, workers in both regions deeply distrust it. Both Jiu Valley miners and Făgăraş workers still argue that television created the image of violent, backward workers in its portrayals of the various *mineriade*. They claim that willful media misrepresentations of workers' lives deny them their humanity and obscure the realities of their lives. A Lonea coalface miner said,

> People don't understand how poor we are because they are manipulated by the government through the press and the mass media. TV comes here and films only when we are going in and coming out of the mine. Why don't they come into the mine and see how hard we work? They don't show us sweating in our underwear.

Although workers note the political effects of television and the press, they feel the media's influence especially in changing perceptions of gender. In a survey conducted by student teams in the Jiu Valley and Făgăraş in summer 2002, Valley women responded more positively than others to television programming with heavy sexual content and advertisements for cosmetics and other beauty products. However, Valley coalface miners were as distressed by such programming as the women were pleased with it. Valley men in other jobs, and Făgăraş men and women both, also disliked it, though less strongly than the coalface miners. (Făgăraş women were as often put out by their inability to afford the products and lifestyles they saw as they were by the rampant sexuality.) Men did not criticize the female degradation depicted by soap opera vixens and by scantily clad models and variety show hosts as much as the sexual and social improprieties that they believe threaten family stability and implicitly free women from their subordination. The Lonea wagon tender was especially pointed about this:

> TV today is really no good, since it encourages inappropriate behavior and increases appetites.[4] And if you try to buy everything that you see, you will have nothing. This is especially true for women. They should still be worried about household things like cooking and cleaning.

After he stopped, however, his wife challenged him and said, "I like elegant things and also like to look pretty, but I am not allowed to have these things." "Not allowed" had a double meaning. It referred both to the cost of such purchases and to her husband's preferences. Similarly, a Lupeni Mine emergency worker, discussing the decline of family life in the Valley, said,

> Part of the problem is television. Sexuality on TV is exaggerated, and most of the stuff on TV is bad, though a very little bit is good. You can learn a little, even though most of the stuff on TV is bad for you. Kids shouldn't learn this stuff on television. TV is where all the foolishness in families begins. Not just TV but from videocassettes, too.

A Lupeni work team leader mirrored this critique:

> Soap operas are all over the place. That's how they make their money in Latin America. But I think that these things hurt marriages. They create false impressions and all have the same theme: People get angry, they get separated, they get back together. It is very unrealistic.

All told, then, television and other media effectively alienate working people from the developing postsocialist market democracy. They feel lied about by the press and TV and distanced from or denied the new objects which define developing postsocialist consumerism. Furthermore, they are disgusted and threatened by the brazenness they confront each time they seek a bit of relaxation. They interpret the images and commodities presented by the media, as they do changing styles, through nostalgic memories of the socialist past and negative feelings about the capitalist present, which they perceive to be rigged. In socialism, though Ceauşescu dominated the airwaves, the few commodities depicted were accessible to all, and other programming offered idealized folk images and moral surety. Today, the broadcast marketplace is a riot of options and possibilities, all of which people must forego if they are to meet even their most basic needs. At the same time, morality has gone out the window (or off the screen), leaving workers with unsettled senses of the world in which they struggle.

Discourse and Distance in Jiu Valley Gender

Though both groups of workers in this study converge on similar understandings of the gendered world, Jiu Valley miners are especially affected by gender-related changes. The charged quality of miners' perceptions of gender is related to the politicization of gendered behavior in the context of *mineriade* and other demands for fair treatment in postsocialist society. Owing to the violence of the marches, the rough physical quality of their work, and their predilection for large families, miners' gender and sexuality (both masculinity and femininity) is constructed by others as animalistic, irresponsible, and violent.[5] These constructions of miners, which they and their families consider slanderous, focus on their gendered behavior and render it problematic, and they distance the miners still more from postsocialist society. In whatever context I spoke with them, they expressed the same concern: that my research be used to help others understand them. They believed, incorrectly, that if others knew how difficult their lives were, they would be treated better.

One critique of miner sexuality concentrates on Jiu Valley marital relations. Non-miners often mention the large numbers of children in mining families and allege high rates of adultery by both men and women, domestic abuse, and fights and other aggression over sexual matters, in both the mine and the home. Children from mining families, boys and girls alike, are also thought to be sexually active at an early age. This rough sexuality is blamed on a lack of self-control. People as diverse as the investigator at the Petroşani general hospital, a local Jiu Valley journalist, and a few owners of commercial establishments all repeated the Orientalist mantra that miners have large families because they often engage in unprotected sex after bouts of drinking. Even the Lupeni Mine safety instructor suggested to Bianca Botea,

> Some miners come home drunk after work, in excited states, so their wives often give in to them then. But they never use any kind of contraception.

Those women are of lower culture even than the men, and creatures of a culture [which never used contraception]. Also, if you speak with your mine buddies about this, they make fun of you. Plus, contraceptives cost a lot of money. My wife knows how expensive they are, though we use them. Many children are made during moments of drunkenness and so are born stupid or handicapped. Many miners have children in times of stress. When a man is angry, when he has troubles at work, what does he do? He makes a baby.

Though some of this rings true, miners see their sexual natures in an essentially opposite light. Instead of feeling that their sexuality is outside their control, they feel that it, and perhaps every part of their physical lives, is decimated by postsocialist forces and constraints. Consequently, miners typically claim their sex lives are practically nonexistent. They say that they come home from the mines totally exhausted and so are often impotent. Furthermore, miners are prudish in their discussion of things sexual, except for empty braggadocio in the mines (*vorba goală*). As well as having clearly separated gender roles, Jiu Valley men and women rarely talked with each other about daily life, let alone about sexual matters. For example, during an interview with a Lupeni miner and his wife, he said that he often worked naked and she responded, surprised, "I didn't know such things went on there!"

Sexuality among miners and mining families in the Valley is decidedly more nuanced than either the outsider critique or miners' denial of it suggests. Miners' gender identities and relations vary as the miner population varies, i.e., by age, education, region of origin, position in the mines, employment status, and even by the particular mine and community where people work and live. The wanton image of Jiu Valley sexuality is mainly based on caricatures of the now-older miners who emigrated from Moldavia after the 1977 strike. Moldavian men and women, people say, desire large families; they abuse alcohol and then act out sexually and physically. Non-miners half-jokingly suggest that if her husband doesn't beat her, a Moldavian woman feels rejected. In contrast, younger miners, even those of Moldavian background, often recognize the folly of large families and forswear sexual violence. Alin Rus related the views of one young miner:

Before the revolution I had a neighbor who was a miner. He had seven children and often beat them and his wife. He was a real dictator. He would even hide food from his children, saying to his wife, "I'm working underground for my country! I need good food!" The family could not challenge him. Nowadays I'm friends with the older child of this man. He is also a miner and married. He has only two children and never beats his wife. He is a good father. After work he rarely goes drinking with his buddies. He told me, "Why should I go drink? I have had more than enough of it [when I was younger]. I'd rather stay at home with my wife and children and watch TV." (Alin Rus, personal communication)

As well as age, education also influences gender attitudes, practices, perceptions, and relationships. With generally more schooling, mine auxiliaries, for example, tend to have more egalitarian relationships with members of their households than do those who dig and load coal at the coalface. Similarly, auxiliaries' wives were more often employed during the socialist years and in the first years of postsocialism than were the wives of coalface miners. An Aninoasa mechanic, speaking of ideal relationships between men and women, said that "men should treat women kindly, and a beautiful woman, to be attractive, must be intelligent, more than anything." He also said that he and many of his colleagues used contraceptives, and if they didn't, it was only because of their expense. In contrast, a Lonea coalface miner echoed his colleagues when he said,

> Contraceptives are the business of women. Maybe the guys will discuss them quietly, at a corner near where rats are scurrying, but basically if you talk about condoms, people will make fun of you.

Miners believe their image, initially formed through media coverage of the *mineriade,* was worsened by the televising of the joint French-Romanian film *Prea Tîrziu,* directed by Romanian filmmaker Lucian Pintilie, based on the novel by Razvan Popescu (1996). The movie depicts mass nudity, the now-infamous Bucharest invasions, alleged murder, and miners' docility in response to police questioning. People in the Valley were either embarrassed or angry about the film. Many miners said it depicted them like animals, as violent and easily manipulated. Some who were extras in the movie said they enjoyed seeing themselves on screen. However, most miners and their wives decried the film, which aired in the Valley to much disappointment and disbelief soon after it was produced. Men and women both, but especially the latter, said that its language was foul and uncharacteristic, that it was wrong to show the miners naked, and that the violent images of miners, in the scenes of both the murders in the mines and the Bucharest *mineriade,* were very far from the truth. The Lupeni Mine safety instructor said,

In the mine it doesn't matter who you are. If the guy who slept with your wife the night before was caught in a cave-in you'd still try to save him. If only one guy has water in a flask, all drink from it. In the mines there have never been big fights or murders. No one was ever hanged over a fiancée's betrayal. How is it possible for there to be murder in the mines? Did you see the film by Pintilie? It was very foul. He made fundamental mistakes and did not understand a thing. No one ever killed anyone else in the mine. I had an old miner's lamp from my grandfather and I gave it to Vasilescu [the actor who played the film's protagonist]. But others from the film crew stole some equipment as souvenirs. The degrading shower room scene was filmed here at Lupeni, and after the film aired, all the women were on the street talking. I even heard some say things like, "Oh my goodness, I saw your husband naked" and other terrible things.

One young woman office worker at National Coal Company headquarters was especially embarrassed and said the film was just an example of how the country views the miners and condemns the Jiu Valley in blanket fashion:

> The movie shows that people think of us as violent and backward. When I travel elsewhere in the country, I don't tell people that I'm from the Jiu Valley, but instead just that I'm from Hunedoara County.

Postsocialism thus widens the gap between how miners and their families perceive their own sexuality and how their sexuality is seen by those outside the mining industry or in other parts of the country. Miners' attitudes toward gender relations are little changed from socialist days. What has changed, however, are their expectations and levels of frustration. As mine salaries fail to keep pace with inflation and some miners lose their jobs altogether, men and women put more pressure on themselves and their partners to find solutions to their troubles and live up to the gender code that originally characterized their partnership. When their efforts largely come to naught, both are humiliated by their incapability, and in their humiliation they feel lessened as men and women. The unemployed perceive this sentiment especially strongly. A forty-seven-year-old former miner, recently bought out from his contract at the Lupeni Mine, spoke to Vasile Şoflău about his frustrations as a man and the provider for his family:

> Since I took the buy-out I've begun to drink heavily. All I do now is think about how I can take care of my child. What can I give him to eat? What can I do now, at my age, now that I no longer have a job? I drink to forget about the dishonor. Often, when my wife and I were both on welfare,

I would think about all kinds of crazy things: hanging myself, throwing myself off some building. If my wife hadn't found a job, we would be desperate.

Miners see strong links between their physical frustrations and concerns and changes in labor. The mine is and has always been an intense physical environment, often even erotic. Men are physically pushed together from the moment they enter the mine's environs. They eat close together at the *cantina*. They undress and dress together in their *vestiari*. They wait in lines together for lamps and other gear. They crush against each other as they ride in the cage (*colivie*) down to their work horizons. They huddle together in the train cars (*cărucioare*) as they travel from mine shaft to worksite. In hot galleries, miners work together naked and in constant physical contact. Their intimacy is palpable as they sit on their haunches and share their food and water. Finally, at the end of their shift they shower, smoke, and drink together. It is partially out of this daily exposure to the rawness of life and flesh that others conjure their baseness. However, to miners, the physical closeness of their working conditions suggests not animalistic sexuality but their true humanity. To them their physicality mirrors their solidarity and commitment to each other in the dangers of the underground, a solidarity and commitment threatened by the extensive changes of contemporary political economy.

Postsocialist processes contribute to miner edginess about, perhaps even outright fear of, the world. The code of the underground, which has long underpinned miners' masculinity, is still followed scrupulously. However, postsocialism plays havoc with the pace, rewards, respect, and security of labor as well as with the structures of brigades and of relationships with one's mates (*ortaci*). Most miners will not admit to fear of or in the underground and shrug off the danger. Still, many in the Valley see miners beginning to be wary. A mine engineer at the Aninoasa Mine suggested that miners are more reluctant to do certain tasks today for fear of cave-ins, a suggestion supported by the head engineer at the Lupeni Mine. Health practitioners working in Jiu Valley mine clinics also claim that miners are more afraid than previously, despite declining rates of death and injury in the mines. The doctor at the Lupeni Mine clinic suggested,

Many more people come to the clinic today with physical complaints and for treatment, since they are more stressed due to the insecurities of their jobs. Because of stress, they feel the dangers of the underground more intensely [*Te leagă pericol de subteren*]. People are much more scared about death at an early age than before. Still, there are fewer requests for medical leave because of their economic difficulties.

Similarly, the former director of the Salvamin, the institution responsible for periodically evaluating miners' health, training mine emergency intervention specialists, and providing and maintaining their equipment, suggested,

> Because of the great stress in miners' lives today there has been an enormous increase in psychologically based illnesses among them, like hypertension, ulcers, and mental illness. Many miners have even become hypochondriacs and worry about their health all the time. But when they come here with an illness, they beg me to not force them to leave their work because they can't afford the time off.

As mine labor and masculine power have long been interrelated, the uncertainty of postsocialist labor intensifies miners' concerns about their sexuality. Sex and the mine are essential yet inverted topics. As so many Valley informants repeat, "When miners are in the mines the chief topics of conversation are women and sex. But when miners are together on the surface sharing a drink after the shift, they mainly speak of the mine and of labor." Thus, the two categories of a miner's life, home and work, are distinct and contradictory, yet potentially complementary and integrated in miners' masculinity. Throughout the socialist years this complementarity was readily achieved. The secure mine job and the well-provisioned home were anchors in a miner's life, between which he traveled and within which he actualized himself by expressing his physicality: the hard, but manly, work of mine labor and the acknowledgment of his sexuality in the large family he fathered and supported. In postsocialism, however, the contradictory demands of each sphere and the impossibility of miners satisfying either now play out as physical challenge instead of satisfaction. These fears and frustrations manifest in changing sexual discourse in the mines and changing mores and practices in the home, both of which index the issue of adultery.

In the "golden period" of the Jiu Valley mining industry, i.e., from before socialism until the strike of 1977, there was an unwritten rule that miners did not speak of sex and women in the mine. The "old-timers" say that doing so diverted attention from the dangerous work at hand. With changes in mining after 1977 and especially with the new work force, sexual banter became ubiquitous and a chief way of relating in the underground. This remains true today, with bragging about sexual skills and conquests and joking about others' questionable potency or unfaithful wives being most common. Though these comments occasionally get out of hand and result in scuffles between miners, they nonetheless testify to the speakers' masculinity and ultimately contribute to male bonding (Gutmann 1997; Herzfeld 1985). Of equal significance, such discourse enables men to exert symbolic control over their dependent wives and thus helps defuse the divisive issue of adultery, itself a major symbol that demonizes miners in Romanian and Jiu Valley political discourse.

There is much debate about adultery in mining families. Again, non-miners often suggest that it is common, because of the uncontrolled, immoral character of miners. The image of randy miners and horny housewives is enabled by the nature of mine housing and labor. Apartment blocks are often occupied by men who work in the same mine, but often during different shifts. Furthermore, miners do not arrive home unexpectedly. They arrive and leave in groups, often on the same bus or worker transport (*tubă*). Once in the mine, they are there until the end of their shift. Consequently, in any apartment building at any given time there are many married women and men whose spouses are absent and who are therefore potentially sexually available. Furthermore, the masculine image of mining supports the idea that miners actualize themselves through physical acts, including both prodigious manual labor in the mine and sexual exploits while off duty. But notwithstanding this received wisdom, most miners suggest that adultery is not common among them and has even declined in recent years because of their physical distress and impotence. Miners even discredit the idea that their wives cheat on them. They say, with some accuracy, that postsocialist conditions limit the free time women have available to engage in extramarital affairs. Many are working black market jobs, while nearly all others are busy stretching declining household incomes to maintain family standards of living.

Despite the humdrum reality of miners' extramarital sexuality, adulterous relationships are possible in the mining community, and they are even more problematic here than in other worker communities because they threaten the most important relationship in a miner's life, between himself and his workmates. Consequently, to defuse this tension miners cathartically joke about adulterous possibilities.[6] However, as a Lupeni Mine work team leader said,

> The constant talk about sex among the miners is really empty speech. Miners talk but don't act. We are such braggarts because we work only among men. In the mine we are all unfaithful to our wives . . . and when we joke about each other's wives, some of the guys get very angry, but that makes us taunt them even more.

Postsocialist threats to miners' identity change the quality and meaning of banter in the mines more than does the possibility of actual adultery, especially of banter concerned with gender and the physical. Postsocialism threatens miners' sense of sexual prowess, domination, and domestic power by attacking the earning power of their labor. Instead of establishing sexual domination as it did in socialist years, sexual banter, intensified by subterranean working conditions and postsocialist stress, now threatens miners' sense of personal control and vitality. This feeling of threat is furthered by changing domestic divisions of labor and the mild subversion of the patriarchal household. That is, when a miner's wife is forced to work, or if he takes on domestic responsibilities to "make ends meet," he believes that he is not living up to the requirements of his gender, and his gnawing sense of personal failure makes the jokes in the underground less funny and more threatening.

Transformation of Gender in the Făgăraş Region

Like the Jiu Valley miners, people in Făgăraş also face the world with significantly transformed outlooks owing to changes in regional political economy. They understand that living their lives the way they would like and achieving their goals for themselves and their families is, and will be for the foreseeable future, impossible. Still, their identities as men and women, drawn from a common mold, remain much the same as during socialism. Both men and women in the region generally think of themselves as self-effacing, hard-working and industrious (*harnic şi vrednic*), and willing to sacrifice and ignore their own needs for the sake of a larger good. These attitudes were especially evident during my visit to a Victoria couple, both still employed at the Viromet plant. Their apartment was a small unit in an older complex that had clearly seen better days. Though the buildings looked dingy and ill-maintained, the inside of the apartment was a veritable greenhouse, with flourishing plants from floor to ceiling around the perimeter of the living room. The couple, in their late forties, were remarkably handsome and clearly very much in love. I had never seen such attentiveness between a husband and wife in all my time in Romania. However, the joy and pride they took in each other was clearly tempered by the times. During our interview a neighbor showed up to return some money he had borrowed. After he left the couple reflected on life's difficulties:

> SHE: Life now is so hard and joyless because of our small wages and high prices. Our neighbor really has a hard time. His wife just died, so he always comes to us for help. We can't complain, because we do much better than others, but we still can't get by. We use half of [the man's] salary just for food. We are both from Victoria so we have no village connections, and have to take care of all our needs ourselves.
> HE: We can't even raise a pig.

This couple's attitude that "we can't complain, because we do better than others" was not uncommon in the region, though such sentiments were rarely heard in the Jiu Valley. Unlike people of the Jiu Valley, Făgărașeni evince moderation in most of what they do and feel, both in their attitudes toward life and in how they act as physical, sexual beings. Sexuality is not an overwhelming concern to the region's workers, as it is to their miner counterparts. Făgăraș families are usually small, with two or three children at most, and the region underwent its demographic transition in the early twentieth century. Whereas Jiu Valley miners decry their declining salaries, which they see as insufficient to maintain their households and gender expectations, in the Făgăraș region people expect to sacrifice for their family's needs. Another Viromet couple I interviewed, who were unlike most couples in the region in having six children (in a three-room apartment), were living truly hand to mouth, on one salary. The woman had recently given up her job to care for both her sick mother, who also lived with them, and her youngest daughter, who suffers from Turner syndrome.[7] As they discussed their large family, their self-effacing, sacrificial identity was obvious, as was the great concern for social approval that characterizes regional life:

> SHE: People spread rumors all the time. If your kids show up at school looking raggedy, they say, "They had six children and aren't even capable of taking care of them." But even with six children, I was never afraid we

would die of hunger. Our children are a blessing from God and they give us pleasure as a family. Whatever we needed [to take care of them], we would find a way to get it. We would work with others in the villages.

HE: I even work the harvest in a village. I would even work for 600,000 [less than half the minimum salary at the time]. It is not much, but next to my salary it is something and helps. All my life I have asked myself how I was able to raise and take care of six kids. We haven't asked for anything from anybody, because if we did, they would laugh at us. Instead we have been able to take care of ourselves.

Făgărașeni's economic behavior has also tended to be conservative. Both men's and women's identities are directly related to economic practice; each is responsible for acquiring resources for the family and for tending them in the most efficacious ways. Even when regional workers received large severance payments in labor contract buy-outs, they often used the money to invest in a small business or to enable a child to emigrate to Italy. Their dress is moderate and their comportment measured. Transylvanians are generally considered taciturn, and they have taken that characteristic to its extreme. Their conservative style also manifests in attitudes toward sexuality and gendered behavior. For example, both men and women define themselves, first and foremost, by their membership in families, households, and social networks and not, as in the Jiu Valley, by their physical qualities and characteristics. A Făgăraș unemployed worker, when asked what it means to be a man, responded by saying,

A man has to be someone with money. He has to be a good worker. He has to be a man involved with his home and family and someone respected by others.

Similarly, an UPRUC worker and union leader responded to the question of what it means to be a man by referring to the responsibility to provide for others:

The most important thing for me is what I can do for my children. They come first and I gladly do for the kids and worry about myself afterward. For example, on salary days I often go out and buy bananas, so that the kids can have this treat.

Women in Făgăraș are considered equal to men in almost all ways, and share the same responsibilities. Whereas in the Jiu Valley men identify with external labor and women with the household, in Făgăraș both men and women identify themselves as household-

Figure 6.2. Woman worker at the UPRUC foundry.
Photograph by the author.

ers first and workers second. In terms of labor, both women and
men believe that women are somewhat less rugged than men, and
have a few additional health needs, but consider them equal to the
same tasks. This was brought out in an interview with a married
couple, both UPRUC workers, when they responded to a question
about whether women or men get sick more frequently:

> SHE: Yes, women are sick more often than men. In our factory for ex-
> ample, I and some other women work where women ought not to. There
> are some workplaces that are particularly difficult for women, but we still
> do the work. Sometimes we lift things that weigh forty kilograms. If there
> is a tool or part that is larger, two, three, or four of us will work together.
> HE: I believe that in our factory all of us are equal.

Sexual discourse and social relations in Făgăraş were also quite
unlike those in the Jiu Valley and again suggest a degree of commonality, if not equality, between men and women. Social groups
in the region were not rigidly single-sex. Though male factory colleagues occasionally gathered at a bar to share a drink, these gath-

erings were neither so critical nor so regular as those of miners and their *ortaci*. When people gathered socially, which was increasingly infrequent, they did so in mixed-sex groups and talked freely with one another. Such companionship and conversation show up constantly in interviews about male-female discourse, especially in relation to work. Thus, in the factories, there was a generally positive, collegial atmosphere between men and women, and women in leadership positions, though rare, were respected. For example, Raluca Nahorniac interviewed a husband and wife, both formerly employed at UPRUC. Speaking of the position of women in the factory, the woman said,

> In our factory sector we have a woman union leader and everyone gets along with her very well. She tells us anything. She announces factory news to us. And we support and assist her. If there is a strike or something, all of us will go out together. For example, at the beginning of this month, when they gave out the rest of the pay from the previous month, they tried to hold back paying our section's workers and said they would pay us later. She said, "We're going out, we are going to the director," and she led all of us on a walkout to the director's.

Also, unlike those of the Jiu Valley, Făgăraş spouses have generally communicated well about family and other matters. For example, when the contract buy-outs were made available to Făgăraş factory workers, they seem to have always consulted with their wives before accepting or rejecting them. A Nitramonia couple interviewed by Vasile Şoflău after the man rejected the contract buy-out made it clear they were equally involved in his decision to remain at work:

> HE: Yes, I probably would have taken the buy-out if I was certain I would have some other work to do after. Of course I consulted with my wife. She said to do what I wanted, but I thought, what would there be for us if neither of us had work? We couldn't find another job here, since UPRUC was near bankruptcy.
> SHE: Yes. What would we do? We don't have heat or hot water in our apartment even now, and they've shut off the water, since many have not paid.

Făgăraşeni's senses of their gendered selves thus have changed little since the socialist or even presocialist years. However, as in the Jiu Valley, postsocialism makes people feel the waning of their physical capacities more sharply (Pine 2002, 96). In some ways this affects Făgăraşeni even more than their Jiu Valley counterparts.

Whereas miners were content with being miners and reproducing the patterns of mine and home over succeeding generations, over the years Făgărașeni developed strategies for social mobility and development, or, as they say, ways to be somebody (*să fie cineva*). Men tend to feel this loss more than women (Carlson et al. 2000), and it is made even more vivid by comparison with the sweeping changes in regional life during socialism. Men especially comment on their sacrifices, implying that they recognize their waning powers and limited ability to regain them. One older Nitramonia foreman suggested,

> We are the generation of sacrifice. In the time of Ceaușescu we were told we had to sacrifice to build socialism. Now we are told that we have to sacrifice for democracy and that life will be better in a few years. But I don't believe it for a moment. The factory equipment is aged and falling apart just like we are.

The analogy between workplace and bodily decline is common in regional discourse. Many Făgăraș workers see postsocialist work conditions as detrimental to their health. Older equipment is poorly maintained, prone to failure, and a cause of workplace accidents. But even more than the miners, whose concerns for survival are more immediate, Făgăraș workers worry about generational continuity: mainly in the factory, but by implication in households and communities as well. As an UPRUC machinist put it,

> So many workers lost their jobs in the restructuring that our team members are now so few that we can't even justify having a work team leader. We used to have twenty-four on our team, and now there are only two from our old troop and one other guy who came from another workshop . . . We often discuss the fact that, after us, there is no one younger than forty. No one thinks about that, that there is no one to replace us and that after ten years there will be no one in the factory. I wanted them to hire my son so he could work with me and I could mold him. But my boss told me that it was impossible, since we can no longer hire anyone. Now there is no one who works near you, who can even bring you a cup of water.

Conclusions: Damaged Gender and Arrested Agency

As the foregoing suggests, the world of gendered certainties for postsocialist workers in Jiu Valley mines and Făgăraș factories is largely unraveling. Men and women are confronted with new, unsettling images that they struggle to integrate into their own lives and to keep at arm's length from their children. They are enticed yet threatened by objects and promises of the good life that they can ill afford and to which they know they would be fools to aspire. Stuck between desire and dread, interest and alienation, workers see themselves as only tentative and handicapped participants in modern culture. This perception is a logical outgrowth of their interpretations of their bodies and sexuality in postsocialism.

Worker sexuality is as uncertain and assailed as their views of media. Their sexual lives are often suspended because of lack of time, space, and energy. They question their own desirability. While women's bodies and sexuality are no longer controlled by the pronatalist state, they remain constrained by other forces. Death from a botched abortion will no longer be the fate of many. Rather, they are confronted with the long, slow (and sometimes not so slow) decline of the new postsocialist labor regime and the special pressures that system places on women for family survival. While women feel the press of postsocialism, men are increasingly alienated from their own sexuality. Their physical ideals are taken from the movies. They are paradoxically distanced from their bodily selves while strongly feeling that labor increasingly threatens their potency and general well-being.

Thus the gendered identities of both men and women are damaged, undermined, and reformed of content and meaning by the particular socio-economic forces that they confront in changing Romanian society. In many ways these forces propel change among men and women. However, we need to ask to what extent such change helps workers to succeed in their plans and projects, or even gives rise to linkages that can combat subordinating postsocialist forces. As the foregoing suggests, the contradictory place of workers' sexuality ultimately obstructs their agency. While on the surface of worker lives there is change aplenty, it is largely directed toward hanging on and surviving, rather than challenging or breaking free of constraints.

Many Jiu Valley women seek gainful employment for the first time in their lives while their men, if employed, give up some of their dominance in the household or, if unemployed, actually take on some heretofore female responsibilities. Other men are unhappy with their loss of power, and react with threats and abuse. Some Jiu Valley women, meanwhile, are simply lost, with no chance of actualizing themselves in consumption practices. In Făgăraş some men and women join together and redouble their efforts to find means to survive by scraping together whatever resources they can possibly access. Others seek to emigrate, or more commonly, enable a child to do so. And, like some of their hapless counterparts in the Jiu Valley, many others quietly and privately descend into abuse, violence, or emotional disintegration.

When I say that these regions' workers are suffering a frustrated agency, I do not mean to suggest that their lives are mainly determined by forces outside themselves (Bartkey 1995, 179–81). Though their free will is certainly crabbed by the conditions in which they live, it is more significant that the choices left open to them are limited in the extreme. Rather than offering solutions, such "choices" actually make it harder for workers to fulfill their possibilities and succeed in their projects, even as they help workers with short-term survival. Each choice is perceived as loss, rather than possibility. Each act is glossed not as resistance but as succumbing to unpleasantnesses not forced on others in their society. Despite the claims of Western feminism, for example, many Jiu Valley women would prefer to stay in their homes (Gal 1997, 90). Făgăraş families suffer significant loss when one of their members emigrates, not to mention the long-term sacrifice required of the émigrés themselves. Postsocialist action is thus not liberating but alienating. Furthermore, rather than allowing then to engage society politically, such plans and actions actually encourage them to reject any conception of politics as reasonable and effective, thus robbing individuals of their agency and identity (Segal 1991, 206–207).

The frustrated agency of the current period is particularly felt at the level of the physical and has significant implications for people's understandings of their possibilities as men and women. Life is burdensome and weighs heavy on people's being. None of them say they are living up to their ideals of masculinity or femininity. As the wife of the Lonea wagon tender said above, "I like elegant things and also like to look pretty, but I am not allowed to have these things." As the aging Nitramonia foreman said, "The factory equipment is aged and falling apart just like we are." Given these problematic realities, it is somewhat beside the point to speak of postsocialist masculinization or even disadvantaged women among workers in the Jiu Valley and Făgăraş region. These people are working class first and foremost, and their agentive possibilities in postsocialism follow that reality.

Thus, the supposedly privileged position of men in the political economy of postsocialism is nowhere to be found in the two regions, at least not among its workers. If anything, men are more threatened than women by the new sexuality that permeates local society, especially through the airwaves. Moreover, transforming the cultural circumstances that have largely placed women in subordinate positions in East-Central European and Romanian society would do little, I am afraid, to change the lot of the working women of these regions. Both men and women, facing limits on their actions and possibilities at every turn, hope only for survival and for the continuity of their families and workplaces. But even these hopes are increasingly evanescent, as they are especially affected by serious threats to the physical health of the regions' peoples, the *coup de grâce* of the economic, social, political, and identity realities which they face.

7

The Embodied Enemy

Stress, Health, and Agency

> The social, cultural, and personal dimensions
> of illness must be understood through other
> means, and one neglected but useful resource
> is narrative.
>
> —**David B. Morris**, *Illness and Culture in the Postmodern Age*

> My head hurts because of the draft. My head
> hurts because of the cold. But mostly my
> head hurts because of my nerves, because of
> all the things that go unfulfilled.
>
> —**TN, Nitramonia chemical operator**

Embodied Distance and Worker Health

Embodied postsocialist distance and fear also affect workers' physical health and well-being, deepening their stress, distress, and inability to act. Like other formerly socialist states (Rivkin-Fish 2003), Romania has recently experienced a steep drop in population because of falling birthrates and life expectancies and high rates of emigration (Cockerham 1999; White and Sporton 1995, 149).[1] However, the declining population is only one indication of the postsocialist worker health crisis. The crisis comes more fully into view when we consider peoples' perceptions, choices, and experiences, and how they use them to make sense of and negotiate the sweeping changes roiling their lives. Jiu Valley and Făgăraş workers' views of what affects their bodies and their health show little variation.[2] Nonetheless, the two groups part company on what they actually do about their health and the degree to which they see their own behavior as efficacious for good health. Differences aside, in the last years both miners and workers have come to see their bodies as under attack, to fear their ensuing physical states, and to feel unable to effectively respond to their decline.

In both regions people ultimately relate their problematic health to their political and economic disenfranchisement. They assume that external factors like work-related stress and corruption and national economic problems directly affect their health. Făgărăşeni recognize a degree of personal responsibility. They generally believe that they can take steps to improve their health. However, they also indicate that, in fact, they do not take such steps! Conversely, people in the Jiu Valley feel they do try to promote their health. However, they believe their actions are meaningless, because of the same external circumstances. In other words, whatever people do or believe they could do, health and health care in both regions flag, whether because of the Făgărăşeni's inaction or Jiu Valley residents' frustration. Taken together, these perceptions and practices, active or aborted, contribute to workers' dread for their corporal integrity, intensifying their fears for economic and social survival.

For the most part, Făgărăşeni have great respect for health care personnel and institutions. They speak of them in awed tones and assume that physicians truly have people's interests at heart. In contrast, Jiu Valley miners view state and local health care institutions and practitioners with anger and suspicion. Even where they express respect for certain institutions, like the Salvamin Mine safety organization, they feel these organizations and their personnel patronize them and condescend to them. Ultimately, both workers and miners believe that society is unconcerned for their physical integrity. They often blame state and local policies and practices for their troubled health. They criticize the January 2000 health care reform that shrank or eliminated many workplace clinics and implemented a capitation payment system, even though the reform was supposed to eliminate the bribes that people were forced to pay for adequate medical treatment. (Complicating the issue, even with the health care reforms, workers believe they must bribe health care personnel to approve their sick leave.) More than these reforms, they decry the practices of factory and mine administrators who, they claim, ignore worker safety and health in favor of production. In these critiques, one can sense the frustrations and uncertainties of workers and miners as they face their shortened lives and threatened bodies.

Postsocialist Stress and the Worker Health Crisis

By all accounts, people feel sicker now than during socialism, and say that the decline in their quality of life contributes extensively to the precariousness of their health (Lakey 1994, 37). Făgăraşeni merely claim this, but Jiu Valley miners act on this belief, as shown by their increased visits to doctors and clinics. Despite their perceptions of ill health, workers and miners take far fewer sick days now than they did in socialist days.[3] This is unquestionably due to job insecurity, falling standards of living, and the felt need to preserve income at any cost. A former director of the Braşov County Public Health directorate confirmed this:

> People don't take sick leave when they should. They work hard at the factory and in the fields until they can't any longer, and then they go to the doctor. There is little concern for prevention. It's not that they can't afford the doctor. They try not to miss work because they need money and fear being forced to take the buy-out.

As this statement implies, working life is a major factor in the downturn in East-Central European health. Until recently, many other explanations for the East European health crisis have contended for pride of place. Some focused on degradation of the health care infrastructure (Watson 1995), others on poor nutrition, smoking, and alcohol abuse (Cockerham, Snead, and DeWaal 2002; Leon et al. 1997), or even on environmental problems (Feshbach and Friendly 1992; Oldson 1996). Increasingly, however, scholars have singled out the social basis of the crisis as its chief cause (Bobek and Marmot 1996; Stone 2000; Weidner 1998). Jiu Valley miners and Făgăraş workers confirm this by their constant references to "stress" when asked to explain their health problems.

Working life is a multidimensional stressor. As miners' pay is tied to production, they are especially stressed by their lack of tools, malfunctioning machinery, unhealthy work conditions, and the actual demands of production. Despite the loss of 60 percent of the mine work force since the buy-outs began, mine production has actually increased over the last years. Clearly people are working harder than ever. Meanwhile, constant worry about mine closures makes the normal stresses of mining's dangers pale in comparison. Stress on the Jiu Valley unemployed is less pronounced, but even more insidious, than that on their active colleagues. For the unemployed, torpor and detachment from all the predictable signposts of one's working life result in loss of self-respect, loss of colleagues, and loss of identity. People sit at home with few resources, feel unwelcome among their former buddies, and are often even rejected by their families. Meanwhile, in Făgăraş stress grows from the need to constantly strategize ways to earn additional income from agriculture or the labor black market. Like the miners, workers are stressed by the increased demands placed on them because of declines in the effective laboring population and the general aging of the work force. Some workers are now expected to handle two or three machines or processes simultaneously.[4] People are also envious of and stressed by the apparent success of families with members who work abroad and send home money.

Workers in both regions also internalize stress resulting from their confused positioning in the new social contexts: the unraveling gendered identities of miners and their wives; Făgăraş parents' fear of new sexual mores; the rejection and derision that older workers encounter for their compromises during socialism, and their own felt loss of power. Stress on women is particularly pronounced. Many Jiu Valley women have lost a main preoccupation in life because of the reduction or loss of their husband's earnings. They can neither maintain their family's standards of consumption nor remain involved in apartment and neighborhood social life. Women whose husbands were bought out must deal continually with their frustrated husbands, who rarely leave home, and with demands to produce income for their households. As one woman said, "When I see him so sick and nervous all the time, it makes me sick and nervous." In Făgăraş, women are pressured to continue to contribute financially to their households even though the jobs and resources are no longer there.

Robert Sapolsky (1997) showed that stress affects a person's entire emotional, physical, and social balance, acting on the hormones, suppressing immunity, and facilitating disease. He says (205) that the key to managing stress is to have some sense that difficult situations are controllable or predictable, and "outlets for frustration, social support, and affiliation." However, not only are postsocialist Romanian workers' lives entirely unpredictable, but nearly all their "outlets for frustration, social support, and affiliation," i.e., labor, Cozma and the union, *ortaci* at the bar, networks, and family rituals, are thoroughly discredited or diminished, leaving them few options but to turn their stress and anger inward on themselves or their families. In this they unfortunately resemble many other peoples who suffer depression and disease due to unemployment or general economic hardship (Catalano, Aldrete, and Vega 2000; Nordenmark and Strandh 1999; Straussner, Ashenberg, and Phillips 1999).

Stress-related diseases and emotional illnesses in the regions are especially on the rise. For example, the number of cases of hypertension and cardiac/ischemic disease reported by the Făgăraş general hospital has grown spectacularly. Such increased numbers may result from greater attention to health statistics in postsocialism. However, diverse health care personnel suggested this is not so. In fact, health budgets, services, and state demands for statistics were more extensive in socialism than today (Lakey et al. 1996, 1048). For example, from 1989 to 2000 the number of beds at the Făgăraş hospital declined from 650 to 375, while sections specializing in emotional illness closed altogether. The director of the Petroşani mental health facility in the Jiu Valley agreed that economic problems are the chief source of his patients' emotional disturbances. He also said that these affect women more than men, since they are responsible for household budgets. Showing me an unused set of admission forms, he claimed a surprising decline in self-admissions, down by a third in the last two years, which he felt was also due to people's fears for their jobs and their precarious economic positions.

Though women were more visible at the facility, I first interviewed a miner from the recently closed Dâlja Mine, who came to the Valley from Moldavia in 1980 and had no prior history of emotional illness. He said he first "broke down" while preparing Dâlja for closing and conservation. He was in a group of ten removing scrap metal from some mine galleries when he felt faint, began to perspire, had trouble breathing, and passed out. After being revived and taken to the surface by his workmates, he had another attack as he dressed to leave work. The man explained his breakdown by referring to his economic fears and obliquely to the disparagement of miners in Romanian society:

> I have been so agitated since they officially closed the mine. My fellows [*ortaci*] helped me then. They were very good. They will even visit me here. We are good guys. We are not crazy like people make us out to be. Our country's leaders know this and so do the mine administrators. Things have been bad for us miners ever since they arrested Cozma.

A woman in the same facility had been hospitalized for a week. This was her third hospitalization, this time because she had hallucinated stabbing her child. She said that her attacks began soon after her wedding, which had been marked by considerable acrimony with her mother-in-law, who opposed the marriage. The woman said she and her husband had a good marriage and were faithful and supportive. However, she was depressed as she feared for her husband's job and his safety at the mine:

> Another of my worries is money. My husband's job is to bring money into the family and my job is to figure out where it goes. We saved and bought a car recently. It is a diesel. We wanted to have it in case of emergencies like this, so my husband can take me to the hospital when I need to go. But if we don't have any money, it will be difficult for us. I am afraid that if I can't get to the hospital, I will hurt my child.

Stress is everywhere in postsocialist workers' lives, from family relations, to gender identity, to employment status, and it takes a constant toll on their daily lives, personal relationships, self-image, and health. Though hospitalizations have declined, this does not mean that workers' health problems, troubled physical identities, and frustrated agency have become less pressing. Though people feel sicker, their economic uncertainly makes them fear the possible consequences of asking for help. And all these stresses ultimately derive from deteriorating health-related circumstances of work and labor.

Labor, Health, and Stress

Of all the conditions of Jiu Valley and Făgăraş life, none is so stressful as labor and its loss and none affects perceptions of health and body as much as changing postsocialist workplaces. Workers' and miners' somatic complaints multiply in direct relation to tensions in work relations, job dissatisfaction, belief in the inefficacy of labor activism, and declines in the extent to which workers feet part of a work collective. I surveyed workers with the Wahler Physical Symptoms Inventory (Wahler 1968), which measures perceptions of physical ailments by means of a forty-two-item inventory. My results suggest that the Jiu Valley miners, both active and unemployed, consider themselves less healthy than do the vast majority of Făgăraşeni. The difference seems due, in the first place, to the stresses of mining, the declining mine industry, and the social conditions of mining communities. Jiu Valley unemployed also feel sicker than Făgăraş unemployed. At the same time, miners are less satisfied with their jobs than Făgăraş workers and are less likely to believe that labor activism is worthwhile, not surprising in the aftermath of the last *mineriade*. Miners resemble Făgăraş workers only in the degree to which they trust their colleagues, but even here their scores were marginally lower.

That miners at the Aninoasa Mine and the Viromet factory had the fewest health complaints, while workers at UPRUC had the greatest, also supports our thesis that work-related stress affects perceptions of health. While we were doing research for this book, the Aninoasa Mine was enjoying a long period of labor stability under consistent management, and miners were very satisfied with their jobs. The same was true at Viromet in Oraşul Victoria, whose workers felt healthiest of all and whose scores in job satisfaction, sense of collectivity, and perception that their actions made a difference were highest. Meanwhile, UPRUC workers perceived themselves to be as ill as Jiu Valley miners did. The UPRUC factory was undergoing a troublesome privatization process and protracted union conflict. Thus, the more tense a labor environment, the greater workers' perceived physical distress.

This simple relationship, unfortunately, can be generalized across postsocialist Romania, where factory environments, especially for workers in the former state sector, are uncertain and problematic. Even more positive situations, like those of Viromet and Aninoasa, don't persist indefinitely. Labor tensions have increased precipitously at both places in the last few years. Aninoasa suffered from a changing administration, then rumors of closure, while Viromet workers had to deal with a new round of labor contract buyouts. The Aninoasa Mine has now closed and Viromet's privatization proceeds apace. I venture to guess that, if they were measured now, perceptions of health at the two institutions would no longer be similar. Similarly, the completion of privatization at UPRUC (Vrânceanu 2004), though more restricted than planned, probably had salutary effects on worker health complaints there.

Worker-Administrator Conflict

Safety issues are a particular source of labor tensions and stress. Workers and administrators typically blamed each other for unsafe work conditions and practices. When they were interviewed, their comments fell into "did so"/"did not" patterns, making it impossible to definitively assign blame to anyone for workplace safety lapses. However, the actual causes seem less significant than the mutual accusations. These grow from workers' perceptions of threat, administrators' pressures to increase production, and the general degradation of postsocialist labor. Workers' perceptions mirror their embodied distance and fear. Though they condemn administrators for lack of concern for their health and safety, workers do little to protect themselves. At the same time, factory, mine, and even union officials shift their own responsibilities and frustrations onto workers' shoulders.

In Romania, occupational safety and health is defined as labor protection (*protecţia muncii,* or PM) and includes remediating unhealthful work conditions, enforcing practices that lessen the effects of unhealthful conditions, making health personnel available in the workplace, establishing clinics and emergency services, providing regular and effective medical examinations, providing good-quality and sufficient safety clothing and equipment, and subsidizing things like meals, vacations, and sick leaves that improve workers' quality of life. Workers' perceptions of PM vary in different mines and factories. Generally, however, since socialism's end, in every institution under study perceptions of PM have declined, despite management's overt commitment to maintaining it. There are various reasons for this. Many requirements, such as that health care personnel be available, have been cut back as the factories and mines restrict production. Quality of life provisions have been taken over by private institutions, whose eye on the bottom line prompts cutbacks in services. But despite these external reasons for declines in PM, workers in the two regions still saw them as evidence of managers' lack of concern for their health.

Perceptions of PM are worse where labor is under stress and social support waning. That PM in Jiu Valley mining is more contentious than in Făgăraş[5] is thus clearly a function of the greater contentiousness of mine labor. No longer able to act politically on their fears of mine closures and falling standards of living, miners internalize these concerns. There is thus a great difference of opinion between miners and administrators over safety practices and responsibility for mine accidents. Administrators say that miners' own behavior and greediness endangers them. They say accidents result from a culture in which miners try to show each other up, ignoring safety rules. They also claim that miners knowingly work in dangerous conditions to increase production and make more money. Administrators maintain they follow all international safety standards, such as ensuring redundancy in electrical, aeration, and water pumping systems. Automatic methane gauges throughout each mine automatically send information to surface stations; when methane levels exceed 1.5 percent alarms sound and miners are evacuated. Electricity to such areas is automatically cut off to force evacuation and help prevent fires. Still, administrators say, miners often ignore these warnings.

Jiu Valley mines are the most dangerous in the country and some of the most dangerous in the world. Deep, folded seams, especially in the eastern region, make it difficult to extract coal and seal off played-out galleries. High levels of methane result in frequent fires and explosions, and unstable strata are prone to cave-ins (*surpare*).[6] Miners thus are right to be concerned about whether administrators are enforcing safe work practices. To their credit, the National Coal Company (CNH) and its constituent mines have had some success in preventing serious accidents over the last years. In the three mines where we did most of our research, the accident rate has steadily declined over the last two decades. Though declines in 1998 and 1999 can be partially attributed to the contract buy-outs and the closing of certain galleries, the improved accident rate is still testimony to administrators' concern for worker safety.

Miners, however, question administrators' commitment to their health and safety. They admit that they often ignore danger while working, because to do otherwise would paralyze them with fear. Still, they suggest that administrative pressure on them to produce contributes to their inattention and negligence, chief reasons for many accidents in Jiu Valley mining. A Lonea electrician referred to workplace rules that require that work stop when the temperature in a gallery reaches 38 degrees Centigrade. However, he said that at Lonea they are regularly told to work in heat that often rises to 40–42 degrees. Another Lonea miner said,

> [Administrators] don't even respect 10 percent of workplace rules . . . If you respect all the regulations you can't do anything. Not only that, if we try to stop these [unsafe] practices, administrators threaten us. They question us and say, "Why don't you want to work?" But if you respond that you won't work in such a methane-rich environment, they'll tell you, "OK. So then we'll meet you outside [i.e., you will lose your job]."

Access to medical care at the factory or mine has become more difficult because of the January 2000 health care reform. The Law on the Social Assurance of Health (Government of Romania 1997a) forced most workplace clinics to close or cut back by creating a capitation system of payment. Staff doctors became "family physicians" with private offices, who receive a small stipend for each of up to two thousand individuals they enroll for basic health care. This stipend is paid by the new Health Assistance Program (Casa de Asigurari de Sanatate, or CAS), to which workers contribute through payroll deductions. Workers are expected to see their family physician for basic health care and for approval of medical leaves of absence. Romanian law stipulates that enterprises with fifty or more employees must also have emergency medical facilities. But because of the reform, the number of workplace medical facilities, personnel, and services throughout both regions has been significantly reduced.

Workers and miners decry the disappearance of these medical institutions and personnel. Their loss is a greater blow because, during socialism and for some years after, the clinics also served workers' families. Făgăraş workers bemoan the loss of affectionate relationships between workers and clinic personnel. At Nitramonia (then the Făgăraş Chemical Combine), the clinic was located on the margins of the plant and served many of those who lived in the dingy barracks just outside the factory grounds. Both workers and health care personnel at Viromet also claim that close friendships existed between them during socialism. Today the Viromet clinic is merely a records repository and referral service. The physician there said she knew most of the workers and their families. Soon to retire, she feared for the health of the community she had served for so long. At UPRUC at the end of socialism, there were two doctors, two dentists, and one dental technician on staff. Now the one remaining doctor is also moving into a family practice. Except in major emergencies, UPRUC workers are sent to the main Făgăraş hospital. All the mine clinicians, too, were hoping to become family doctors, and managers debated whether they should replace them with other emergency medics or allow the physicians to work half-time at the mine.

The clinics are not universally lauded. Miners and workers criticize their personnel for demanding bribes (*şpaga, ciubuc*) for quick and effective treatment. Miners were especially incensed about this, since they more frequently requested sick leave and nonemergency treatment. According to miners, approval of sick leave (*foia de boală*) cost from fifty thousand to one hundred thousand lei at the Aninoasa Mine and was twice as expensive at Vulcan. Health officials and workers alike assume that such bribery will be less likely because doctors will be better paid under the capitation system. Still, work-site clinics and dispensaries will only provide emergency medical care, dispense treatments prescribed by family doctors, and orga-nize periodic medical tests for workers. Also, given the disarticula-tion of medical care from the workplace, these changes are unlikely to improve workers' self-protective behavior or their perceptions of their health in the near future.

The changing organization of health services may also limit the frequency and effectiveness of factory medical tests, previously un-der the purview of the workplace clinics. Such tests have been con-tentious, but have mainly served worker interests. In Făgăraş work-ers have comprehensive health exams when they are first hired, including EKGs and Wasserman tests. Lately, however, only work-ers in sections with critical responsibilities, like the UPRUC crane section (*macaranje*), receive exams after that. One UPRUC worker complained about a serious and long-standing cough (though he was working without a mask in the factory foundry), but said he hadn't had a medical exam for almost two years. According to his foreman, foundry workers should be examined twice a year, but there haven't been any exams in months. The man himself said, "I would go if I were called, but they haven't called me. It would make no sense for me to ask them to call me, since they will not listen to me in any case."

Jiu Valley miners go through more stringent medical exams than do Făgăraşeni. However, a bad test result can mean a loss of in-come. The examinations take place at the mine clinics themselves, but are administered by the Salvamin Institute, itself a specialized, though partially privatized, health and safety sector of the CNH. Comprehensive medical exams are given miners when they are hired and again after five years. The Ministry of Health stipulates that all mine employees should be reexamined every three years, or annually for those who work underground. Those suffering from discrete (grade I) pulmonary fibrosis (*fibroza*), one of a variety of chronic obstructive pulmonary diseases, must also have an X-ray every two years. Fibrosis is caused by breathing coal dust.[7] Those with moderate fibrosis are X-rayed every year, and those with criti-cal fibrosis every six months. In addition, those in critical jobs, like rescue workers (*salvatori*) and explosives experts (*artificieri*), are re-quired to have annual EKGs, EEGs, and audiologic and ophthalmo-logic exams.

Depending on test results, mine administrators can remove active miners from the underground and place them in less taxing, less well paid positions. Though their base salary remains the same, a change in worksite may cost a miner up to half his monthly income, because he loses the supplements (*sporuri*) that come with underground work. Thus, miners often attempt to manipulate information about their health. Some try to keep their ailments secret, and so will skip scheduled exams or bribe examiners for clean bills of health.[8] As the Lupeni Mine safety instructor told Bianca Botea,

> There are many cases where sick miners try to stay working in the underground. There was a young miner who was twenty-one years old who had a slight heart attack. So I told him, "Hey, don't you think it would be better for you to work for slightly less money on the surface than to risk your life every day in the *subteren*?" I sent him to a cardiologist in Petroșani to evaluate whether he could continue to work underground. Usually Ministry of Health regulations say that even with a slight heart attack you cannot continue in the underground. However, this guy came back from the doctor with approval to begin his work again. So I told him, "Your health is more important." But he said, that the money for surface work is too little, that he is young, and he needs to make money. A little later, however, he came to me and told me that he could no longer work underground, that the administrators set his team to work at level 400, where there is a 60 degree incline, and when he tried to work there his heart was beating like crazy. It was only then he asked me to ask the doctor in Petroșani to prepare the papers to get him a surface position.

The conflicts between health and money also appear in workers' and miners' use or nonuse of protective clothing and equipment. Workers and miners also complain about lack of access to such items. For example, a Lonea miner, describing (incorrectly) how a miner gets new work clothes, turned the process into a metaphor for the poor treatment miners receive at administrators' hands:

> They are supposed to give you protective clothing twice a year, but it is sometimes so hard to secure it, so why bother. Think about coming out of the mine, completely dirty, needing new equipment. First you have to go to the sector chief, who writes you up a ticket to attest that you need the stuff. Then you have to go to the aeration section to get permission from the Protecția Muncii supervisor. Then you go to the financial section to fill out a form and attest whether this is one of the free suits you get or you have to pay for it. Then you go the head accountant to register. Then you even have to go to the mine director to get his signature. Sometimes he is sitting there with visitors and drinking coffee and he sees you and says,

"Please wait outside a bit. Can't you see I am busy?" . . . all this after coming out of the mine where you have been working on your knees for six hours.

Still, such complaints seem *pro forma,* and many workers do not even use the materials provided them. They explain that safety equipment restricts their movements, making it difficult to meet production targets, and is of poor quality anyway, among other reasons. At Viromet not a single worker in the deafening methane production section wore hearing protection, though all acknowledged receiving headphones. Workers say they are uncomfortable and that others would make fun of them if they wore them. In the UPRUC polyester section, workers, mainly women, were constructing large vats and storage bins by covering molds with resinous materials and fibers, while men ground materials at lathes. Of the ten women I spoke with, only one wore protective gloves, and not a single man wore a mask to filter out the particles their work was generating. The women claim that factory administrators put them in a double bind by threatening them with fines if they do not wear gloves, but then demanding increased production, which requires them to set their gloves aside. Făgăraş chemical workers are regularly given milk to combat the toxicity of the factory's gaseous environments. However, though they complain of insufficient supplies, they often don't drink the milk even when it is available. A former UPRUC equipment manager corroborated this:

> Before the revolution they used to give one-half kilogram of milk per day to each worker, but after it they only gave milk to certain workers, especially those in the vat section. But even though people often didn't drink it, those who worked outside wanted the same as those who worked inside, so they complained. There were also problems about getting the right type of clothing. We always talked about our illnesses at the factory, because there was always loud noise and large amounts of dust. Hey, look at this. [She showed me a face mask taken from a drawer.] I kept this when I left the factory. I thought I might as well keep one. But they don't work so well. They are not the right kind, so I never used it.

Another worker, however, explained that the milk was used to express work-team solidarity against the administration in the declining economic environment:

> To protect us against the toxicity of the gas, they used to give milk more often and in larger amounts. It was about three or four kilograms per shift

of seven or eight guys, or about 250 grams per person. Now, it's about one hundred grams . . . one single glass. We pretty much look out for each other, so some people don't drink what they get, so others will be able to drink more. Workers who live in the villages also don't usually drink their share, so that people who live in the city can take the milk home to their children. You only drink if there is a gas event and something bad happens in the factory.

Workers' fears for and passivity about their health and their antipathy for national politics are mutually reinforced when treatment for work-related illness is held up by politics. In 1999 the national budget to remediate occupational illnesses was left hanging because of a disagreement between the Ministry of Health, which administered those programs, and the Ministry of Labor, which sought to take them over. In this conflict the miners were temporarily deprived of access to ten beds per month at two sanatoria for fibrosis and silicosis treatment. They had fought for these beds in a strike led by Miron Cozma, but were again put out in the cold. Even after the conflict was resolved, a highly placed administrator at the Salvamin health service said that miners still wait a long time for admission to those facilities, and some miners say admission requires large bribes. Miners' belief that action to get their health needs met is futile was reinforced, as was their sense that the system conspired against them.

Workers and the Health Care System

Miners' and workers' attitudes toward and relationships with the health care system and its personnel mirror their paradoxical views on labor protection. Făgărășeni mainly respect the health care system but rarely avail themselves of it. They do little about their health until they become sick. Miners are attentive to the point of paranoia to their bodies and health, and are uncertain that medical personnel share their concerns. They demand attention from health care personnel, but then often reject their advice and prefer to look after themselves. These stances are little changed from socialist days, except in their intensity. Thus, Făgărășeni claim they visit doctors more rarely today than in the past and miners aver that clinic health care was better during socialism. This greening of past health care, like so many other aspects of workers' lives, is certainly a direct response to the distance and dread of postsocialist experience. But the fictionalization of the socialist past, both here and in their rose-tinted memories of past labor conditions, only makes it more difficult to negotiate and get by in the postsocialist present.

Miners are particularly frustrated by the medical care they receive, or rather, feel they don't receive. In interviews at the Lupeni Mine and elsewhere their disaffection was as much existential as about practical matters. Some feared their health was failing because their work had grown harder. Others complained that medical care wasn't available when it was needed. Still others were confused by the health care reforms. Finally, many said that clinical care was irrelevant and that the doctors didn't understand how to treat miners, and claimed that medical treatment today only made one sicker. A Lupeni miner summed up this view:

> If you go to the doctor when you have a cold, when you come home you are worse. But if you put forth a bit of extra effort working, the time goes by and you are not harmed by it. In fact, if you just work hard, you will probably get better.

A Lonea miner confirmed the opposition of the clinic and self-treatment:

> I won't go to the doctor even if I have a problem. About five years ago my right hand was paralyzed and the doctor sent me to physical therapy. I took the treatment but it didn't help very much. But one day when I was collecting blueberries with my family in the sun, the paralysis just passed away. The doctor sent me again to physical therapy, but I remembered my grandfather, who was also a miner. His hand was also paralyzed, but he would tie his scythe onto his belt and cut hay, and it worked pretty well for him. So I said to myself, through movement, through doing things, you can treat yourself.

Făgărașeni, unlike the miners, believe that modern medicine works. However, they only go to doctors when an illness has progressed significantly, and perhaps not even then. Their economic concerns push health care to the bottom of the list of ways discretionary income might be spent. They try not to purchase medicine because of its cost, while miners say they avoid buying medicine because they don't think it will work. Perhaps because of their greater and more recent ties to rural communities, Făgăraș workers and their families make greater use of natural medicines (*leacuri babești,* or "old lady" cures) like herb teas and poultices. Many also believe in the evil eye (*ochiat*), and claim that more curses have been cast lately, as many people are invidious and blame their misfortunes on others.

Health personnel respond in kind to workers' sentiments. Jiu Valley doctors are highly critical of miners' medical beliefs and practices. Like other outsiders to the mining industry, they hyperbolize and mythologize miners' behavior. For example, they claim miners are excessively fearful of injections and medication and patronize them when they come to the clinic in emergencies. More positively, the paternalism of clinic personnel means they will sometimes treat miners' wives and children, and even an occasional bought-out miner down on his luck. Făgăraş doctors, meanwhile, have greater respect for local workers, but still see them as inarticulate and unconcerned for their own health needs. In both regions, disconnects between workers and health care practitioners mirror the workers' estrangement from society. The aches and pains of Jiu Valley and Făgăraş labor are thus amplified by the laborers' knowledge that neither they themselves nor medical personnel can mitigate them.

Neither the stance of the Făgăraşeni nor that of the Jiu Valley miners means that they have fatalistically accepted their lot. On the contrary, postsocialist workers know their life, health, and work is threatened by other forces, and that there are steps that they can and should take to counteract those forces. However, they also believe that anything they do will likely be frustrated by those same forces arrayed against them, or at least will cost them scarce resources and have uncertain results. Consequently, their plans and actions are often stopped in their tracks. Such reluctance to work for change is also due to ongoing behaviors that intensify workers' health crises, like eating a poor diet and using alcohol and tobacco.

Diet and Drink, Again

Earlier I described how changing diets relate to changes in the postsocialist organization of domestic labor. Changing postsocialist diets also affect workers' health and perceptions of their bodies, though less because of their poor quality than because of what they signify about declining social lives and the increased stress involved in obtaining food. Although more kinds of food are more available in the postsocialist marketplace, food costs more, is harder to come by, and demands a greater proportion of people's budgets, attention, and concern. Furthermore, most miners and a good number of workers in the Făgăraş region lack both gardens and ready access to rural resources. Consequently, they must buy most of their food in town markets. Even workers with rural connections must often work for that pig or sack of peppers, which drains their time, energy, and labor power.

For some workers, albeit not for most, the situation borders on dire. In a nutritional survey organized in summer 2002 we examined the source, amount, and quality of food eaten by families in the two regions over one week's time. In the Jiu Valley, more than 90 percent of food is acquired at the local market. Of eighty-two sample households, forty-four went without at least two meals in that week, and three missed seven or more. Missed meals were clearly related to food costs. Of the forty-four households that missed meals, ten had both spouses actively employed and yet could not always put food on the table. Eighteen households had only one person actively employed, and neither spouse was employed in sixteen households. In Făgăraş the student research team completed a dietary survey for a limited sample of ten households. However, even here five households went without two or more meals in the week, and of these five, three had both spouses employed. In addition, workers' diets are remarkably repetitive and spare. Jiu Valley family meals (including the main midday meal) often consisted of only tea and bread, or perhaps potato soup and bread, tomato soup, fried potatoes, or other similar fare. Făgăraşeni generally had a more varied diet, since more households get some food by working for others in the countryside.

More than in Făgăraş, health in the Jiu Valley is threatened by lack of meat. But meatlessness is more a social and political issue than a strictly dietary one. Like the Yanomamo, with their concept of "meat famine" (Chagnon 1968), miners claim they need meat at every meal to be able to work as they do. However, few miner households today eat meat more than once a week. Given production levels in the mines, lack of meat does not seem to have too great an effect on miners' labor power. However, the long-term effects of this diet on health are unknown. Furthermore, miners' perceptions of their dietary shortfalls continually prompt them to contrast life in socialism with the problematic political economy today. Thus, when asked about his diet, a Lonea wagon-tender discussed it in relation to shortfalls that all miners face:

> For a healthy diet we should eat meat at least twice a week, but now we are lucky if we eat meat twice a month, and that is usually chicken . . . But like I say, we're lucky because other miners have no food to bring with them [for their shift], but only food from the mine cafeteria. But food there is so terrible. It is like the food they give you in the army. Probably it is left over from stores,[9] then given to us. That causes so much of our sickness.

Though miners crave meat and fat, health professionals criticize them and their spouses for their poor diet. The head doctor at the Lupeni clinic said,

> These guys are as sick as they are also because of their diet, which consists of at least two or three beers a day plus much fat, bread, sugar, and salt. They don't know any better than to eat this way.

A staff social worker at the Petroşani general hospital adopted a more sympathetic tone, but largely concurred with the Lupeni doctor:

> Miners' health is also threatened by their high-fat diets. They must eat it for energy in the mines. But the problem is their families eat it too, resulting in high rates of cardiovascular diseases. Now life expectancy is 50–60 years for men in the Jiu Valley and 65–70 for women. Colon cancer is also on the rise.

Excessive alcohol use and alcoholism also continue to damage workers' (especially miners') health. However, as with diet, the connection between drinking and ill health is more complicated than a simple correlation (Cockerham 1997; Watson 1995). People's choices, including the choice to drink, must be understood in a larger context. In fact, drinking itself is not a significant problem for workers' health. Drinking played a major role in forming individual and group identities (Kideckel 1985) and, in the past, even facilitated social control (Ames, Grube, and Moore 2000). Postsocialism, however, has changed alcohol practice, pushing much drinking out of the bar and into solitary venues. Furthermore, postsocialist malaise encourages female alcoholism, especially in the Jiu Valley, and intensifies alcohol-fueled domestic abuse in both regions.

This was not always the case. Effective worker and miner social relations were largely crafted through drinking. For all miners, those who lived in the Valley before the 1977 strike and those who arrived after it, postshift drinking with one's workmates was an important symbolic activity, an affirmation of life itself. Drinking reinforced work-team solidarity and cemented the underground code according to which no one who is in danger is an enemy. The cohesion of mine work teams and the respect others gave them were also solidified by public drinking. Miners say that you could tell a true and effective work brigade (*o brigadă adevarată*) because when they entered a bar all the other patrons left. When "true brigade" members drank together, they did not ask others to join them. The Lupeni safety instructor reaffirmed the social importance of drinking:

If you are a miner and don't drink with others, it causes your partial exclusion. If you won't drink on payday, people really become suspicious. "Who is that?" they would say. "Why doesn't he drink with us? What kind of a big-shot does he think he is? Is he better than us?"

Drinking was also a way that miners demonstrated their masculinity. Talk at the bar centered on the work day just completed, conditions in the mine, and interesting or unforeseen events that had transpired. Thus, in drinking men demonstrated mastery over the mine and their work, the essentials of their lives. There was little talk about women, children, or household matters, and there was also no sexual bragging. All those discourses were reserved for the underground. Domination of wives and households was left assumed and unstated, though many a miner's wife showed up at the mine or bar on payday to limit the money her husband had to drink away.

Miners also claim that their labor justifies a fondness for drink. They say that work in the mines is so hard and dangerous, more so lately, that they need something to calm them after work: hence the mug of beer with a cigarette chaser. Some miners say that drinking even cures health problems caused by the mines. A Lonea miner said,

I'll tell you why miners drink so much. When you enter an atmosphere of more than 3 percent methane, it screws up your head. You can't see and you have strange sensations. The only way to escape these symptoms is to drink a hundred grams of strong drink. Vodka or plum brandy, it doesn't matter. No pills or anything else can help; only alcohol. Now this has not been proven medically, but we know it from the old-timers.

Social norms and other rationales to the contrary, drinking behavior is greatly influenced by postsocialism. For example, many miners dispute images of themselves as hopeless alcoholics and say that what appears to be drunkenness is really exhaustion from their increasingly rigorous and nerve-wracking occupation. In both regions people also say that drinking is on the decline since they are less able to afford it. Still, my sense is that alcohol use has remained fairly constant. Now, however, people drink less expensive things and more often drink at home, where they avoid the costs of buying for others. Some miners even say that "bar talk" has changed, and now focuses on the physical challenges of mine work after the buyouts, their concerns about mine closures, and the latest economic or political scandals besetting their industry. This modified discourse further clouds their perceptions and the possibility of miner agency. As communal drinking is limited and solitary drinking increases,

workers and miners feel more cut off from their groups. The Lupeni
Mine safety instructor lamented,

> Miners should not drink alone. Miners say, "Only cattle drink alone and
> have nothing to say to one another." Miners drink in groups, and beer
> from the house does not have anywhere near the value of beer from the
> bar. Drinking beer at home is not good for miners.

Over time, however, declining incomes have caused declines in
public drinking. The bars still fill up on payday and the day or so
after, but empty out more quickly. More disconcerting, miners find
fewer drinking buddies there; the shifting around of mine personnel as a result of the buy-outs has thrown together at the bar people
with little loyalty to one another. The unemployed, meanwhile,
lose nearly all opportunities to drink with their former workmates.
Many working miners are uncomfortable having former colleagues
around, while many of the bought-out can't afford to buy rounds
and are occasionally embittered toward their former mates.

Many claim that female alcoholism is on the increase in both
regions. In the Jiu Valley health care personnel, social activists,
and even some miners say this. Women's drinking in the Jiu Valley
owes more to their increasingly solitary lives, along with declining
incomes, troubled husbands, fearful neighbors, and changing standards of beauty and accomplishment. A Lupeni Mine rescue worker
and his wife often brought up the issue of women's drinking while
discussing problems that husbands and wives face in postsocialism.
Speaking first, the woman said,

> There are some women who can't get enough money [to drink]. They do
> domestic work for others . . . wash a carpet or help with housecleaning
> and then, with the money they get, they go and drink. Some others, when
> they get money [from their husband's pay], they eat and drink for two or
> three days and after that they don't even have money for bread.

Her husband interjected,

> There are men who go drinking far too much and there are also women
> who out of confusion are also heavy drinkers.

But his wife then responded,

> Hey, if the guys drink, why shouldn't I? But this just isn't the case with us
> [in the Jiu Valley], it's found everywhere. Drink is a female disease too.

There are women who were raised in families of drunks and there are some women here who drink more than their husbands. When a woman drinks, and her husband's mother drinks, well, the kids suffer from a lack of attention and remain uneducated and uncivilized.

People evaluate women's drinking more harshly than men's. Male drinking is still thought integral to male, especially miner, identity. Domestic abuse, missed or shoddy work, and physical ailments are fair trade-offs for their work in the mines or, if they have been bought out, their frustrations at not working. A woman drinking, however, does so out of personal weakness, low character, and refusal to accept the responsibilities of a wife and mother. Women are more culpable for their actions, which ramify and injure others around them.

Făgăraş workers have also changed their drinking habits in postsocialism. Good *rachiu,* the local mixed-fruit brandy, is less available than in the past. Copper boilers (*cazane*) made by Roma craftspeople are in disrepair, and few Roma are willing or able to fix them. Meanwhile, distilling costs at open *cazane* are often prohibitively high. Some *cazan* owners now just make a batch for themselves and then shut down the boiler. Instead of *rachiu,* workers drink Western whiskey and gin, or foreign and Romanian beers. Whatever the libation, social drinking (though perhaps not drinking in general) is less common in the region, as are alcohol-related diseases.

Alcohol use in both regions thus both indexes and contributes to declines in worker agency. As the spheres in which people drink become restricted, their feelings of being connected to and supported by others evaporate. Always a barometer of social change in Romanian society (Kideckel 1985), relationships and discourse in the context of drinking have grown fewer, coarser, and rife with complaint. Instead of crafting social relations, alcoholism among women and youth contributes to a view of the world as in disarray, a view that is reaffirmed by family breakdown and physical hurt. Furthermore, whether actual alcohol use has decreased, stayed the same, or increased, stress-related drinking both magnifies alcohol's negative effects on body, health, and spirit and fuels people's passivity. Definitions of problem drinking need to be revised to recognize that alcohol can serve positive functions in the formation of communities. Still, one young unemployed Făgăraş worker reflected that his drinking, ill-health, and unemployment went hand in hand, despite the satisfactions of community they offered:

All my illnesses come from drinking. Last month I was hospitalized for nine or ten days. Because of alcohol, I suffer from rheumatism, anemia, and circulatory problems. I drank a lot until I began to feel bad. I mainly drank *rachiu* at bars with my friends. I drank about one liter a day for two years straight. When I drank I felt neither bad nor good. I just liked to go and tell stories with my friends. I liked drinking. Half the time people were lying, but they were such beautiful lies.

Gender and Health

Women have more health problems in postsocialism, and they also feel their ill health more intensely, as suggested by their high scores on the Wahler Physical Symptom Inventory. Of all the postsocialist practices and conditions influencing women's health, stress seems especially significant. In particular, the stress of maintaining one's household in challenging circumstances falls disproportionately on women (Dobrescu, Rughiniş, and Zamfir 2000). Perhaps because of this, postsocialist Romania is unlike most places in the world in that more women than men die of circulatory problems, especially cerebrovascular diseases. It is true that Romanian women have a higher life expectancy than men (73.3 years for women and 65.5 for men, as of 1998), and in postsocialism this figure has even increased slightly. Nonetheless, since 1995 growth in female life expectancy has slowed, and there is some indication of its reversal (UNDP 2000, 45, 43).

In both regions concern for women's health is a particular metaphor for workers' distance from the care and concern of the state and society. In the Jiu Valley women are usually thought weaker than men and more susceptible to illness bred of their difficult living conditions. Valley people often consider the lack of hot water in their apartments especially deleterious to women's health. Jiu Valley men also claim that women are more likely to suffer nervous conditions today because they are increasingly worried about their husbands' safety in the mines. Furthermore, both men and women recognize that women's increasing health problems are due to the difficulties of managing a household with shrinking funds. However, the wife of a recently bought out Lonea miner said, more correctly, that ill health was everyone's lot in the Valley:

Here ill health doesn't depend on your sex. Our children are even born with rheumatism. Our air is completely polluted. Until last year all apartments were heated only by coal-fired central heating, and these [systems] still predominate. Petrila and Lonea only get their heat from these coal-burning central furnaces. There are many toxic gases in the air, so we have many asthmatics in the region.

In Făgăraş, as might be expected given the rough equality of their domestic and working lives, people see fewer differences between the health of women and men. However, the health problems of both sexes are still widely blamed on deteriorating conditions at the factories. Thus a Nitramonia foreman suggested,

> Women are usually more resistant to the various illnesses brought on by work in toxic gas zones. But this depends on where you work. Still, women are more affected by work in cold environments than are men. Generally speaking, people in our factory are healthier now, but that is only because the factory doesn't operate at full capacity, but only at about 20 percent.

Whatever the particulars of postsocialist morbidity, there is no doubt that women are increasingly pressured to fill the roles that their culture expects of them. Consequently, when things fall apart in families and households, or when children perform poorly in school, it is the woman who is blamed. Also, in a complete about-face from socialist conditions, little health care is available for working women. During the last decades of socialism, women's health care was largely designed to support state pronatalism. Though this policy and its goals were egregious, some of what was done in its service did contribute to better overall health for women—that is, if they survived the numerous illegal and unsafe abortions into which they were forced. Not so today. As the lone medical assistant left at the Nitramonia factory suggested, many more women than men apply for sick leave. She went on to say,

> Conditions for women workers are much worse. They try to do the same things that men do to earn more money, and they have to work as hard as men to keep their jobs in the factory. A few things are done to help pregnant women, but it is nothing like it was during the time of Ceauşescu. Now, after four months of pregnancy a woman can be excused from night work, heavy work, or can even have her workplace switched if necessary. But most women don't do this because they might lose money and they don't want the men to make fun of them. Hey, there even used to be a midwife [*moaşă*] at the factory, but not any longer.

Women's reproductive health in Romania has clearly improved from the dark days of pronatalism, even if too few people still use effective contraception (Hord et al. 1991; Magyari-Vincze 2004; Şerbanescu et al. 1995). However, people believe just the opposite. In the Jiu Valley, talk of miscarriage was rife and appeared to intensify women's sense of threat and dread. We visited a number of homes where young couples were frustrated about interrupted pregnancies and worried that they would never carry a child to term. Their concern was palpable, as were their suspicions that social forces conspired to prevent their successful pregnancies. Ioan and Maria Munteanu were one such couple. He was a union activist from Lupeni, and she long unemployed. Her latest scheme to make money was selling fancy cookware on commission, but her neighbors had no money, so that fell apart, leaving the family in debt for the cookware samples. More than a job, Maria wanted a child. She was on the verge of tears as she and her husband recounted her recent miscarriage while she held on to her "baby," a large, fancily dressed doll standing rigid on the couch:

> SHE: I lost my pregnancy after one and half months.
> DAK: What do you think was the cause?
> SHE: I had a cold. It was the end of April. I wasn't working. But I lost the baby at home. When I started to bleed, I went to the Lupeni hospital emergency ward, but when I found out that this guy, Dr. M, was the one on call that day, I left and didn't get my problem taken care of right away. But the bleeding continued, so I returned even though I was scared. Dr. M is feared by all the women. He speaks to us dirtily and treats us poorly. Other women also say this. I know he harmed me. After curettage, I knew things weren't right. Now I am afraid that I can't have any children.
> HE: I believe environment has a lot to do with the miscarriages. Not just pollution from the mines, but Chernobyl especially affected us and the food we eat.
> SHE: We know many people who have had miscarriages.
> HE: I know three or four people at the mines whose wives have lost their pregnancies in just the last few months. Our birth rate is low and falling.
> DAK: How many children would you like?
> HE: The ideal family today is two or three, but four would be great. In the past miners had a lot of children because we had large salaries and didn't worry about the cost of things. Today only Pocaiţi [members of Evangelical Protestant sects] have many children.
> SHE: Yes, but many people like us have none when they want to have children.

Miscarriage, unemployment, and declining ability to maintain home and children match the feelings of psychological loss that Heather Carlson and her colleagues found among Romanian women (Carlson et al. 2000). However, her interviews with forty

Romanian women aged thirty-five or over in the late 1990s showed their remarkable resiliency in the face of vast and inescapable personal, financial, and other losses. Our informants in the Jiu Valley and Făgăraş suggest the same; they've no choice but to go on. Thus, women persevere in the postsocialist storm even though their perceptions of their health and fertility, and of the reproductive and medical care they receive, are ever worsening. (Inadequate care is typically provided to people to whom a "reproductive stigma" is attached [Schneider and Schneider 1996, 9–11].) Moreover, demands on their time are increasing, their husbands' physical condition is threatened, and their children's prospects are disappearing. The pressures of postsocialism produce situations in which family and social life hang on the thread of female fortitude. However, increasing domestic abuse, alcoholism, family abandonment, and loss of every kind have begun to erode this fortitude. Without women's power to act, Romanian worker families are increasingly frozen into the frustrated agency in which they find themselves. It is no wonder that TN, the worker quoted in this chapter's epigraph, feels ill. His wife is downtrodden, and without her, he is lost.

Conclusions: Postsocialist Health, Embodied States, and Frustrated Agency

Sick workers make a sick society. The veneer of modern Romania may be promising, but the promise is hard, if not impossible, to realize with society's backbone so troubled. Though other groups, like intellectuals, may have escaped what Andrei Pleşu (1996, 561) termed the neurasthenia of socialism, in which people "lived from day to day in the shadow of a diffuse anxiety . . . swinging between despair and brute force," workers are only more trapped in it today. Pleşu was sanguine about Romania's future. He saw intellectual work and practice, like garlic, as able to equilibrate society's blood pressure (564), to help Romania as a whole "get by." However, the physical state and embodied perceptions of labor work against such equilibration. Most socialist contradictions have turned into the despair of postsocialism or the brute force of anger at a fixed game. These postures obscure labor's possibilities by hedging workers' lives around with problematic health circumstances and bodily perceptions. Working people and their families find their options blocked at every turn. Many people, women in particular, are bogged down in struggles for mere survival. Others have the sinking sense that they are physically incapable of even beginning a plan of action, let alone bringing it to fruition. To update Confucius for postsocialist times, "A journey of a thousand miles will certainly end without a first step."

The troubled state of Jiu Valley and Făgăraş workers and their class contemporaries throughout the country is by no means hidden from view. Health care workers with whom I spoke, especially those connected to the public health services in Braşov and Hunedoara counties, affirmed the distressed physical state of workers and families in the regions. But, like working people generally, they also felt ineffectual, blocked by structural and budgetary limitations. Some, like the Lupeni physician and Petroşani hospital sociologist quoted above, "blamed the victim." They saw medical care as largely irrelevant in a mining population of such limited culture and learning. Further complicating labor's health, preventative medicine is rare in Romania, and public health–related social marketing campaigns (e.g., against tobacco, alcohol, domestic violence, unsafe sex) typically fail, because authorities promote them only half-heartedly and workers are alienated, uninterested, and distrustful. More certainly could be done to inform miners, workers, and the unemployed of how to preserve and improve their health (e.g., by boiling unpurified water and properly disposing of domestic waste). However, even these relatively low-cost measures are unlikely to change health conditions, practices, and perceptions largely shaped by the frustrations and paralysis of postsocialist political economy, because they largely avoid the political issues in which such frustrations ferment (Baer 1996).

Workers' terror that their bodies are failing is, after all, correct, though the decline is less the product of improper health practices, failing institutions, or even increased disease vectors than of daily stress. As workers observe shuttered factories, closed mine galleries, media distortions, the luxury cars and villas of the moneyed classes, and the outstretched hand of the family physician, they raise a number of pointed questions. If factories don't hire and mines will close, why have children? If our legitimate demands are met only with truncheons or broken promises, why stand up and make them? If my spouse's efforts to secure a small income are negated at a whim, why work harder? If our children's attempts to secure an education are made irrelevant by others' bribes, why learn? And if our attention to our health and bodies is rendered useless by defective plumbing, heating, housing, and diet, why stay sober, why stay clean, why struggle? Why, indeed!

8   **What Is to Be Done?**

> We will take all necessary measures to extract value from the region's resources to certainly improve people's living conditions.
>
> **—Ion Iliescu, campaign speech to Jiu Valley miners, Miners' Day, 1999**

> Romania basically has only three things of value for the global economy: scrap metal, raw timber, and women.
>
> **—CN, Jiu Valley journalist, 2004**

At the beginning of this book I quoted extensively from interviews with two workers, a bought-out miner from the Petrila Mine in the Jiu Valley and an employed worker and union activist at the UPRUC chemical fittings factory in Făgăraş. Their tales conveyed both the diversity and commonality of the stress with which workers have lived since the fall of socialism and the fear and alienation with which they face the present. Subsequent chapters explored the many dimensions of this stress and these embodied emotions, as they are expressed by workers. The onslaught of postsocialist forces atomizes and commodifies them at their workplaces (when they are lucky enough to have a job). The restructuring of society neutralizes and anathematizes their political identities and practices. Their families and communities are wracked by massive emigration, deterioration of their housing and diet, and the unraveling of networks, and these processes are spurred on by the lash of new consumption demands, which they are ill able to meet. Their identities and practices as men and women are buffeted, and must be intensively reworked if they are to survive. Their bodies, health, and emotional strength and stability paradoxically suffer from both too much anger and too much apathy. Struggling in every sector of their lives, workers look back to and fictionalize the heyday of socialism as a model of the good life, which further dampens their ability to plan for, act on, and achieve their desires. This arrested and distorted state bodes ill for both them and society. Clearly, change is called for.

The title of this chapter consciously echoes V. I. Lenin's famous question, posed a decade or so before the Russian Revolution. At that time the Bolshevik leader offered a revolutionary prescription for the ills plaguing Russia. However, neither society nor workers in postsocialist Romania and East-Central Europe today can challenge the global neo-liberal order into which the former socialist states have rushed headlong. On the contrary, workers, like others, see no solution but to survive within the current system. They know their memories of socialism will remain only memories, even as their fear and alienation deprive them of what little influence they might have on the deluge of policy and practice transforming the post-socialist lands. Still, although workers are unable to play a major role in regional social change, postsocialist states must still address the diminishing of their lives, bodies, and souls. Though workers' stresses and struggles may favor East-Central European economic development in the short run, over the long haul they can only provoke confrontation and society-wide challenges and costs.

Certainly, the lives of postsocialist workers and their families are not without joys and satisfactions, even in these uncertain times. However, the various transformations confronting miners, workers, and their families have emptied life of much of its content and meaning. Many Jiu Valley men—miners of great renown, former socialist heroes, and scourges of socialist and postsocialist governments alike—sense that they are now superfluous, their lives mocked as animalistic anachronisms. In Făgăraş, meanwhile, many look out at the crumbling factories, deteriorating housing, and emigrating youth and fear for their individual and collective futures. Women in both regions, employed or not, complain of unremitting labor, isolation, declining family status, denigration of their and their husbands' lives, and their children's crabbed life chances. Moreover, current social forces make it difficult to define new possibilities. Money is short. Jobs are scarce. Alternatives are lacking. Friends and family are in similar or worse predicaments. People withdraw into themselves and their homes, at best distancing themselves from society and social action, and at worst falling prey to personal and domestic pathologies. Social alienation and fear for the future contribute to the popularity of angry politicians like Andrezj Lepper in Poland, Vladimir Meciar in Slovakia, and ultra-nationalist Corneliu Vadim Tudor and his Greater Romania Party in Romania. Vadim's support in the 2000 and 2004 presidential elections was due in large part to his campaign's masculine symbolism of violence and power, and his vague promises to eliminate corruption and revive the nation—by violence, if necessary. As gruff as his message was, it nonetheless touched some of the deep-seated sensibilities troubling workers today.

Numerous programs have recently been developed to remedy the distress of populations in East-Central Europe, in Romania, and even in the Jiu Valley and the Făgăraş region. These include national policy interventions such as wage and price indexation, phase-ins of new labor contract buy-outs, and legal protections against summary layoffs. Interventions also include more targeted practices, such as laws enabling special investment zones, special provisions for workers at industrial complexes undergoing privatization, and job training programs and public works employment in hard-pressed regions. These programs are developed and funded both by the national government and by international bilateral and multilateral institutions such as the EU and the World Bank. However, the programs that specifically target workers seem motivated less by concern for effective change in these communities than by the desire to avert political activism. Thus, though these policies have some positive effects, most come up short in practical ways and, more problematically, in the logic of their design, implementation, administration, and evaluation. Though generally well-meaning, ultimately they also heighten workers' fears, uncertainties, and perceptions that society is unconcerned for them.

One example of such a policy is the Law on Disfavored Zones (Romanian Government 1998), which gives incentives for investment in regions like the Jiu Valley, defined as "disfavored" because of their mono-industrial character or high unemployment. The law mandates, among other things, duty-free import of capital equipment, special financing and government credit for approved investments, tax reductions on income earned from investment properties in a disfavored zone, and favorable tax status for enterprises hiring unemployed workers from disfavored zones. Still, despite these salutary provisions, the law has brought only limited investment and few jobs into regions like the Jiu Valley and Făgăraş and, worse than that, it exacerbates worker disaffection because of the way it articulates with critical postsocialist phenomena.

The law was quickly applied to mining zones, but its application in numerous other areas was obstructed, although they clearly met the law's specifications. A team from Făgăraş spent months trying to have the region designated a disfavored zone under the law, making numerous trips to Braşov and Bucharest, only to have their application denied. The former vice-mayor of the city wondered whether the law was intended to actually produce results at all. He suggested that it was passed only as a sop to the miners, to defuse some of their political volatility. Others who have heard of the law, including workers, say that many of its provisions are manipulated to the advantage of politicians and investors and the disadvantage of labor. For example, one provision requires investors to hire the local unemployed for qualifying projects. This requirement, however, is often ignored. For instance, when I asked a group of ten workers building the road from Petroşani to the Banat resort Băile Herculane where they were from, most indicated Timişoara, where their company, SARTEX, was located. Two said they were from Deva, the capital of Hunedoara County, in which the Jiu Valley is located. Only one was from the Valley itself, and he was not a former miner.

The Law on Disfavored Zones is only one example of how the deck of positive initiatives is stacked against the interests and possibilities of postsocialist workers. More destructive have been the mainly irrelevant job training programs developed by international aid agencies and financial institutions and the false promises—of new jobs, new homes, new resources for their children—made regularly to workers. Thus, to answer the question posed at the head of this chapter: much needs to be done, and leaders of all political persuasions are professing commitment and showing evidence of movement. However, such things seem mainly window-dressing for the benefit of international agencies monitoring and evaluating the East-Central European states to see whether they meet global or EU standards; the leaders are not actually implementing EU requirements. Meanwhile, at home, workers, politicians, businesspeople, and others know such policies are to be taken with a wink and a nod.

Interventions for Labor throughout the Postsocialist Lands

Though Romanian workers have generally fared more poorly in postsocialism than others in East-Central Europe, the Jiu Valley and

Făgăraş cases echo throughout the region. Workers generally, and particularly current and former employees of large state industrial complexes (Crowley 1997, 2004; Crowley and Ost 2001; Gardawski, Gąciarz, et al. 1999), have been largely left to fend for themselves, despite the *Sturm und Drang* of state and international interventions. Since the fall of communism, the East-Central European region has been a vast sinkhole for foreign assistance, partly intended to cement the West's victory in the Cold War. Aid from multilateral organizations like the World Bank, bilateral organizations like the United States Agency for International Development (USAID) and EU-PHARE, and private-sector organizations like the Institute for Civil Society Development has mainly been earmarked for infrastructure development, industrial restructuring, privatization, and democratization. Benefits to workers are supposed to "trickle down" from these projects.

Like foreign assistance programs generally (Ferguson 1994; Wedel 1998a), such interventions as job training and health education have a generic or all-purpose, "cookie-cutter" quality to them that renders them irrelevant to the needs of particular regions and groups. Thus, for example, the World Bank assisted the Romanian government in developing and applying a poorly thought through assistance program for the unemployed in the Jiu Valley in 1998–2000. Coming on the heels of the equally problematic labor contract buy-out, the program barely touched crushing Valley unemployment and, like the Law on Disfavored Zones, contributed to workers' senses of abandonment. For example, job retraining was only offered to those recently let go from their work, excluding most Valley women on the spot. Similarly, public works jobs offered to formerly highly paid miners offered only minimum wage and often required expensive commutes to and from work. Furthermore, corruption in the program's local implementation waylaid some of the monies and favored certain individuals over others.

Problematic support for organized labor adds to workers' inability to press for effective policies and programs. Although trade unionism is in steep decline elsewhere in the capitalist world, labor union membership in East-Central Europe is still extensive, with unions highly visible in national political economic events and processes. On closer examination, however, the prominence of unions in the postsocialist world seems less an affirmation of worker power than an example of inertia in the development of globalized capitalism out of late socialism. With few exceptions (including Poland's Solidarity and Romania's Cartel Alfa), the region's dominant unions, now renamed to avoid socialist taint, are the same out-of-touch behemoths that handled socialist policies and benefits "before the fall." Their structures and leadership scramble to cope with salary negotiations, occupational health and safety problems, and the like. Even where unions have changed to better address current labor issues, they often are compromised by interunion competition to increase membership rolls or by the confused regulations determining how unions may affiliate with each other, what I elsewhere called "disorganized organization" (Kideckel 2001, 98). Finally, national legislation prevents East-Central European labor unions from taking up the causes of the unemployed (many of whom are former members), preventing them from playing an effective role in an issue that involves every aspect of society, including the lives of union members and their families.

Despite its numbers, in many respects organized labor is in disarray throughout the postsocialist world, and trade union membership is declining both in absolute numbers and in diverse economic sectors. Union membership has remained steady only in the state sector and in large enterprises (Gardawski, Gąciarz, et al. 1999, 259), but even here unions have lost power and authority as members' identification with their union has declined. Additionally, East-Central European unions poorly represent women, who continue to constitute almost 50 percent of workers throughout the region (Occhipinti 1996; Pollert 2001a). Most significantly, unions have not been effective in their work. Polls show workers in union-represented sectors are less satisfied with nearly every aspect of their working life than are their colleagues in other, mainly non-unionized, sectors (Gardawski, Gąciarz, et al. 1999, 260). This dissatisfaction is due not only to problems with their unions, but also to the fact that it is the industries most disadvantaged in the growth of regional capitalism that are most heavily unionized.

Though factors affecting workers' employment and other life conditions vary throughout the region, the issues facing workers are largely similar. In an interview in the *Multinational Monitor,* Jasna Petrovic, editor-in-chief of the International Confederation of Free Trade Unions' Central and Eastern Europe (ICFTU-CEE) Network Bulletin and regional coordinator of the ICFTU East European Women's Network, points out a general decline in respect for labor rights and notes that it correlates with a similar decline in union effectiveness, vastly increased unemployment and poverty rates, and the failure of governments to counter the ascendancy of private capital throughout East-Central Europe:

> MM: To what degree are labor rights respected in Central and Eastern Europe?
>
> JP: Labor rights are under attack in all countries in the region. There are still some countries . . . in which labor legislation has actually not been changed since the Communist era . . . a real campaign of the World Bank and the International Monetary Fund is currently under way in almost all countries of the region, aiming at urgent new revisions in labor laws . . . to ensure the liberalization of the labor market, flexibilization of labor relations and reduction of workers rights. This is an attempt to attack trade unions, and motivated by a desire to reduce their influence.
>
> Overall, workers' rights are least observed in countries with a more intensive entry of international and foreign capital, that is, in Baltic and Central European countries.
>
> MM: What are some of the common problems in the region related to respect for labor rights?
>
> JP: The basic problem . . . is the growing poverty, disastrous unemployment levels and massive non-payments of wages due to business's lack of liquidity. Add to this mass redundancies in the state sector (military, police, education) and the public sector in general, as well as hundreds of thousands of companies undergoing bankruptcy and liquidation procedures; plus delays in payment of pensions and state employees' salaries, as well as the limitation of wage growth in the public sector. It is clear that there is an incredibly large number of problems.
>
> Laws are still relatively proworker and socially sensitive, but the reality is not. A large number of workers are in the street and have no prospect of finding a new job. Many find themselves in court demanding unpaid severance pay or unpaid wages, or are in labor disputes over the issue of their return to work.
>
> Courts . . . have not been transformed, and an average court case lasts between three and ten years. This is a major problem . . . because employers have an advantage . . . due to the inefficient and slow judiciary.
>
> Lately, a major problem has been the instability of employment contracts. Private employers are increasingly employing workers with fixed-term agreements or hiring them illegally. It is estimated that the informal economy involves 50 percent more workers than the official figures show, and these are unprotected workers, even if they are registered as employed, receiving minimum wages and having no rights. Collective bargaining agreements most often do not cover them. (Petrovic 2002)

Thus, the problematic conditions faced by workers across the region are broad, deep, and consistent regardless of the level of national development. Where wages are higher, so is the cost of living. Where jobs are plentiful, unions are in retreat. It is clear workers have lost some benefits since the fall of socialism: attention from the state, a legal regime that afforded and enforced some basic rights, symbolic capital, security, and the effectiveness of their own representatives, to name a few. In their place capitalism promised that hard work and sacrifice would rapidly improve standards of living, give workers a real voice in their life and labor and in national politics, and free their children from the want and fear they had known much of their lives. The extent to which the former socialist states' participation in the global market will actually promote these improvements remains unclear. There is ample reason to be concerned.

Europe and Postsocialist Workers

Despite the concerns of union leaders like Jasna Petrovic and the difficulties confronted by postsocialist workers in East-Central Europe, some recent salutary developments may presage improvement in their welfare. These include steadily increasing Western investment, the transfer of highly paid West European factory jobs to well-educated East-Central European workers who can be paid less, better chances of controlled, contract-based labor migration (seasonal, temporary, and even permanent), and the increased application of EU labor regulations in East-Central European workplaces. These possibilities are echoed by the International Labor Organization:

> Opportunities have emerged with the introduction of new forms of work organization and technologies, demanding high levels of skill and flexible working attitudes. As aspirations for high educational attainment remain strong across the region, there are good prospects for high "social and economic return" on future investments in human resource development and training. (ILO 2002, iii)

Still, despite these new opportunities, it is uncertain whether such developments can serve as vehicles for improvement in workers' lives, families, and physical capacities. In fact, a review of these "positive" developments shows them often balanced or negated by other factors. Thus, the "entry into Europe" must be understood as the equivocal event that it actually is, rather than as either panacea or problem. The lower wage rates of East-Central European workers are also equivocal. Positively, they have attracted a wide variety of Western investment and facilitated a new range of employment possibilities in the postsocialist countries. As the ILO implies, they may have also spearheaded improvement in working conditions. Some new factories and service centers, like the spanking clean

Volkswagen plant employing about 2,500 people on the outskirts of Poznán, Poland, and the new Peugeot-Citröen plant outside Trnava, Slovakia, employing 3,500 (Landler 2004), rival those in Germany and France. However, they have negative consequences as well, for workers across the breadth of Europe.

The out-migration of West European jobs produces backlash among both workers and governments in the non-accession EU, i.e., the EU states prior to the addition of Poland, Hungary, the Czech Republic, and Slovakia (Buechsenschuetz 2004). To appease West European workers, countries in the non-accession EU are considering legislation that would restrict the economies and workers of the entering states. Over time, these will lessen any advantages East-Central European workers will have as a result of lower labor costs. Furthermore, not only are out-migrating jobs a concern of West Europeans, but so too are in-migrating East Europeans, glossed in the West as the "Polish plumber." Such workers are seen as a threat not only to Western wage and benefit packages but to the moral fiber of the EU countries. Thus, despite open border policies, immigration restrictions that specifically target workers may become more stringent in the future, as suggested in a recent RFE Research Report:

> For the broader populations so often influenced by the low-brow reporting of tabloid newspapers, the opening of the borders presents a threat to their jobs—and not only among states bordering the acceding countries, such as Austria or Germany. Ed Vulliamy noted in "The Observer" of 11 April: 'Suddenly, our new partner citizens in the EU—those same people whose deliverance from Communism, wrought by their own bravery, we celebrated 14 years ago—have become potential 'benefit tourists' (Daily Mail), agents of 'social upheaval' (Financial Times), a 'menace' (the Mail again) to our social services, a horde of gypsies, or a 'flood tide' (Daily Express) of 'millions of immigrants' (the Mail again). Government talk is not of liberty or union, but of 'habitual residence requirements' and 'employment registration certificates.' (Buechsenschuetz 2004)

Like emigration, foreign investment, privatization, and capitalist development are also not without their downsides for workers, their families, and their communities. Privatization facilitated by foreign investment is one of the reasons that East-Central European labor has fragmented into diverse and mutually uninterested labor forces (Pavlinek 2004). This fragmentation was especially severe in Romania, where large-scale manufacturing particularly suffered in the first years of postsocialism (Anton and Cimpoeasu 1996). Workers lucky enough to secure employment in the large, foreign-financed manufacturing sector, such as at the Volkswagen and Peugeot plants, have better job security, better working conditions, and better wages than workers in both the state and small-capitalization private sectors. According to Michał Buchowski (personal communication), at one Volkswagen plant in Poland trade union membership is high and average wages are 20 percent more than the national average.

Such workers, however, are a small minority, and their labor unions tend to concentrate on local issues. I have seen little evidence that they are jealous of or angry at their more fortunate colleagues working in the large foreign-controlled industries. East-Central Europeans are no longer committed to the socialist ideology of forced equality in pay rates and living standards and accept social differentiation in their ranks. Nonetheless, the development of a large foreign-controlled manufacturing sector has in effect freed these workers from the concerns faced by the majority of employed and unemployed in the postsocialist world, thus lessening the presence and power of workers as a class. In fact, workers in the foreign sector are the least visible of all in local and national labor actions.[1]

Western investment also redivides the postsocialist states. Socialist development policies, especially those in Ceauşescu's Romania, often spread industry around the country to equalize regional development and living standards, often with uneven results (Hoffman 1972; Sampson 1984; Tsantis and Pepper 1979). Today, abetted by Western capital, that process is largely reversed. Capital is again concentrated in major urban centers, which are more accessible to Western markets and organizations, and marginal regions again bear the brunt of economic imbalance. Areas that have again become centers of rural poverty, such as Moldavia in Romania's northeast, furnish many of the youth, women in particular, who end up trafficked for sex and labor, though victims of this trafficking come from other areas as well (Allnut 2004; Fisher 2004). The macroeconomic effects of population and resource transfer are another cost that must be borne in order for the postsocialist states to develop within the fabric of the EU. East-Central European host countries are deprived of productivity, profit, and people, all of which are transmitted westward at a time when such resources are critically needed at home to improve the economic future of the developing postsocialist state.

Entry into the EU also appears as a mixed blessing in the narratives of Jiu Valley and Făgăraş workers. Though Jack Friedman suggests that the miners are concerned about being "expelled from inclusion in the global" (2003, iv), this suggestion needs to be unpacked. For the most part, miners are worried that integration into "Europe" will force them to limit their production or will not recognize the quality of Romanian workers, resources, or production processes. They see entry into Europe as a threat to existing coal production. As a Lupeni miner suggested,

> We have the best coal quality in Europe, but mining as an industry still keeps losing ground. In five years the mines will be full of water and impossible to exploit, and that way the Poles will be able to come here and sell coal to us.

They also blame Europe for destroying Jiu Valley production by raiding its labor. An Aninoasa miner suggested that

> many Jiu Valley miners have left to work in Hungary. The Hungarians steal our workers because the Jiu Valley is the best school for miners in all Europe. Our miners go to Hungary to work, and produce twice as much as the Hungarian miners do. Because of this the Hungarians are being hassled by their own miners who want jobs.

Făgăraş workers are also concerned about the possible effects of EU accession on Romania generally, though they do not think accession will especially affect their own industries and occupations. Furthermore, owing to their greater familiarity with Western Europe, often gained through emigration, they are also somewhat more equivocal about the role of foreign capital. Still, incidents like the recent theft of much of Nitramonia's capital in an American entrepreneur's faux privatization scheme (Şelaru 2004) are bound to popularize wild theories, like that of a former Nitramonia worker who suggested that

> Western commercial interests actively work to keep Romania down. Just think about how the price of Coca Cola is low compared to the price of milk. This certainly suggests there is a conspiracy to wreck the Romanian economy and agriculture in particular. The West only wants to make sure that Romania doesn't get too good at producing. The money they give for aid disappears like it went into a black hole. This is done deliberately.

Workers' Bodies, Workers' Health

Changes in the conditions of labor contribute to pressures on workers' bodies and health throughout the postsocialist zone, not merely in Romania. Worker health is certainly not as dire as in the years immediately after the fall of socialism, and life expectancy and morbidity have stabilized. However, conditions will remain difficult. Issues relating to worker health differ mainly in their magnitude throughout the region; they include declines (both absolute and relative to budgets) in national and local funding for public health, the reduction or elimination of safety and health programs in the workplace, and the constant choice workers must make between health care and other needs, such as food and housing. Other health issues confronting East-Central European workers were defined in a report commissioned by the International Labor Organization:

> Among the causes [of poor worker health care] are cuts in public funding which leave many local authorities without the resources or administrative capacity to meet new obligations . . . Total spending on health in Central and Eastern European countries ranges between 2.6 percent in Romania and 7.2 percent of GDP in the Czech Republic. The Central and Eastern European average is 5.3 percent compared to the European Union average of 8.5 percent.

"All of this has surely contributed to the catastrophic fall in life expectancy rates in Russia, Ukraine and some other countries in the region." . . . The crisis has been worsened by rapidly increasing rates of sexually-transmitted diseases, HIV/AIDS, tuberculosis and numerous other chronic illnesses. (Afford 2003)

The causes of increased mortality in postsocialist East-Central Europe, especially among middle-aged men, have been hotly debated. Lately, transformations in labor (production demands, unemployment, insecurity) and the related intensification of social inequality have been recognized as critical causes of decreases in life expectancy. Marmot and Bobek (2000a) even suggest that poverty plays less of a role in morbidity and mortality than do inequality and workers' perceptions of it. Jozan and Forster (1999) echo these findings in their study of mortality and social disadvantage in Budapest in 1980–83 and 1990–93. Here, though mortality was higher among disadvantaged and impoverished groups than among the better off even in socialism, with the end of socialism the differences between the two groups' rates of both death and preventable death have increased. Furthermore, Jozan and Forster's data imply greater pressure on the health of men, who are typically workers of varying skill levels, either employed, unemployed, or underemployed:

> Within the group of most disadvantaged districts, the ratio of standardised mortality ratios in 1990–3 compared with 1980–3 increased significantly in males for all causes . . . As the free market economy and health insurance based services replace previous systems in Hungary, and as income

distribution becomes more inequitable, urgent research and intervention will be needed to control the social inequality in all aspects of health, as identified by the World Health Organisation's Health for All 2000 initiative. (Jozan and Forster 1999, 915)

The distancing of labor has profound effects on health and life expectancy, and this is painfully clear in the contrast between Romania and the Czech Republic. The Czech democratic experience is exceptional throughout the postsocialist world. Here life expectancy, including male life expectancy at birth (LEB), has increased during postsocialism. But most telling, according to Blazek and Dzúrová (2000, 305–306), is the fact that in the Czech Republic the conditions of labor are generally good. Throughout postsocialism unemployment in the Czech Republic has been relatively low, service sector jobs have rapidly multiplied, an extensive system of social security and state oversight has been maintained, and poverty rates have risen only moderately. Meanwhile in Romania the distancing and stress of labor take their toll especially on workers' health and life expectancy. As Cornelia Mureşan shows, not only do males in the 30–60 age cohort show the greatest decline in LEB, but

the economic crisis of the last years has led to the continuous deterioration of real income . . . and continuous growth in unemployment. These issues have had serious repercussions on the population's health conditions. (Mureşan 1999, 191)

There are some dissenters from this view. For example, Marmot and Bobek (2000b, 128) suggest that Romanian LEB statistics show steady increases in mortality both before and after "regime change" in 1989 and 1990. They therefore assume that more general social conditions, not specifically postsocialist ones, account for the increase. However, their logic is not compelling. The postsocialist differentiation of Romanian society has meant that diverse social strata, which it had been the socialist state's policy to forcibly homogenize, today diverge in their health and life expectancies. Better medical treatment and living conditions for politicians, businesspeople, and middle-class professionals accompany steep declines for those in less fortunate social groups, especially workers. In fact, even Marmot and Bobek (131) note the role of income differentials and the importance of relative deprivation in East-Central European mortality. These factors most likely operate across regional, ethnic, gender, and age groups.

Labor, Culture, Belonging, and Agency

Ill health is thus yet another factor pushing East-Central Europe's once-powerful industrial labor force from its commanding position in the newly capitalist region. Loss of physical power combines with loss of political power and loss of purchasing power to contribute to embodied distance and the disastrous frustration of worker agency. Individually or collectively, workers are less and less able to influence change and development at national, regional, or local levels. More significantly, they are less able to shape the course of their own and their families' lives. Their ability to plan and act falls prey to an acceptance of their decline: a habitus of resignation, if you will. Such perceptions of loss of control are rife in the postsocialist world. For example, Michał Buchowski's discussion of the new proletariat in the west Polish village of Dziekanowice shows that people there have "a self-perception of the reality of being losers in the new system [that] creates an ideological community and fortifies resignation" (Buchowski 2001, 152).

Caroline Humphrey considers the dispossessed in the former Soviet Union, including "temporary contract workers," "out-workers at home," and the growing legions of others increasingly found "outside . . . primary unit[s] of society" (2002b, 21–39). According to Humphrey, such people experience a "nightmare of chaos" through their loss of or decline in position. Not only are their income, education, and health care limited, their identities are unhinged and their senses of belonging destroyed. Humphrey's discussion also obliquely addresses the declining significance of the state (27) and its protective, though all-encompassing, control over workers' lives. The elimination or diminution of state power does not, however, provide workers with opportunities to act in and on their own behalf. Rather, their days are spent in devising short-term strategies to cope with the myriad problems of daily life. Only rarely, in attempting to cope with the forces that pressure them, do a few manage to take control of their own lives and futures.

Workers' Coping Strategies

As Humphrey and others show, the strictures that the postsocialist system places on workers and their families make life planning more reactive than proactive. For workers throughout the postsocialist world, many aspects of "getting by" are transformed. Practice and planning are limited by the scarcity of resources, by the break-down in social networks, by intense competition for jobs, and by the divisions between employed and unemployed. As a consequence, people mainly devise short-term strategies to satisfy their basic and immediate needs. However, though their physical survival is en-sured, they do not have the time and energy necessary to plan for and enact more extensive change.

Even workers' short-term strategies are less viable than those of other groups. In a case study from Novosibirsk, in Russia's "far east," Tchernina (2000, 151) suggests that unemployment and un-deremployment force people to act much as they did in socialism. They try to improve their lives by "penetrating all levels of the in-formal economy, and intensifying their efforts in their home econ-omy." However, in socialism everybody did so; such strategies were as available to workers as to the next person. Today, even workers' coping practices and contexts are more restricted than those of their middle-class peers. The scientific-technical intelligentsia are more likely to succeed in substituting informal and domestic economic practice for formal employment than are industrial workers. Thus Tchernina lists six coping strategies used by Novosibirsk people, but several of them seem particularly ill-suited to those with the skill levels and training possibilities of former industrial workers: 1) get-ting an additional job similar to one's current one; 2) using equip-ment from one's permanent place of employment to earn additional income; 3) getting trained to provide newly demanded services; 4) shuttle-trading (purchasing goods abroad for resale at home); 5) supplementing existing employment with manual labor; and 6) en-tering other irregular occupations. Workers and their families are likely to be able to effect only numbers 1, 5, and 6, which are not only very much alike, but also limit long-term possibilities even further. Numbers 2, 3, and 4 are usually beyond the physical and financial capabilities of working families. Even more significantly, as Tchernina (167) points out, many of the disadvantaged (and here she specifically includes workers) possess no coping strategies what-soever with which they can confront unemployment.

Throughout the postsocialist world, the growing mass of unem-ployed and underemployed workers are often blamed for their own dispirited lives and their failure to cope with, let alone succeed in, the new world of market capitalism. They are criticized for their in-ability to take a chance, their refusal to tighten their belts, and, like the Lupeni hunger strikers discussed earlier, for making outsized demands which their countries can ill afford. But few or none of the options allegedly available to them, whether state-sponsored interventions or other local employment or entrepreneurial possibilities, are in fact available (Dobrescu, Rughiniş, and Zamfir 2000). Many interventions are hopelessly irrelevant even before they are implemented, and they often exacerbate the problem of narrowed worker agency rather than providing a way out.

Still, though solutions for most are still wanting, some people do adapt and even thrive. Some escape from postsocialist strictures though retraining. Others have families that assist them. Increasing numbers opt for emigration, either within their home country or to legal or illegal labor in West European locales.[2] And some can even marshal the resources to start a business or otherwise reposition themselves in the changed postsocialist market. But these few individual successes are the exceptions to declining worker agency. Their very rarity shows how limited most workers' ability is to plan and determine their life course. The stories of two former miners, one whose striving enabled his great success, and another whose efforts turned to dust, illustrate two postsocialist patterns. Unfortunately the latter is by far the more common.

Lotzi M, a Magyar Romanian originally from the Cluj region, is the rare success. Lotzi left a twenty-year career in the Lupeni mines as a machinist (and a member in good standing of the Communist Party) shortly after the Revolution. He was inspired to leave the mines by a fading Communist Party slogan on a building that said, "Whoever wants to create something looks for the means to do so. Whoever doesn't, looks for excuses." He bought a supply of penny candy, balloons, and the like to sell on the street in his home town. Lotzi worked for two years both in the mines and in his new business. Finally, as he began to earn sufficient profit, he moved from table to kiosk to storefront, and left the mines for good in 1995. He now works full-time running two successful businesses: a general store selling cigarettes, soap, cosmetics, liquors, and the like, and a bakery and delicatessen.

Though proud of his success and glad of the choices he made, Lotzi readily acknowledges their costs. He faced withering criticism from former mine colleagues, though it was often couched in a joking manner. When they saw him on the street they asked how he could leave his colleagues (*ortaci*) behind in the mine. Some called him "Sweet Lotzi," or said things like "Oh, aren't you ashamed, businessman?[3] You go and sell things with gypsies in the marketplace. You should hear how people laugh at you behind your back." Maintaining the business also comes at great personal cost. He travels several times a week between the Jiu Valley and Bucharest, a twelve-hour round trip, plus the time he needs to do business in Bucharest. He takes few, if any, vacations and says he has neither friends nor the time for them. He sleeps four hours a night, worries constantly about his "bottom line," and sees no end in sight to his frenetic pace. "Still," he says, "everyone wants to leave something behind, and this will be our legacy to our daughter."

Unlike Lotzi's, Gheorghe R's attempt at remaking his life was a failure. Gheorghe, a Romanian ethnic originally from Arad, on the Hungarian border, was a union leader at the Petrila Mine, a confidant of Miron Cozma, and a participant in all the *mineriade*. After the last march, during which the miners were beaten by police, Gheorghe was fed up with the mine and miner politics. So he and his wife, Elena, opted to take the first buy-out and buy a small van to start a cartage business. That business was difficult, however, as there were many bureaucratic hurdles and much competition. After a few months, with less than half their original stake of US$4,500 remaining, Gheorghe gave up that venture and bought a small bar and dance club in town, where Elena also worked, cooking and cleaning. Like Lotzi's, Gheorghe and Elena's success prompted jealousy and insults from former colleagues. One evening during a dance, a fight broke out between two men Gheorghe didn't recognize. However, he believes they were put up to it by powerful people in the Valley because, soon after the fight, amid complaints from neighbors about the raucous environment, Gheorghe and Elena lost their dance and music license, their patrons deserted them, and they were forced to sell. Today the bar, again offering music and dancing, is a Valley hot spot. But Gheorghe remains unemployed, at home most days, and thoroughly miserable. The family's savior has been Elena, who secured work as a night security guard and combines that with her normal household duties.

Lotzi's story, inspirational as it is, is rare in the postsocialist world. Gheorghe and Elena's story is repeated over and over. Few workers have Lotzi's single-minded determination to change and capacity to endure. Many who, like Gheorghe and Elena, try to overcome postsocialist conditions fall prey to corruption, conflict, or merely the lack of markets for their ventures. Thus, few workers cut loose from their former occupations are likely to brave the uncertainties and insults of striking out on their own. The question remains, then, how to intervene most effectively with a population whose suspicions and fears are rampant and whose belief in their own abilities has been trampled by a decade and a half of postsocialist change. Millions of dollars and euros and thousands of person-months have been devoted to retraining and reemploying those who have lost their livelihoods. Yet much of this effort has gone for naught, and few programs have generated the results they looked for. Thus we need to ask what it is about such interventions that keeps them from living up to their promise to remake the postsocialist labor force and what their actual effects and consequences are, intended or not?

On Sponsored Intervention

State-sponsored intervention for retraining the unemployed takes various forms, though I will collectively term such efforts "reemployment interventions." These include general outplacement measures (mainly counseling for redundant workers), vocational training, entrepreneurship courses, and public-sector employment. In Romania, according to Dobrescu, Rughiniş, and Zamfir (2000, 9–13), such interventions have come up short because they have been based on faulty premises. They first assumed that a normal capitalist economy would shortly develop. Market forces would quickly reintegrate the redundant workers of postsocialism. Interventions were thus designed to ease short-term dislocations in the labor market. However, reemployment interventions never succeeded enough to truly make a difference in the postsocialist landscape. The unemployment avalanche in the 1990s meant that most programs were eclipsed by the necessity for the state to fund direct assistance (Alexandrova, Chagin, and Struyk 2004).

Interventions were often funded by international agencies, and consequently tended to be all-purpose and generic, "cookie-cutter" programs barely related to the social conditions of specific regions and populations. Additionally, they were beset by problems of quality, simplistic and marginally relevant curricula, lack of resources, and—as always—corruption:

> The problem was not so much in the objective of these policies . . . but rather in their poor design and targeting. For example, training was offered for professions and skills not in actual demand in the labour market, or its quality was so low that employers had no incentive to hire trainees. In contrast, redundant workers were frequently not provided with sufficiently intensive assistance in redeployment or with measures to increase

their competitiveness, and professional or territorial mobility. (Nesporova 2000, 216)

Dobrescu, Rughiniş, and Zamfir (2000, 9–13) show how these problems beset interventions in the Jiu Valley and the city of Braşov, the capital of the county in which Făgăraş is located. They point to the "gap between the curricula and the labor market requirements" (10), and many other factors as well. For example, Jiu Valley reemployment intervention programs had virtually no possibility of success, as they really weren't intended to succeed. Coming on the heels of the 1997 labor contract buy-outs, they were intended to stave off the deluge of unemployment-fueled anger. The problems associated with Valley reemployment schemes were legion, and any miner could speak at length about them. The World Bank funded them, together with the Romanian National Agency for Professional Organization and Formation (ANOFP), now renamed the National Agency for Occupying the Labor Force (ANOFM), and aside from one sociological survey of the local population (Lamaraso Group 1998; Larionescu, Rădulescu, and Rughiniş 1999) it largely ignored local knowledge in designing its interventions. A woman who managed to secure a spot in one retraining program said,

> The teacher is incompetent. He spends most classes talking about his family and does not know any of the material. He is very insulting if we ask a question. I think he is a friend of someone at the Labor Directorate. Besides, there are virtually no accounting positions open in the Valley, so I don't even know why I go.[4]

Interventions were only slightly more successful in the Făgăraş region, although local agencies were more involved in their coordination and the number of participants was slightly higher. The major problem in that region was the overall lack of intervention programs; there were too few applicants for diverse programs to be organized.[5] At the same time, whatever retraining was offered was also plagued by irrelevant curricula, lack of necessary technologies and course materials,[6] and little chance for student graduates to secure employment in any case. The irony is that the one set of programs designed to make a difference in redundant workers' lives, to help them cope, really only drove home that escape from their situation was unlikely.

The faltering economy and lack of successful reemployment interventions in the two regions have left most workers and their families to their own devices as they attempt to cope with the conditions they face. The particular strategies they adopt depend on a host of factors, including family size, community of residence, proximity of relatives, educational background, and the like. Coping strategies are also seasonal and regional. But whatever the characteristics of workers and families, coping mainly consists of devising strategies to hang on, to ensure basic survival, and rarely looks to the long term (except when a family member emigrates).

These practices, what Tchernina (2000, 167) terms "passive survival strategies," take a diversity of forms. People do odd jobs on local black and grey labor markets, pick mushrooms or other wild foods for consumption or resale, sell their possessions and move to less expensive housing, reconfigure their households by sending people elsewhere for a while,[7] or move in with relatives. Though each practice makes survival a little easier, none is without cost. Again, as Tchernina indicates, such strategies have two negative effects:

> [Because they increase] the proportion of survival decisions aimed for the immediate improvement of the current level of income . . . these decisions [often] entail engaging in illegal activities, participation in the informal economy . . . professional degradation and family dissolution. [Also,] planning for the future becomes very short term; long-range objectives are ignored, no long-term decisions are made, so that these families do not have the experience to adapt smoothly to the on-going economic changes. (2000, 168)

Thus, today's survival, or at least the strategies aimed at ensuring it, impedes the possibilities of tomorrow. Activism is encumbered and passive coping costs individuals and families both physically and spiritually, furthering embodied distance and draining individuals of energy and commitment. This contradiction sits at the base of the problem of postsocialist change and must especially be taken into account in developing programs to both help worker families hold firm today and facilitate their choices for their and their society's future.

Making a Difference in the Jiu Valley and Făgăraş

The general conditions of postsocialist workers thus seem clear. To varying degrees, the former workers in the socialist industrial complexes, and others now employed (or formerly employed) in restructured industries, large and small, struggle to retain their balance, to cope with uncertainty, to remain on their feet. But employed or unemployed, in the state sector or privatized, workers are painfully aware of the precariousness of their circumstances. Whether they are healthy or not, they feel infirm. Whether their families are stable or not, their fears for continuity are overwhelming. This burden presses down on their sense of what is possible in the present and future, even as it weighs them down physically, helping produce their typical habitus of resignation with occasional outrage. As a friend recently suggested, "There is no longer any joy or gaiety in life here [in the Jiu Valley]. There is no laughter on the street, and people just walk aimlessly."

Postsocialist states, under the tutelage of international finance institutions and bilateral donors, have thus far largely addressed these sad circumstances with stop-gap interventions like public works employment and minimal monetary or in-kind assistance. Where the postsocialist states have sought to facilitate long-term change, they have done so largely through interventions designed to qualify unemployed workers for occupations supposedly solicited in their new market economies (Asociaţia Valea Jiului 2004). However, despite the host of interventions and assistance measures, workers have generally not responded with enthusiasm, acceptance, or engagement. Their resistance has prompted many to question whether any intervention on their behalf will succeed. Others throughout the region claim that "they just don't want to work," as interventions also fail due to lack of entrepreneurial energy, long-term commitment, and capitalization (Christopher Troxler, personal communication).

In keeping with the theme of this book, however, I suggest that most attempts to address postsocialist workers' circumstances have been piecemeal, designed less to make a real difference than to provide political cover. State efforts thus far have been cheap, utilitarian window dressing intended to allow the government to avoid dealing with the dominant problem affecting Romanian society: the remarkably unequal distribution of resources in a system protected and maintained by breathtaking corruption. Because of this, millions of dollars earmarked for local development and improvement projects find their way into the pockets of officials and managers, their families and underlings. Workers' disenchantment, lack of effort, and belief that little will make a difference are thus highly realistic, growing from their recognition of the vast theft of their possibilities with every misapplied program, diverted loan tranche, and spurious local investment project.

The gap between state employment or social intervention programs and workers' responses is thus one not just of structure but of meaning. Though many workers still seek the securities of socialism in the new labor market, most know those days are largely past. All would settle for something slightly less: minimal predictability, so they might plan, so they might more systematically provide for their children's futures, so they might attend a relative's wedding and not have to go without food or clothing to do so. Furthermore, despite what many of their critics claim, workers do not ask the state or its agents to provide solutions to their various and myriad social and physical problems. What they want is something more: possibility. The possibility of an evening out at a restaurant or cinema. The possibility of eating well and regularly, and thus addressing their health concerns. And above all, the possibility of trusting in the efforts of local, national, and international lenders to develop programs for meaningful, continuous, reasonably well paid employment.

As well as individual projects, then, interventions must promote change in meaning and signification, to counter people's immediate suspicions, fears, and shortfalls. Simultaneously, they must provide evidence of growth and future possibility; they must show themselves to be not merely stop-gaps or political sops designed to defuse worker resentment and alienation, but programs with long-term staying power. Furthermore, it is not sufficient to merely create a general strategy of development. Approaches must be devised that address inter- and intraregional cultural variation, that are tailored to particular populations. Without fine-grained approaches based on local need and meaning, national and international agencies run the risk of either implementing wildly inappropriate policies (Ferguson 1994) or allowing assistance to be hijacked by groups of self-interested partisans (Wedel 1998a, 1998b).

Future development initiatives in the two regions under study require different structural emphases. To the extent that development planning has moved forward, this fact seems to be recognized, and attempts have been made to avoid the "cookie cutter" approach that has often characterized such efforts in the past.[8] The enforcement of laws designed to limit the abuses of the black market, important across the board, seems to be a greater problem in Făgăraş than in the Jiu Valley. Conversely, infrastructure investment is needed more in the Valley than in Făgăraş. Similarly, entirely new kinds of employment must be created in the Jiu Valley, while privatization and retooling would likely be more effective in Făgăraş, whose citizens are also more receptive to job training programs than their Jiu Valley cousins. However, whatever the particular mix of activities to be started or enlarged, the first task in each region is to spur agency by creating enabling environments and engaging local energies and ideas in projects from their conception. Especially given people's alienation from and suspicion of postsocialist structures, local people must not be treated merely as the targets of plans hatched elsewhere.

Even before this, however, the first task in both regions is to address the social malaise of worker families, which often underlies frustrated agency and which is reflected in and reinforced by narrative (Gupta 2005). Social problems in worker communities are multiple, seemingly intractable, and clearly on the increase. They include domestic abuse, alcoholism, fraying family life, and the concomitant increase in psychological and physical ailments. These problems can only be addressed when we see the precise vectors and stresses under which diverse Romanian workers operate. Loss of identity and the angry group life of miners and bought-out miners bring about different sorts of personal crises than the never-ending strategizing for resources, the personal jealousies, and the stress of black market labor do for Făgăraş workers.

Numerous programs have been instituted in both regions to address these problems, though usually to little effect. Their failure is partly due to the mutual suspicion of workers and officials and functionaries, respectively the targets and purveyors of development programs. Still, despite this suspicion and distance, people long for meaningful ways to address obstacles in their lives. For example, women in both Făgăraş and the Jiu Valley complain about the dearth of agencies and programs to deal with their concerns. When they are abused they have no refuge, and existing agencies often do not even consider their claims legitimate. Though women are generally more group-oriented than men and many have stated their desire for personal, sexual, and domestic counseling services, they often find themselves on the bottom of the list for services provided from local budgets. Few regional NGOs focus on women's issues, especially in the Jiu Valley. There is little doubt that women's groups will have a difficult time achieving the influence necessary to make a difference in the regions. However, there are still ways to expand women's possibilities without relying on aid from unwilling or uncertain local authorities. In the Jiu Valley, for example, unemployed women in diverse neighborhoods could be organized into volunteer groups to improve housing and neighborhoods or provide domestic and labor counseling, and offer low-cost entrepreneurial advice. All that is necessary is for those empowered in regional development to identify two or three outspoken, dedicated women per neighborhood, offer training in group development, and provide meeting space and refreshments for the first few meetings. Though some male heads of household would no doubt keep their wives from attending, others would be interested in the program, and still others would succumb to group pressures. Results can be impressive if local people are given the means to use their own initiative.

Beyond social programs, local development can only be effective if it expands the institutional structures and capacities in which local citizens participate and through which they enunciate their own needs and desires. There are already diverse nongovernmental organizations in both regions, though they are often mainly designed to attract funding from outside sources to benefit their principals. For example, associations for unemployed people dot the Jiu Valley, but they attempt to ameliorate existing problems rather than being forward-looking and employment-oriented. Such associations could readily be used as starting points for neighborhood improvement projects or as the core of small business development. Some younger people, in particular, have excellent ideas and abundant energy for such businesses. Some lack capital, but their most significant problem is their inability to negotiate Romania's complex bureaucracy. Local associations could help with this. Down the road, microloans might be made available for business development. Romanian workers generally are skeptical of these organizations and practices, which they somewhat pejoratively call a "Gypsy wheel" or "Gypsy lottery" (*roată ţiganilor*). However, if such loans were accompanied by help overcoming bureaucratic obstacles, they would certainly be more attractive.

Still, microcredit schemes notwithstanding, the potential of small businesses and entrepreneurialism to create jobs has been overemphasized in both regions. Neither is likely to significantly promote regional development, especially given the lack of disposable income, the distrust between workers and others, and the predatory practices of state and regional bureaucracies. There is thus a need to think on a larger scale and for the relevant agencies to both increase and target their resources in both regions to spur significant transformation. Eco-, agro-, and industrial tourism hold considerable promise for employment in both regions. Both are extraordinarily rich in natural resources and their uplands are ideal for hiking, skiing, horseback riding, and similar activities. Tourism, in fact, is touted by many as a near panacea. However, the focus on the employment possibilities of tourism is somewhat ludicrous given the generally low quality of infrastructure in both regions, especially in the Jiu Valley. For tourism to make a difference, then, investment in it needs to be combined with simultaneous and intense infrastructural improvement. Individuals must be trained for jobs in tourist-related occupations, and local organizations must be helped to develop and expand touristic advertising. Furthermore, such activities must strictly conform to the Law on Disfavored Zones by employing, as far as possible, individuals from each region.

One such multidimensional project, which has the expansion of tourism as its goal, is the planned reconstruction of the thirteenth-century Făgăraş fortress (*cetate*).[9] The restored fortress will be primarily occupied by a museum chronicling the region's anticommunist resistance (Fundaţia Culturală "Negru Vodă" 2004), covering the period from the aftermath of World War II through the campaign to collectivize agriculture, 1945–62. This project was to be funded by a multimillion-dollar grant from the World Bank, and would have combined the efforts of thirteen institutions across Romania. However, the project has currently been put on hold owing to uncertainties about the funding and problems between the local Făgăraş administration and the Romanian Ministry of Culture. If it is completed, the restored *cetate,* a remarkable architectural and historic resource, should draw tourists from throughout Romania, and perhaps Europe and the world. Together with the planned Museum of the Romanian Diaspora, it could serve as an anchor for regional development—not to mention pride—for years to come.

Though each type of program has promise, the ultimate challenge in postsocialism is to provide workers with hope and skills for the future and a sense of personal responsibility; to overcome their sense of not belonging, which is bolstered by close to two decades of alienated practice. There are few, if any, answers for this challenge at the moment. One program that I want to highlight does, however, provide an interesting model, though its true successes are still some years off. In summer 1999, as this research project began, I was fortunate to make the acquaintance of Dana and Brandi Bates. The Bateses are Americans who, motivated by their religious and service commitments and training in outdoor education, began a program in social and environmental education for underprivileged children from Lupeni on Straja Mountain, just above that Jiu Valley town. Despite a series of problems over the years, including the theft of all their equipment the first summer, accusations that they were spies for militant Protestantism, and the theft of $30,000 by a trusted employee, the Bateses' persistence has paid off in the establishment of their Viaţa Outdoor Education Program, held every summer, and over forty "Kaizen[10] Clubs" throughout Romania. The Viaţa program brings groups of children to Straja Mountain for a week, at a nominal cost, to learn various outdoor skills, all of which have a social and group component. The tasks the children are set cannot be accomplished unless they are done collectively by the whole group. The campers' last day is spent in "sweat equity" projects on the mountain or in town: picking up trash, helping invalids, refurbishing public parks. In this way, social responsibility is encouraged, but contextualized as fun.

Viaţa works in part because it is multidimensional, much as the social problems in the Valley are multidimensional. Furthermore, that program addresses the needs of body and spirit and meaning as much as, if not more than, it does the needs of the social structure and tax base. Its impact, however, is but a drop in the bucket, and illustrates by juxtaposition the persisting high levels of stress and related declines in health and general well-being that remain in the mining communities from which children for the program are drawn.

Viaţa also contrasts with the general mood of Valley miner communities in its emphasis on life, which is, after all, what its name means. People in both the Jiu Valley and Făgăraş regions increasingly fear untimely death—which has, in fact, become more likely. Death here has yet to be remade into the failure of biomedicine, as it has been in more developed capitalist societies (Lock 1997, 219); it is still considered the result of societal failure. Death's specter haunted these postsocialist communities, and the discourse of death was everywhere in the two regions. Such overwhelming concerns particularly cry out for ethnographic understanding and practical intervention. However, to be ameliorative, critical social science must go beyond mere depiction of funereal practices and cemetery art and articulate death's connections with the changing conditions and social relations of the living. The Jiu Valley miners, of course, know sudden death as a condition of their labor and live with it as a matter of pride. Miners are more distressed by the possibility of early death after retirement than by the risks of working in the mines. To retire after twenty or more years in the underground and then die within one or two years, a not uncommon experience, was considered by miners the ultimate illustration of the futility of their lives and of their denigration and abandonment by society. For Făgăraşeni, however, death is not the same constant companion. They are more concerned about the death of their region itself, and the loss of generational continuity. But whatever the concern, their stress about the present and uncertainty about the future is written on their bodies in anger, resignation, ill health. The day when their renewed labor slakes their anger, strengthens their bodies, and turns their resignation to purpose and practice is yet overdue.

Notes

1. Getting By in Postsocialism

1. Victor Ciorbea, former mayor of Bucharest and former president of Romania's largest postsocialist trade union confederation, the National Council of Free Romanian Trade Unions—Brotherhood (CNSLR-Fraţia), was prime minister in the right-center Democratic Convention government from 1996 until 1998.

2. A lung disease treatment facility is located in the town of Geoagiu, in northern Hunedoara County. The Jiu Valley miners received access to five beds per month at the facility, largely through the protests of their former union president, Miron Cozma.

3. Uzine pentru Utilaj Chimic, or Factory for Chemical Industry Fittings and Tools.

4. Centralized plants that depend on the main factories for power and fuel heat most Făgăraş apartments. Throughout the autumn of 1999, because of the precarious economic situation in the factories, these plants were not functioning, so there was no central heating in the city's apartments. The Făgăraş unions planned a general strike for mid-November (see chapter 3) if the plants had not begun to operate by then. Heat was restored a day before the planned walkout, but operated only sporadically for the rest of the winter.

5. The Combinat is the main Făgăraş chemical factory, of which much more will be said throughout the book.

6. Descriptions of fieldwork in postsocialism invariably consider issues other than labor. For example, in two important publications (Berdahl, Bunzl, and Lampland 2000; DeSoto and Dudwick 2000), inequalities of class and labor are considered in only one (Lemon 2000b) of nineteen contributions.

7. I am indebted to Gabriel Troc of the European Studies Faculty at Babeş-Bolyai University for his comments about the indifference to and impossibility of class measurement in Romania today.

8. The recent strikes in the transportation and education sectors have prompted a wave of union resignations.

9. A search of AnthroSource (http://www.anthrosource.net) using the keywords "agency" and "resistance" turned up close to 1500 entries.

10. Crowley and Ost 2001 offers an excellent overview of the contradiction between East European union militancy and the unions' lack of political effectiveness.

11. In a late 1997 poll, for example, only banks and bankers scored lower in public confidence (Muntean 1997, 21). Similarly, in polls conducted for the Soros Open Society Foundation in June 1997 and by the Open Society Foundation in May 2001 (Center for Urban and Regional Sociology 1997, 29–30; Open Society Foundation 2001, 56) only 21 percent of those polled expressed confidence in unions, the lowest score among all institutions.

12. Between 1996 and 1999, for example, there were an average of 320 illegal wild-cat strikes per year and another 30 or so major national labor actions (Comisia Naţională pentru Statistică 1999).

13. When I asked Romanians if they could stand the conditions under which they lived, they often responded, "Yes, and even worse!" (*Da, şi mai rău!*).

14. The word that refers to demands in labor, *revendicări*, is an artifact of bargaining between unions and management, and largely absent from workers' daily vocabulary.

15. See also Nelson 1999, Scheper-Hughes 1992, and Silverman 2001 for this perspective.

16. Many people from the Valley, non-miners especially, now refuse to identify themselves as such when they speak with Romanians from other parts of the country. They say that they are not embarrassed, but that their origin affects the way that others relate to them. They generally say that they are from Hunedoara County and leave it at that.

17. The only miners who were skeptical of our work and refused to sit for interviews were some of those at the Aninoasa Mine. Their community was somewhat smaller and more insular than the other mining towns, which, I feel, encouraged their suspicions.

2. How Workers Became "Others"

1. Precise data supporting this estimate are hard to come by. It is largely derived from what I was often told by diverse "responsible" people in the Jiu Valley, including officials of the National Coal Company, representatives of urban governments, and employees of the Labor Directorate who were responsible for administering unemployment payments.

2. At the Făgăraş Chemical Combine in 1970, for example, 57 percent of the workers lived in village communities in the region and only 43 percent in the city of Făgăraş itself (Herseni et al. 1972, 247).

3. I have engaged in a protracted debate with Indian-Australian anthropologist Kuntala Lahiri-Dutt (Lahiri-Dutt 2006; Lahiri-Dutt and Macintyre 2006) on the role of women in mining. Prof. Lahiri-Dutt quite accurately points out extensive activities by women in diverse mining regimes, such as in West Bengal, India. However, this does not mean that women are active in all mining systems.

4. The term Momârlani is derived from the Hungarian for "those left behind" (*maradvány*, residue or remnant), in reference to their autochthonous status. Momârlani are conceptually distinguished from Barabe, roughly meaning "outsiders." According to Mircea Baron (1998, 41) the terms came into use when workers in the late nineteenth century built the railroad linking Simeria and Petroşani, the main Jiu Valley town. The workers coined the term "Momârlani" for the peasants, and the peasants bastardized the term *Bahnarbeiter* (road worker) into "Barabe" when speaking of outsiders to the Valley. However, some families of Barabe have lived there for over a hundred years and worked in the mines for generations. "Momârlani" is not a precise regional term. Though the term refers to rural provenience, Vasile Şoflău indicates that it is not restricted to the Jiu Valley but is also used by and about other mainly rural populations in the larger southwest Transylvania region. Momârlani have also worked in the mines since the late 1970s. However, regional received wisdom suggests that they often bribe mine officials with gifts of local produce to secure auxiliary posts and avoid work on the coalface.

5. The border between Habsburg Transylvania and Romanian Oltenia ran through the Jiu Valley town of Vulcan.

6. Herseni's career serves as a testimony to the political history of twentieth-century Romania. Born the son of an Austro-Hungarian local bureaucrat in a village outside Făgăraş in 1907, Herseni was influenced in his youth by contact with fascist Iron Guardists, who were strongly represented in the Făgăraş zone. He received his doctorate in 1934 in Berlin, where he was exposed to National Socialist ideology. After his return to Romania he was a member of the highly regarded sociological school headed by Dimitrie Gusti, and was a principal contributor to the multivolume interwar study of Drăguş village. During the Iron Guard period in Romania, he was appointed secretary general in the Ministry of National Education, Religion, and the Arts. Because of his Guardist background he was arrested by the new communist government in 1952 and spent ten years in prison, being released on the ascension of the nationalist communist government of Gheorghe Gheorghiu-Dej. With the rise to power of Nicolae Ceauşescu in 1965, sociol-

ogy, banned during the early years of the communist state, returned to favor as a practical discipline and Herseni resumed his career. He died in Bucharest in 1980.

7. See Lascu 2004 for a more detailed discussion of Momârlani traditions.

8. For Poland, which did not collectivize agriculture, and for Hungary, which adopted economic reforms early in the socialist period, there is a particularly vibrant literature on this topic (Buchowski 1997; Nagengast 1991; Słomczyński and Krauze 1978; Szelényi et al. 1988).

9. The literature on the nature, causes, and significance of class relations in socialist society is extensive and spans the socialist years, from Djilas (1955) to Bahro (1977) to Konrád and Szelényi (1979) to Burawoy (1985).

10. This is only one interpretation. Many others suggest that the workers fired first, or were provoked to fire first.

11. Workers' health, of course, was assured by the bounteous harvests brought in by the equally caricatured peasants.

12. See Creed 1999 for an extended discussion of the theory of household strategies and of diverse household strategies in socialist communities.

13. Each such ordinance offers workers a large payoff based on the number of years worked. For Jiu Valley miners, Ordinance 22/1997 established that those who had worked more than fifteen years could receive a severance package worth twenty-two months' salary, which averaged about 44 million lei or over US$3,000 in 1997 exchange rates. For other workers, severance packages totaled less than one year's salary.

14. Workers employed for six months or more can qualify for eighteen months of unemployment compensation (*ajutor de şomaji*) and nine months of welfare (*ajutor social*).

15. State regulations on hiring, remuneration, and employment benefits are extensive. Employers typically pay an additional 40 percent of a worker's salary for benefits, about 38 percent tax on profits, and annual interest rates of 65–85 percent on business loans. This compels many to avoid such costs by hiring at least a portion of their workers illegally.

16. Though this book deals mainly with workers in Romania, the experience of the other formerly socialist states is not dissimilar. At a conference titled "Trade Unions in East-Central Europe after Communism" held May 1999 in Warsaw, Poland, the Polish union representatives frequently complained that workers' opinions were never polled, nor were their situations considered in policy development. This opinion was echoed by other conference participants from Hungary, the Czech Republic, Bulgaria, and Ukraine. See also Ost 2002 for an excellent discussion of the difficulties of Polish workers during postsocialism.

17. Not all who held symbolic capital in socialism are bereft of it today. Martha Lampland (2002) shows that former socialist cooperative farm managers are able to retain power and prestige in their local communities by granting favors and assistance to fellow villagers.

18. The term *mineri mineri* has two meanings. It refers to the "full miners," the most qualified in the hierarchy of mine labor. However, when used by miners the term also means "real" miners, those who exhibit the essential qualities of the miner. Perjovschi's use of the term here also conjures that essential miner.

19. For example, one woman, married to a worker at the Lonea Mine who had been born in the area and was not participating in the marches, said that participants were fools (*proştii*).

20. *Adevărul*, a national newspaper, is the heir of the former leading Communist Party paper, *Scînteia*, and is widely seen as a mouthpiece for Ion Iliescu and the Romanian Social Democratic Party.

21. Costeşti is the Oltenian town where the last of six miner marches ultimately ended, in February 1999.

3. Postsocialist Labor Pains

1. Of late Ceauşescu images have multiplied in theaters, museums, television programs, and other odd places, such as in a Făgăraş garage.

2. "Ce înveţi la tinereţi, aceea ştii la bătrîneţe."

3. However, he used the more pejorative and vernacular term, "Ţigan," instead of the accepted "Rom."

4. *Huilă* is a coal midway between anthracite and bituminous, especially effective in steel blast furnaces and for generating electricity.

5. Most are from Lonea, Livezeni, Val de Braz, or Uricani.

6. Illegal removal of scrap metal from Jiu Valley mines, Făgăraş factories, and other industrial areas is a major problem. While filming at the Vulcan Mine in August 2002, I watched two men and a woman cart some off. Two security guards also watched from afar. There is so much theft, the guards no longer even try to stop it.

7. "Drujbă e drujbă, slujbă e slujbă." He used the Russian word for friendship. In Romanian, a *drujbă* is a chainsaw.

8. To minimize dust, coal should be sprayed with water at various stages of its extraction and processing.

9. Contract buy-outs continue in dribs and drabs; 1,500 miners were bought out in late 2004.

10. Bianca Botea and Vasile Şoflâu contributed a great number of ideas, comments, and critiques to this section.

11. All miners and auxiliaries received supplementary pay for underground work, dangerous work, night work, special training, seniority, and vacation, and even received a "fidelity supplement" (*spor de fidelitate*) for union loyalty.

12. These numbers appear worse than they are. The Făgăraş and Victoria combines each spun off a second enterprise, and their payrolls shrank accordingly. Nitramonia is now paired with Arsenalul Armatei ("Arsenal of the Army," formerly Rompiro) and Viromet with the Victoria Chemical Works. Both are special sections for explosives. When I was there, Arsenalul had about eight hundred employees and the VCW fewer than three hundred.

13. In 1989, 1,858 of the 4,210 Viromet employees (44%) were women; in 1998, 916 of 2,398 (38%) were women. Nitramonia in 1989 had 8,283 workers, of whom 3,184 (38%) were women; in 1998, it had 2,168 workers, of whom 880 (41%) were women. In 1999, UPRUC had 1,070 workers, of whom 292 (27%) were women.

14. Moldavian immigration to Făgăraş and Braşov County was extensive in the 1950s and '60s. Unlike immigrants in the Jiu Valley, many Moldavians integrated into local communities by marrying and buying homes.

15. The minimum guaranteed salary at the time of this interview was 700,000 lei per month.

16. That is, they receive money from both pensions and other work. Pensioners can be paid at a lower rate than those with active work contracts (Codin and Zecheriu 1992; Prisăcaru 1996).

4. The Postsocialist Body Politic

1. I discuss this nostalgic belief in earlier labor unity below.

2. The Independence Union at UPRUC was dissolved in 2001.

3. In 1999, when this interview took place, 1,070 people were employed at UPRUC, meaning that about 300–400 were non-union workers.

4. UPRUC was the only one of the factories and mines where we carried out re-

search where the union council asked to meet with us, questioned us closely about our purposes and planned activities, and also requested access to our findings so that they could use them in their own activities.

5. The Cielo is a prestigious automobile made by the Korean-based Daewoo Corporation in its plant at Craiova in southwestern Romania. Until Daewoo went into receivership, it made South Korea the largest single provider of foreign direct investment in Romania.

6. He referred here to a scandal involving Miron Cozma, who is alleged to have killed a woman and wrecked an expensive automobile. Hush money was paid for the charges against Cozma to disappear.

7. In 2001, Beja founded the Miron Cozma League, whose purpose was to press Iliescu, who had been reelected in 2000, to pardon Cozma. Iliescu first refused, then assented, and then reversed himself again.

8. Since Iliescu's reelection, the restructuring of the mine industry has continued, though at a slower pace than under the previous Constantinescu government.

9. *Adevărul* is the main mouthpiece for Ion Iliescu's Party of Social Democracy. Allegations that it distorted the miners' actions are thus significant, since Iliescu allegedly was one of their chief political allies. This, then, perhaps partially explains the miners' voting for ultra-nationalist Corneliu Vadim Tudor in both rounds of the 2000 presidential election.

10. Cornel Coposu was head of the National Peasant Party—Christian Democratic. He died in 1995.

11. Cozia Monastery, near the Oltenian village of Costeşti, was the site of the January 1999 negotiations between the government and the Liga. Some commentators laud these talks (Croitoru 1999), while others consider them a grave mistake (Dinescu 1999).

12. The UDMR is an officially recognized cultural interest group comprising ethnic Romanian Hungarian citizens. Though not formally a political party, it acts like one: it elects representatives to parliament and sometimes allies itself with other parliamentary forces. In 1996 it cooperated with the Democratic Convention, but with the change in government in 2000, it generally supported the policies of Iliescu and Prime Minister Adrian Nastase.

13. In fact, hiring of retirees has become a problem. Pensions are low, and so pensioners seek work on the labor black market.

14. These countries were not, of course, randomly listed. Rather, they were mainly problematic areas in which the US and UN are involved. The listing implies not only that their own lives in Romania are worse than those of workers in these other places, but also that only with international help can East European governments meet their people's need for jobs.

5. Houses of Stone or of Straw?

1. The name is taken from the American TV show of the same name and contrasts the splendor of the Ewing family ranch with the degraded conditions under which Romanian mining families live. Some people in Vulcan now term the housing complex "Kosovo," because of its bombed-out appearance.

2. This is particularly the case in Romania, where people often describe their national character by referring to the story of a peasant who, granted a wish by a good spirit, asks for the death of his neighbor's goat.

3. Rumor had it that what coal there was to run the heating plant was purchased from Mozambique, as Romanian coal had become too expensive.

4. Inexpensive Turkish-made cardboard shoes have become common as burial wear over the last decade.

5. Mihail Sadoveanu (1880–1961) was a Romanian author and a favorite of communist authorities.

6. Casa Ajutor Reciproc is a public loan facility; loans are repaid by payroll deductions. People claim that all larger purchases today must be financed with CAR loans as, unlike in the socialist years, families have no savings on which to rely.

7. This conclusion is based on a one-week dietary survey conducted among families in the Jiu Valley town of Vulcan and in Făgăraş, as well as impressionistic data and interviews.

8. Chronic obstructive pulmonary disease and cardiovascular disease are the most frequent causes of death in the Jiu Valley.

9. Though the population of the Jiu Valley declined by 6 percent, from 174,263 in 1997 to 163,859 in 1999, there has been a slight increase in the number of divorces, from 463 in 1993 to 473 in 1998, and a large decrease in marriages, from 407 in 1997 to 230 in the first ten months of 1999. Despite declining population, cases of abandonment almost doubled, with 63 in 1998–99, compared to 67 in the previous four years. According to cooks at two mine cafeterias, greater numbers of homeless children have begun to show up for hand-outs, indicating the dissolution of mining families.

10. For example, there were 27 corporal crimes (many family-based), such as felonious assault, in 1998–99, compared to 32 cases in the previous five years.

11. From 1976 to 1989, an average of 212 divorces per year were registered at the Făgăraş judiciary. This increased in 1990–96 to 308 per year, but declined again from 1997 to 1999, to an average of 265 per year. There were 24 cases of abandonment per year between 1976 and 1989; the average fell to 14 per year between 1989 and 1996, and to 5 cases per year from 1997 to 1999 (Judecătorie Făgăraş 1999).

12. In 1992 there were 442 marriages in Oraşul Victoria, Făgăraş, and nearby villages, and in 1998, 424 (Direcţia de Statistica 1999). Other statistical indicators of Făgăraş social conditions have stayed consistent. Thus the rate of violent crime in the region has remained unchanged since 1976, the first year for which I have these data, varying from 14 per year in the period 1976–89 to 17 per year in 1990–96, to 19 per year in 1997–99 (Judecătorie Făgăraş 1999).

13. The Făgăraş hospital closed its psychiatric facility in 1992. Psychiatric patients needing hospitalization are sent to Braşov, but as the wait for space there is long, few people seek treatment.

14. She used the term *dezgheţat* (de-iced) to describe this quality of youth, and was not referring specifically to political freedom.

15. Jiu Valley women scored highest of all groups surveyed on the Wahler Physical Symptoms Inventory, administered as part of my research.

6. Strangers in Their Own Skin

1. Susan Rogers's (1975) seminal article on the illusion of male power among the French peasantry serves as the intellectual foundation for my discussion here.

2. Romanians distinguish soft-core pornography (called *sexi*) from hard-core pornography (*porno*).

3. The word *pregătire* means appropriate training for a career, in this case for that of a proper woman, or proper wife.

4. Ironically, just as he made this comment, a Rexona deodorant ad was playing on the TV while a can of Rexona was visible on a shelf behind him.

5. In an analogous case, Butchart (1998) shows that European political hegemony in Africa was constructed by depicting those whom one seeks to control as animalistic, wild, and uncivilized.

6. In Kideckel 2004a I relate a number of these jokes and stories.

7. This condition affects females who, having a missing or damaged X chromo-

some, are typically short, suffer delayed puberty and infertility, and have other physical distortions and medical problems.

7. The Embodied Enemy

1. Preliminary results of the March 2002 census show a 5 percent decline in Romania's population over the previous decade. Romania's population was measured at 21.7 million, down from almost 23 million in 1992. According to Aurel Camara, director of the National Statistics Institute, the two main reasons for the decline are migration and the excess of mortality over fertility (Mato 2002).

2. This discussion is based on a survey in summer 2002 of fifty Făgăraş and eighty-seven Jiu Valley families. The sample included the same proportions of employed and unemployed workers and miners as existed in the communities as a whole.

3. In Viromet in 1976, 3896 workers took 76,216 sick leave days, averaging 19.56 days per worker. In 1982, during years of increased forced labor, this figure declined to 14.55 (4258 workers, 61,975 sick leave days). By 1989 it had fallen to 10.14, but it increased after the revolution to 14.51 (3922 workers, 56,898 sick leave days), and then dropped immediately in 1991 to 5.76. Since then the figure has hovered around 5–6 sick leave days per worker per year, with a high of 6.42 in 1995 and a low of 4.85 in 1998, the last year for which data are available. Much the same is true of Nitramonia, where in 1990, 7980 workers took 105,270 sick leave days, averaging 13.19 per worker, while in 1999, 2113 workers took 20,587 days, averaging 9.74 per worker. At the Petroşani hospital there has been a staggeringly large drop-off in sick leave days from the first to the most recent years of postsocialism.

4. Făgăraş workers' discussion of these requirements virtually duplicates the descriptions of work and stress under the socialist piece-rate work regime cogently described by Miklós Haraszti (1978).

5. In the summer 2002 survey Făgăraş male workers and both men and women in the Jiu Valley considered bosses unconcerned for worker health. Jiu Valley men and women also thought union leaders unconcerned. Făgăraş men were equivocal about union concern, and Făgăraş women mainly thought their union leaders supportive, but were equivocal about bosses.

6. Explosions are a problem where closed mine galleries are improperly conserved, causing methane build-up, fires, and explosions. This occurred three times in less than a year (August 2001 to June 2002) at the Vulcan Mine, killing twenty-one miners.

7. The semihard coking coal (*huilă*) of the Jiu Valley does not cause much silicosis, which is more prevalent among miners of minerals and nonferrous metals.

8. Additionally, miners' desire to keep their health problems secret may have influenced their responses to our questionnaire.

9. This appears to be a reference to a corrupt practice in which mine administrators and union leaders contract with private stores to purchase food for mine cafeterias. The food is always of the worst quality, thus providing the store owners (often related to or connected with highly placed mine or union officers) with hefty profits and the mine administrators and union leaders with kickbacks.

8. What Is to Be Done?

1. I emphasize that I am speaking here of a particular moment in time, the early 2000s, as the labor activism of workers in this sector can and no doubt will change considerably. The entry of the East-Central European nations into the EU and increased foreign investment will especially propel such changes.

2. Next to Spaniards themselves, there were more Romanian casualties among the

victims of the Madrid subway bombings of March 11, 2004, than any other nationality (Campbell 2005).

3. The term for businessman/businessperson in Romanian, *bişniţar,* is still laden with negative connotations. Some are a residue of socialist disapproval. The word also connotes manipulation of others, corruption, disregard for social commitments, and the like.

4. She quit the course soon after this conversation and returned to university, which she could afford only thanks to a substantial loan from her elder brother, a successful Bucharest businessman.

5. According to the head of the local office of the state Labor Directorate (Consorţiul Făgăraşeana 1997), in the late 1990s, in order for a job retraining course to be offered, local employers had to have requested at least fifteen people trained in that way. However, the costs of legally hiring labor often kept employers from officially requesting workers. In summer 1999, according to the local journal *Ţara Făgăraşului,* in Făgăraş the state employment board listed jobs for two carpenters, two tailors, two machinists, two welders, and two manual laborers. This list of available positions was addressed to over 2,500 people who were receiving unemployment compensation, and about 10,000 other unemployed people who no longer qualified for state assistance.

6. In 1999 a course on basic data processing skills for business was offered at the Făgăraş Chamber of Commerce. However, none of the dozen computers worked correctly, all had either 386 or 8088 processors (which were then ten years out of date in the West), and the seven male and female students sat around talking among themselves for most of the two-hour class.

7. Such absences must be distinguished from emigration. Whereas the latter implies a lengthy period away from one's home community, the household reconfiguration I discuss here involves short-term absences, lasting a season or two at the longest. Household members are often sent elsewhere to lower the household's liability for water bills and other utility costs, often levied on a per capita basis.

8. The Jiu Valley social sector was surveyed intensively, but to questionable effect, prior to the implementation of World Bank development planning activities (e.g., Lamaraso Group 1998; World Bank 2004).

9. The *cetate* has a long and checkered history. During the Middle Ages it was the bastion of local princes, including for a time Vlad Ţepeş, the historical Dracula. It served as an armory in World Wars I and II, and afterward as a notorious prison where many political, military, and intelligence officials of the presocialist regimes were interned and executed. During the 1970s the fortress became the region's main ethnographic and historical museum and was combined with a hotel and wine cellar, now mainly fallen into disuse.

10. *Kaizen* is Japanese for "constant improvement."

Works Cited

Abraham, Dorel. 1990. "Post-revolutionary Social Phenomena in Romania: 'The University Square' and the Violent Collective Behavior of June 13th to 15th." *Romanian Journal of Sociology* 1(1–2): 121–30.

Afford, Carl Warren. 2003. *Corrosive Reform: Failing Health Systems in Eastern Europe.* Geneva: ILO Publications.

Agence France Presse. 2000. "HIV/AIDS Epidemic Is 'Exploding' in Eastern Europe: Official." November 28. http://www.aegis.com/news/afp/2000/AF001189.html.

Alexandrova, Anastasia, Kirill Chagin, and Pavel Struyk. 2004. "The Effectiveness of Local Government Active Labor Programs: The Case of the Benefits-to-Wages Program in Russia." *Review of Urban and Regional Development Studies* 16(1): 33–45.

Allison, Christine, and Dena Ringold. 1996. *Labor Markets in Transition in Central and Eastern Europe, 1989–1995.* World Bank Technical Paper no. 352. Washington, D.C.: The World Bank.

Allnut, Luke. 2004. "Inflows to the East Are a Problem Too: The EU Migration Debate." *International Herald Tribune*, April 21.

Ames, Genevieve M, Joel W. Grube, and Roland S. Moore. 2000. "Social Control and Workplace Drinking Norms: A Comparison of Two Organizational Cultures." *Journal of Studies on Alcohol* 61(2): 203–19.

Anon. 1994a. "A Romanian Restructuring." *Mining Journal* 322(8268) (March 25): 212.

———. 1994b. "Romanian Strike Intensifies." *Mining Journal* 323(8287) (August 5): 93.

———. 1999a. "Government's Last Chance." *In Review: Romania's Magazine for Business* (October): 6–13.

———. 1999b. "Striking Romanian Miners Clash with Police on March." *New York Times*, January 20.

———. 2005. "Atenţie se închide România." *News Café: Sete de Ştiri*, November 16.

Anton, Ion, and Mihaela Cimpoeasu. 1996. *Romania's Industry Moving into the EU: A Study Based on Three Industries.* LICOS Centre for Transition Economies. Leuven, Belgium: Katholieke Universiteit Leuven.

Appadurai, Arjun. 1996. *Modernity at Large: Cultural Dimensions of Globalization.* Minneapolis: University of Minnesota Press.

Ashwin, Sarah. 1999. "Redefining the Collective: Russian Mineworkers in Transition." In *Uncertain Transition: Ethnographies of Change in the Postsocialist World,* ed. Michael Burawoy and Katherine Verdery, 245–71. Lanham, Md.: Rowman and Littlefield.

Asociaţia Valea Jiului. 2004. *Raport de activitate 2003.* Petroşani: Asociaţia Valea Jiului.

Baban, Adriana, and Henry P. David. 1997. "The Impact of Body Politics on Women's Bodies." In *Women and Men in East European Transition,* ed. Margit Feischmidt, Enikö Magyari-Vincze, and Violetta Zentai, 156–70. Cluj-Napoca: Editura Fundaţiei pentru Studii Europene.

Bacon, Walter M., Jr., and Louis G. Pol. 1994. "The Economic Status of Women in Romania." In *Women in the Age of Economic Transformation: Gender Impact of Reforms in Post-Socialist and Developing Countries,* ed. Nahid Aslanbeigui, Steven Pressman, and Gale Summerfield, 43–58. London and New York: Routledge.

Baer, Hans. 1996. "Bringing Political Ecology into Critical Medical Anthropology: A Challenge to Biocultural Approaches." *Medical Anthropology* 17(2): 129–42.

Bahro, Rudolf. 1977. *The Alternative in Eastern Europe.* Trans. David Fernbach. London: NLB.

Bărbat, Alexandru. 1938. *Desvoltarea şi structura economică a Ţării oltului cu un plan de organizare.* Cluj: Tipografia Naţională Societate Anonimă.

Barbu, Daniel. 2004. *Republica absentă: Politică şi societate în România postcomunistă.* Bucharest: Biblioteca de Politică.

Bârgău, Valeriu. 1984. "Oamenii subpămîntului." In *Gligor Haşa,* ed. Planeta Cărbunului, 115–70. Bucureşti: Editura Eminescu.

Baron, Mircea. 1998. *Cărbune şi societate în Valea Jiului: Perioada interbelică.* Petroşani: Editura Universitas.

Bartkey, Sandra Lee. 1995. "Agency: What's the Problem?" In *Provoking Agents: Gender and Agency in Theory and Practice,* ed. Judith Kegan Gardiner, 178–93. Urbana: University of Illinois Press.

Beck, Sam. 1991. "Toward a Civil Society: The Struggle over University Square in Bucharest, Romania, June 1990." *Socialism and Democracy* 13:135–54.

Berdahl, Daphne. 2000. "Introduction: An Anthropology of Postsocialism." In *Altering States: Ethnographies of Transition in Eastern Europe and the Former Soviet Union,* ed. Daphne Berdahl, Matti Bunzl, and Martha Lampland, 1–13. Ann Arbor: University of Michigan Press.

———. 2005. "The Spirit of Capitalism and the Boundaries of Citizenship in Post-Wall Germany." *Comparative Studies in Society and History* 47(2): 235–51.

Berdahl, Daphne, Matti Bunzl, and Martha Lampland, eds. 2000. *Altering States: Ethnographies of Transition in Eastern Europe and the Former Soviet Union.* Ann Arbor: University of Michigan Press.

Birtalan, Laura. 1999. "Munca la negru atinge dimensiuni fără precedent." *Adevărul,* July 26, p. 8.

Blazek, J., and D. Dzúrová. 2000. "The Decline of Mortality in the Czech Republic during the Transition: A Counterfactual Case Study." In *The Mortality Crisis in Transitional Economies,* ed. Giovanni Andrea Cornia and Renato Paniccia, 303–27. London: Oxford University Press.

Bobek, Martin, and Michael Marmot. 1996. "East-West Mortality Divide and Its Potential Explanation: Proposed Research Agenda." *British Medical Journal* 312:421–25.

Boboc, Ion. 2000. "Costurile sociale ale restructurării mineritului în România. Studiu de caz: Valea Jiului, Part I." Bucharest: Institutul de Cercetări Sociale Protector AS. Report.

Bolger, Andrew. 1998. "Management Violence at Work." *Financial Times* (London), July 20.

Borneman, John W. 1997. *Settling Accounts: Violence, Justice, and Accountability in Postsocialist Europe.* Princeton: Princeton University Press.

———. 1998. "Narrative, Genealogy, and Historical Consciousness: Selfhood in a Disintegrating State." In *Subversions of International Order: Studies in the Political Anthropology of Culture,* 125–52. Albany: SUNY Press.

———. 2004. Introduction to *Death of the Father: An Anthropology of the End in Political Authority,* 1–32. New York: Berghahn Books.

Bourdieu, Pierre. 1977. *Outline of a Theory of Practice.* Cambridge: Cambridge University Press.

———. 1984. *Distinction: A Social Critique of the Judgement of Taste.* Cambridge, Mass.: Harvard University Press.

Braiţ, Petre. 2001. "Cronica unei restructurări anunţate." Unpublished typescript.

Brehoi, Gheorghe, and A. Popescu. 1991. *Conflictul colectiv de Muncă şi Grevă.* Bucharest: Forum.

Briggs, Charles L. 2004. "Theorizing Modernity Conspiratorially: Science, Scale, and the Political Economy of Public Discourse in Explanations of a Cholera Epidemic." *American Ethnologist* 32(4): 164–87.

Brown, K. S. 2000. "Would the Real Nationalists Please Step Forward: Destructive Narration in Macedonia." In *Fieldwork Dilemmas: Anthropologists in Postsocialist States,* ed. Hermine G. DeSoto and Nora Dudwick, 31–48. Madison: University of Wisconsin Press.

Brubaker, Rogers. 1985. "Rethinking Classical Theory: The Sociological Vision of Pierre Bourdieu." *Theory and Society* 14(6): 745–75.

Brues, Alice M. 1959. "The Spearman and the Archer." *American Anthropologist* 61: 458–69.

Buchowski, Michał. 1997. *Reluctant Capitalists: Class and Culture in a Local Community in Western Poland.* Berlin: Centre Marc Bloch.

———. 2001. *Rethinking Transformation: An Anthropological Perspective on Postsocialism.* Poznán, Poland: Wydawnictwo Fundacji Humaniora.

———. 2004. "Between Stigmatization and Resistance: A Creation of 'Victimized Groups' Identity in Poland." In *Performing Identities: Renegotiating Socio-cultural Identities in Post-Socialist Eastern Europe,* ed. Enikö Magyari-Vincze and Petruţa Mîndruţ, 25–36. Cluj-Napoca: Editura Fundaţiei pentru Studii Europene.

Bucur, Maria. 2002. *Eugenics and Modernization in Interwar Romania.* Pittsburgh, Penn.: University of Pittsburgh Press.

Buechsenschuetz, Ulrich. 2004. "EU Welcomes New Members, but Where Is the Enthusiasm?" *Radio Free Europe/Radio Liberty Newsline* 8(81) (April 30), part 2.

Bunzl, Matti. 2000. "The Prague Experience: Gay Male Sex Tourism and the Neocolonial Invention of an Embodied Border." In *Altering States: Ethnographies of Transition in Eastern Europe and the Former Soviet Union,* ed. Daphne Berdhal, Matti Bunzl, and Martha Lampland, 70–95. Ann Arbor: University of Michigan Press.

Burawoy, Michael. 1985. *The Politics of Production: Factory Regimes under Capitalism and Socialism.* London: Verso.

Bush, Larry S. 1993. "Collective Labor Disputes in Post-Ceauşescu Romania." *Cornell International Law Journal* 26(2): 373–85.

———. 2004. "Trade Unions and Labor Relations." In *Romania since 1989: Politics, Economics, and Society,* ed. Henry F. Carey, 419–38. Lanham, Md.: Lexington Books.

Butchart, Alexander. 1998. *The Anatomy of Power: European Constructions of the African Body.* London: Zed Books.

Campbell, Duncan. 2005. "A Year On from Train Bombs, Pain Is Still Etched on Streets of Madrid: Families Grieve While Anger Is Directed at Politicians and Media." *The Guardian,* final edition, March 11, p. 3. Lexis-Nexis Academic Universe.

Carey, Henry F., ed. 2004. *Romania since 1989: Politics, Economics, and Society.* Lanham, Md.: Lexington Books.

Carlson, Heather R., Alex Johnston, Aurora Liiceanu, Cristina Vintila, and John H. Harvey. 2000. "Lessons in the Psychology of Loss: Accounts of Middle-Aged Romanian Women." *Journal of Personal and Interpersonal Loss* 5(2–3): 183–201.

Cartwright, Andrew. 2001. *The Return of the Peasant: Land Reform in Post-Communist Romania.* Burlington, Vt.: Ashgate Publishing.

Catalano, Ralph, Ethel Aldrete, and William Vega. 2000. "Job Loss and Major Depression among Mexican Americans." *Social Science Quarterly* 81(1): 477–87.

Center for Urban and Regional Sociology. 1997. *National Public Opinion Poll.* Bucharest: CURS.

Central Intelligence Agency. 2007. *The World Factbook: Romania.* https://www.cia.gov/cia/publications/factbook/geos/ro.html#Econ.

Cesereanu, Ruxandra. 2003. *Imaginarul violent al Românilor.* Bucharest: Humanitas.

Chagnon, Napoleon A. 1968. *Yanomamo: The Fierce People.* New York: Holt, Rinehart and Winston.

Chiriac, Marian. 2000. "Desperation Fuels Romanian Sex Trade." Inter Press Service cited on Lexis-Nexis World News, August 28.

Cockerham, William C. 1997. "The Social Determinants of the Decline of Life Expectancy in Russia and Eastern Europe: A Lifestyle Explanation." *Journal of Health and Social Behavior* 38(2): 117–30.

———. 1999. *Health and Social Change in Russia and Eastern Europe.* London: Routledge.

Cockerham, William C., M. Christine Snead, and Derek F. DeWaal. 2002. "Health Lifestyles in Russia and the Socialist Heritage." *Journal of Health and Social Behavior* 43(1): 42–55.

Codin, Mihaela, and Mirele Zecheriu. 1992. *Starea de Şomaj şi Comportamentul Şomerilor.* Bucharest: Institute for Research on the Quality of Life of the Romanian Academy.

Cohen, Roger. 2000. "Poverty Drives East's Women to Sex Trade." *International Herald Tribune,* September 20.

Comisia Naţională pentru Statistică. 1996. Anuarul statistic al României 1996. Bucharest: Comisia Naţionala pentru Statistica.

———. 1999. Anuarul statistic al României 1999. Bucharest: Comisia Naţionala pentru Statistica.

———. 2002. *Participarea la forţă de muncă pe sexe şi medii.* http://www.insse.ro/Statistici/ forta_munca/site_AMIGO_evol_ani.htm.

Consorţiul Făgăraşeana. 1997. Program of Active Employment Measures. Făgăraş: FIMAN/PAEM.

Constantinescu, Olga. 1973. *Critica teoriei România—Ţara eminamente agricolă.* Bucharest: Editura Academiei.

Cook, Joe. 1999. "Miners' Victory Sets Back Reform Hopes in Romania." *Financial Times* (London), January 23, third London edition.

Cornia, G. A. 1994. "Income Distribution, Poverty, and Welfare in Transitional Economies: A Comparison between East Europe and China." *Journal of International Development* 6(5): 569–92.

Cornia, Giovanni Andrea, and Renato Paniccia, eds. 2000. *The Mortality Crisis in Transitional Economies.* London: Oxford University Press.

Creed, Gerald. 1995. "An Old Song in a New Voice: Decollectivization in Bulgaria." In *East European Communities: The Struggle for Balance in Turbulent Times,* ed. David A. Kideckel, 25–46. Boulder, Colo.: Westview.

———. 1999. *Domesticating Revolution: From Socialist Reform to Ambivalent Transition in a Bulgarian Village.* University Park: Pennsylvania State University Press.

———. 2002. "Economic Crisis and Ritual Decline in Eastern Europe." In *Postsocialism: Ideals, Ideologies and Practices in Eurasia,* ed. C. M. Hann, 57–73. London: Routledge.

Croitoru, Adina. 1999. "Reforma in minerit a fost negociata." *România Libera,* January 20.

Crowley, Stephen. 1997. *Hot Coal, Cold Steel: Russian and Ukrainian Workers from the End of the Soviet Union to the Post-Communist Transformations.* Ann Arbor: University of Michigan Press.

———. 2004. "Explaining Labor Weakness in Post-Communist Europe: Historical Legacies and Comparative Perspective." *East European Politics and Societies* 18(3): 394–429.

Crowley, Stephen, and David Ost. 1999. "Class Dismissed: Labor Quiescence in Post-Communist Transformations." Unpublished symposium proposal.

———, eds. 2001. *Workers after Workers' States: Labor and Politics in Postcommunist Eastern Europe.* Lanham, Md.: Rowman and Littlefield.

Das, Veena, and Arthur Kleinman. 2000. Introduction to *Violence and Subjectivity,* ed. Veena Das, Arthur Kleinman, Mamphela Ramphele, and Pamela Reynolds, 1–18. Berkeley: University of California Press.

David, Henry P., and Adriana Baban. 1996. "Women's Health and Reproductive Rights: Romanian Experience." *Patient Education and Counseling* 28(3): 235–45.

DeSoto, Hermine G., and Nora Dudwick, eds. 2000. *Fieldwork Dilemmas: Anthropologists in Postsocialist States.* Madison: University of Wisconsin Press.

Dinescu, Mircea. 1999. "Incordarea puterilor în stat." *Academia Caţavencu,* 6(1–2) (February 2).

Djilas, Milovan. 1955. *The New Class: An Analysis of the Communist System.* New York: Praeger.

Dobrescu, Angela, Cosima Rughiniş, and Cătălin Zamfir. 2000. "Coping Strategies in Three Regions of Romania Affected by Mass Redundancies." SOCO Project Paper no. 82. Vienna: Institut für Wissenschaften vom Menschen.

Drazin, Adam. 2002. "Chasing Moths: Cleanliness, Intimacy, and Progress in Romania." In *Markets and Moralities: Ethnographies of Postsocialism*, ed. Ruth Mandel and Caroline Humphrey, 101–26. Oxford: Berg.

Dunn, Elizabeth C. 2004. *Privatizing Poland: Baby Food, Big Business, and the Remaking of Labor*. Ithaca, N.Y.: Cornell University Press.

Earle, J. S., and G. Oprescu. 1995. "Romania." In *Unemployment, Restructuring, and the Labor Market in Eastern Europe and Russia*, ed. Simon Commander and Fabrizio Coricelli, 233–88. Washington, D.C.: World Bank.

Earle, J. S., and C. Pauna. 1996. "The Incidence and Duration of Unemployment in Romania." *European Economic Review* 40(3–5): 829–38.

———. 1998. "Long-Term Unemployment, Social Assistance and Labor Market Policies in Romania." *Empirical Economics* 23:203–35.

Emirbayer, Mustafa, and Ann Mische. 1998. "What Is Agency?" *American Journal of Sociology* 103(4): 962–1023.

Fekett, Şofron S. 1956. *Istoria Uniunii uşe şi Ligii Societăţilor Româneşti din America*. Cleveland, Ohio: The Union and Leagues of American Romanian Societies.

Ferguson, James. 1994. *The Anti-politics Machine: "Development," Depoliticization, and Bureaucratic Power in Lesotho*. Minneapolis: University of Minnesota Press.

Feshbach, Murray, and Alfred Friendly, Jr. 1992. *Ecocide in the USSR: Health and Nature under Siege*. New York: Basic Books.

Fisher, Ian. 2004. "Eastern Europe's Immigration Challenge." *International Herald Tribune*, April 27, p. 2.

Foucault, Michel. 1978. *The History of Sexuality: An Introduction*. New York: Random House.

———. 1980. "Body/Power." In *Power/Knowledge: Selected Interviews and Other Writings, 1972–1977*, ed. Colin Gordon, 55–62. New York: Pantheon.

———. 1984. "'The Body of the Condemned' (Discipline and Punish)." In *The Foucault Reader*, ed. Paul Rabinow, 172–75. New York: Pantheon.

Freese, Barbara. 2003. *Coal: A Human History*. Cambridge, Mass.: Perseus Publishing.

Friedman, Jack R. 1999. "Betrayal and Anger in Romania's Jiu Valley." Paper presented at the annual meeting of the American Anthropological Association, Chicago, November.

———. 2003. "Ambiguous Transitions and Abjected Selves: Betrayal, Entitlement, and Globalization in Romania's Jiu Valley." Ph.D. diss., Duke University.

Fuller, Linda. 1999. *Where Was the Working Class? Revolution in Eastern Germany*. Urbana: University of Illinois Press.

Fundaţia Culturală "Negru Vodă." 2004. Muzeul Rezistenţei Anticomuniste Făgărăşene. Rosturi şi Rostiri, no. 2. Făgăraş: Fundaţia Culturală "Negru Vodă."

Gâf-Deac, Ion. 1994. "The Strategy of Restructuring the Mining Industry in Romania." In *The Mining Industry on the Threshold of the XXI Century: Proceedings of the 16th World Mining Congress*, 90–99. Sofia, Bulgaria: World Mining Congress.

Gal, Susan. 1997. "Feminism and Civil Society." In *Women and Men in East European Transition*, ed. Margit Feischmidt, Enikö Magyari-Vincze, and Violetta Zentai, 89–99. Cluj-Napoca: Editura Fundaţiei pentru Studii Europene.

Gal, Susan, and Gail Kligman. 2000a. *The Politics of Gender after Socialism: A Comparative-Historical Essay*. Princeton: Princeton University Press.

———, eds. 2000b. *Reproducing Gender: Politics, Publics, and Everyday Life after Socialism*. Princeton: Princeton University Press.

Gardawski, Juliusz, Barbara Gwąnciarz, et al. 1999. *Rozpad Bastionu? Związki zawodowe w gospodarce prywatyzovanej*. Warsaw: Institute for Public Affairs.

Garton Ash, Timothy. 1989. *The Uses of Adversity: Essays on the Fate of Central Europe.* New York: Random House.

Gheorghe, Gabriela, and Adelina Huminic. 1999. "Istoria mineriadelor din anii 1990–1991." *Sfera Politicii* online, no. 67. http://www.dntb.ro/sfera/67/mineriade-5.html.

Gledhill, John. 2005. "States of Contention: State-Led Political Violence in Post-Socialist Romania." *East European Politics and Societies* 19(1): 76–104.

Good, Mary-Jo Delvecchio. 1992. "Work as a Haven from Pain." In *Pain as Human Experience: An Anthropological Perspective,* ed. Mary-Jo Delvecchio Good, Paul E. Brodwin, Byron J. Good, and Arthur Kleinman, 49–76. Berkeley: University of California Press.

Gorun, Gheorghe. 2004. "Un crâmpei de istorie: Revolta minerilor de la Motru—1981." *Memoria* 46(1): 17–27.

Gupta, Akhil. 2005. "Narrating the State of Corruption." In *Corruption: Anthropological Perspectives,* ed. Dieter Haller and Cris Shore, 173–93. London: Pluto Press.

Gutmann, Matthew C. 1997. "Trafficking in Men: The Anthropology of Masculinity." *Annual Review of Anthropology* 26:385–409.

Hall, Ray, and Paul White, eds. 1995. *Europe's Population: Toward the Next Century.* London: UCL Press.

Hann, C. M. 1993. "From Production to Property: Decollectivization and the Family-Land Relationship in Contemporary Hungary." *Man* (n.s.) 28:299–320.

———. 1996. "The Skeleton at the Feast: Contributions to East European Anthropology." CSAC Monographs 9. University of Kent at Canterbury.

———, ed. 2002. *Postsocialism: Ideals, Ideologies and Practices in Eurasia.* London: Routledge.

Hann, C. M., and Elizabeth Dunn, eds. 1996. *Civil Society: Challenging Western Models.* London: Routledge.

Haraszti, Miklós. 1978. *A Worker in a Worker's State.* New York: Universe Books.

Harsanyi, Doina P. 1994. "Romania's Women." *Journal of Women's History* 5(3): 30–54.

Hegland, Mary Elaine. 1995. "Shi'a Women of Northwest Pakistan and Agency through Practice: Ritual, Resistance, Resilience." *PoLAR: Political and Legal Anthropology Review* 18(2): 65–80.

Herseni, Traian, et al. 1972. *Combinatul Chimic Făgăraş: Cincizeci Ani de Înfiinţare.* Sibiu, Romania: Intreprindera Poligrafica.

Herzfeld, Michael. 1985. *The Poetics of Manhood: Contest and Identity in a Cretan Mountain Village.* Princeton: Princeton University Press.

———. 2004. *The Body Impolitic: Artisans and Artifice in the Global Hierarchy of Value.* Chicago: University of Chicago Press.

Hobsbawm, E. J. 1984. "Man and Woman: Images on the Left." In *Workers: Worlds of Labor,* 49–65. New York: Pantheon.

Hoffman, George. 1972. *Regional Development Strategy in Southeast Europe: A Comparative Analysis of Albania, Bulgaria, Greece, Romania, and Yugoslavia.* New York: Praeger.

Hoffman, Oscar, Simona Raşeev, and Dinu Ţenovici. 1984. *Clasa muncitoare din România în condiţiile revoluţiei tehnico-ştiinţifice.* Bucharest: Editura Academiei.

Holmes, Douglas. 2000. *Integral Europe: Fast-Capitalism, Multiculturalism, Neofascism.* Princeton: Princeton University Press.

Hord, Charlotte, Henry P. David, France Donnay, and Merrill Wolf. 1991. "Reproductive Health in Romania: Reversing the Ceauşescu Legacy." *Studies in Family Planning* 22(4): 231–40.

Humphrey, Caroline. 2002a. "Does the Category 'Postsocialist' Still Make Sense?" In "Introduction: Postsocialism as a Topic of Anthropological Investigation," introduction to *Postsocialism: Ideals, Ideologies and Practices in Eurasia,* ed. C. M. Hann, 12–15. London: Routledge.

———. 2002b. *The Unmaking of Soviet Life: Everyday Economies after Socialism.* Ithaca, N.Y.: Cornell University Press.

International Labor Organization. 2002. "Training Policies for Vulnerable Groups in Central and Eastern European Countries." On-line Seminar Report, http://www.ilo.org/public/english/employment/skills/disability/download/prague.pdf.

Iordăchel, Ion. 1993. "Relaţii între salariu, bugetele de familie, şi conflictele colective de muncă." *Muncă şi Progres Social* 13–14(1–2): 29–33.

Jozan, P., and D. P. Forster. 1999. "Social Inequalities and Health: Ecological Study of Mortality in Budapest, 1980–3 and 1990–3." *British Medical Journal* 318:914–15.

Judecătorie Făgăraş. 1999. *Dosarele de statistica a le Judecatoriei Făgăraş, 1976–1999.* Unpublished.

Judecătorie Petroşani. 1999. *Dosarele de statistica a le Judecatoriei Petroşani, 1989–1999.* Unpublished.

Kideckel, David A. 1985. "'Drinking Up': Alcohol, Class, and Social Change in Rural Romania." *East European Quarterly* 18(4): 431–46.

———. 1988. "Economic Images in the Romanian Socialist Transformation." *Dialectical Anthropology* 12(4): 399–411.

———. 1993. *The Solitude of Collectivism: Romanian Villagers to the Revolution and Beyond.* Ithaca, N.Y.: Cornell University Press.

———. 1999. "Storm and Stasis: The Paradox of Labour in Post-socialist Romania." *EMERGO: Journal of Transforming Economies and Societies* 6(2): 24–46.

———. 2000a. "Labor, Health, and Politics in Two Romanian Regions. Part I: Labor and Society in the Jiu Valley and Fagaras Regions; Variations in Definitions and Responses to Crisis." Washington, D.C.: National Council for Eurasian and East European Research Working Paper Series.

———. 2000b. "Labor, Health, and Politics in Two Romanian Regions. Part II: Health Perceptions and Labor Conditions." Washington, D.C.: National Council for Eurasian and East European Research Working Paper Series.

———. 2001. "Winning the Battles, Losing the War: Contradictions of Romanian Labor in the Postcommunist Transformation." In *Workers after Workers' States: Labor and Politics in Postcommunist Eastern Europe,* ed. Stephen Crowley and David Ost, 97–120. Lanham, Md.: Rowman and Littlefield.

———. 2002. "The Unmaking of an East-Central European Working Class." In *Postsocialism: Ideas, Ideologies and Practices in Eurasia,* ed. C. M. Hann, 114–32. London: Routledge.

———. 2004a. "Miners and Wives in Romania's Jiu Valley: Perspectives on Postsocialist Class, Gender, and Social Change." *Identities: Global Studies in Power and Culture* 11(1): 39–63.

———. 2004b. "Two Little Americas: Labor and the Global in Two Romanian Regions." Paper presented at the Conference on Globalism, Globality, and Globalization: Ten Years of European Studies in Cluj. University of Babeş-Bolyai, Cluj-Napoca, Romania, October.

———. 2004c. "The Undead? The Death and Rebirth of Nicolae Ceauşescu and Patriarchal Politics in Post-Socialist Romania." In *Death of the Father: An Anthropology of Closure in Political Authority,* ed. John W. Borneman, 123–47. New York: Berghahn Books.

Kideckel, David A., Bianca Elena Botea, Raluca Nahorniac, and Vasile Şoflău. 2000. "A New 'Cult of Labor': Stress and Crisis among Romanian Workers." *Sociologie Româneasca* 1 (n.s.): 142–61.

Kideckel, David A., and Alin Rus. 2003. *Days of the Miners: Life and Death of a Working Class Culture.* Video documentary. New York: CMI Productions.

Kleinman, Arthur, Veena Das, and Margaret Lock. 1997. Introduction to *Social Suffering,* ix–xxvii. Berkeley: University of California Press.

Kligman, Gail A. 1988. *The Wedding of the Dead: Ritual, Poetics, and Popular Culture in Transylvania.* Berkeley: University of California Press.

―――. 1998. *The Politics of Duplicity: Controlling Reproduction in Ceauşescu's Romania.* Berkeley: University of California Press.

Knapp, Bernard, and Vincent Pigott. 1997. "The Archaeology and Anthropology of Mining: Social Approaches to an Industrial Past." *Current Anthropology* 38(2): 300–304.

Konrád, George, and Ivan Szelényi. 1979. *The Intellectuals on the Road to Class Power: A Sociological Study of the Role of the Intelligentsia in Socialism.* New York: Harcourt Brace Jovanovich.

Kornai, János. 1980. *Economics of Shortage.* Amsterdam: North-Holland.

Kovács, Katalin, and Mönika Váradi. 2000. "Women's Life Trajectories and Class Formation in Hungary." In *Reproducing Gender: Politics, Publics, and Everyday Life after Socialism,* ed. Susan Gal and Gail Kligman, 176–99. Princeton: Princeton University Press.

Kubik, Jan. 1994. *The Power of Symbols against the Symbols of Power: The Rise of Solidarity and the Fall of State Socialism in Poland.* College Park: Pennsylvania State University Press.

Kurti, Laszlo. 1991. "The Wingless Eros of Socialism: Nationalism and Sexuality in Hungary." *Anthropological Quarterly* 64(2): 55–67.

―――. 2002. *Youth and the State in Hungary: Capitalism, Communism, and Class.* London: Pluto Press.

Laba, Roman. 1991. *The Roots of Solidarity: A Political Sociology of Poland's Working-Class Democratization.* Princeton: Princeton University Press.

Lahiri-Dutt, Kuntala. 2006. "Kamins Building the Empire: Class, Caste, and Gender Interface in Indian Collieries." In *Mining Women: Gender in the Development of a Global Industry, 1670–2005,* ed. Laurie Mercier and Jacy Gier, 71–87. New York: Palgrave Macmillan.

Lahiri-Dutt, Kuntala, and Martha Macintyre, eds. 2006. *Women Miners in Developing Countries: Pit Women and Others.* London: Ashgate Publishing House.

Lakey, Cynthia Kay. 1994. "Quality of Life and Health Status in the Romanian People." Master's thesis in nursing, MGH Institute of Health Professions.

Lakey, Cynthia Kay, P. K. Nicholas, K. A. Wolf, and J. D. Leuner. 1996. "Health Care and Nursing in Romania." *Journal of Advanced Nursing* 23(5): 1045–49.

Lamaraso Group. 1998. *Social Assessment of Mining Sector Restructuring in Romania: Monitoring Social Impacts and Mitigating Adverse Impacts.* Bucharest: World Bank.

Lampland, Martha. 2002. "The Advantages of Being Collectivized: Cooperative Farm Managers in the Postsocialist Economy." In *Postsocialism: Ideals, Ideologies and Practices in Eurasia,* ed. C. M. Hann, 31–56. London: Routledge.

Landler, Mark. 2004. "Slovakia Vies to Create 'Detroit' of Europe." *International Herald Tribune,* April 14, p. 11.

Lane, David. 1997. Review of *Varieties of Transition: The East European and East German Experience,* by Klaus Offe. *Europe-Asia Studies* 49(6): 1106–1107.

Larionescu, Maria, Sorin Rădulescu, and Cosima Rughiniş. 1999. *Cu ochii minerului: Reforma mineritul în România.* Bucharest: Editura Gnosis.

Lascu, Ioan. 2004. *Tradiţii Care Dispar: Comunitatea Momârlanilor din Zona Petroşani.* Craiova: Editura Craiova.

Lechanu, Doina. 2003. "'Whatever Doesn't Kill You, Makes You Stronger': How Romanian Women Became Powerful and Controlling in Spite of a Dominating Patriarchal Society." Unpublished paper, Central Connecticut State University.

Lemon, Alaina. 2000a. *Between Two Fires: Gypsy Performance and Romani Memory from Pushkin to Postsocialism.* Durham, N.C.: Duke University Press.

―――. 2000b. "Talking Transit and Spectating Transition: The Moscow Metro." In *Altering States: Ethnographies of Transition in Eastern Europe and the Former Soviet Union,* ed. Daphne Berdhal, Matti Bunzl, and Martha Lampland, 14–39. Ann Arbor: University of Michigan Press.

Leon, David A., Laurent Chenet, Vladimir M. Shkolnikov, Sergei Zakharov, Judith Shapiro, Galina Rakhamanova, Sergei Vassin, and Martin McKee. 1997. "Huge Variation in Russian Mortality Rates, 1984–94: Artefact, Alcohol, or What?" *Lancet* 350: 383–87.

Lloyd, John. 1999. "The Last Bandit King: The Plight of Romania's Miners and Their Arrested Leader, Miron Cozma." *Financial Times* (London), February 20, Saturday W Edition 1, p. 1.

Lock, Margaret. 1993. "Cultivating the Body: Anthropology and Epistemologies of Bodily Practice and Knowledge." *Annual Review of Anthropology* 22:133–55.

———. 1997. "Displacing Suffering: The Reconstruction of Death in North America and Japan." In *Social Suffering,* ed. Arthur Kleinman, Veena Das, and Margaret Lock, 206–44. Berkeley: University of California Press.

Lukić, Jasmina. 2000. "Media Representations of Men and Women in Times of War and Crisis: The Case of Serbia." In *Reproducing Gender: Politics, Publics, and Everyday Life after Socialism,* ed. Susan Gal and Gail Kligman, 393–423. Princeton: Princeton University Press.

Lukose, Ritty. 2005. "Empty Citizenship: Protesting Politics in the Era of Globalization." *Cultural Anthropology* 20(4): 506–33.

Magyari-Vincze, Enikö. 2004. "Le patriarcat d'en haut et d'en bas en Roumanie." *Nouvelles questions féministes* 23(2): 29–49.

Mandel, Ruth, and Caroline Humphrey, eds. 2002. *Markets and Moralities: Ethnographies of Postsocialism.* Oxford: Berg.

Marcus, George. 1995. "Ethnography in and of the World System: The Emergence of Multi-sited Ethnography." *Annual Review of Anthropology* 24:95–117.

Marmot, Michael, and Martin Bobek. 2000a. "International Comparators and Poverty and Health in Europe." *British Medical Journal* 321:1124–28.

———. 2000b. "Psychosocial and Biological Mechanisms behind the Recent Mortality Crisis in Central and Eastern Europe." In *The Mortality Crisis in Transitional Economies,* ed. Giovanni Andrea Cornia and Renato Paniccia, 127–48. London: Oxford University Press.

Marody, Mira, and Anna Giza-Poleszczuk. 2000. "Changing Images of Identity in Poland: From the Self-Sacrificing to the Self-Investing Woman?" In *Reproducing Gender: Politics, Publics, and Everyday Life after Socialism,* ed. Susan Gal and Gail Kligman, 151–75. Princeton: Princeton University Press.

Matei, Horia C., Marcel D. Popa, et al. 1972. *Chronological History of Romania.* Bucharest: Editura Enciclopedică Română.

Matinal. 1997. *După 20 de Ani sau Lupeni '77–Lupeni '97.* Petroşani: Imprimeria Grapho Tipex.

Mato, Zsolt-Istvan. 2002. "Preliminary Census Results Show Considerable Decline of Population." *RFE/RL NEWSLINE* 6(125), part 2, July 8.

McMahon, Robert. 2000. "UN: Foreign Investment in Eastern Europe Remains Steady." RFE/RL Research Report. http://www.rferl.org/features/2000/10/04102000162241 .asp.

Mihailescu, Vîntilă. 2004. "Institutional 'Transition' and 'Post-Communist' Changes in Romania: Notes for an Anthropology of Transparency." Paper delivered at the Conference on Globalism, Globality, Globalization. Babeş-Bolyai University, Cluj, Romania, October.

Milosz, Czeslaw. 1953. *The Captive Mind.* New York: Knopf.

Morris, David B. 1997. "About Suffering: Voice, Genre, and Moral Community." In *Social Suffering,* ed. Arthur Kleinman, Veena Das, and Margaret Lock, 25–45. Berkeley: University of California Press.

———. 1998. *Illness and Culture in the Postmodern Age.* Berkeley: University of California Press.

Muntean, Georgeta. 1997. *Atitudini Politice, Civice, şi Morale ale Populaţiei României Faţă de Procesul de Tranziţiei: Fază Unică.* Bucharest: Research Group Romania Ltd.

Mureşan, Cornelia. 1999. "The Decrease of Life-Expectancy at Birth in Romania and Some Crisis Contributing Factors." *Health and Place* 5(2): 187–92.

Nagengast, Carole. 1991. *Reluctant Socialists, Rural Capitalists: Class, Culture, and the Polish State.* Boulder, Colo.: Westview.

Nagy, Beáta. 1997. "New Career Perspectives—Women Entrepreneurs in Hungary." In *Women and Men in East European Transition,* ed. Margit Feischmidt, Enikö Magyari-Vincze, and Violetta Zentai, 100–109. Cluj-Napoca: Editura Fundaţiei pentru Studii Europene.

Nash, June. 1979. *We Eat the Mines and the Mines Eat Us: Dependency and Exploitation in Bolivian Tin Mines.* New York: Columbia University Press.

Nelson, Diane M. 1999. *A Finger in the Wound: Body Politics in Quincentennial Guatemala.* Berkeley: University of California Press.

Nemoianu, Alexandru. 1997. *Cuvinte despre Românii-Americani.* Cluj-Napoca: Clusium.

———. 2001. *În America la "Vatra Româneasca."* Bucharest: Editura Minerva.

Nesporova, Alena. 2000. "Fighting Unemployment and Stress: Labour Market Policies in Central and Eastern Europe." In *The Mortality Crisis in Transitional Economies,* ed. Giovanni Andrea Cornia and Renato Paniccia, 204–24. London: Oxford University Press.

Nicolaescu, Madalina. 1994. "Post-Communist Transitions: Romanian Women's Responses to Changes in the System of Power." *Journal of Women's History* 5(3): 117–28.

———. 1997. "The Representation of Women's Bodies in the Press for Women: Desire and Identification in the Romanian Women's Journals." In *Women and Men in East European Transition,* ed. Margit Feischmidt, Enikö Magyari-Vincze, and Violetta Zentai, 144–55. Cluj-Napoca: Editura Fundaţiei pentru Studii Europene.

Nordenmark, Mikael, and Mattias Strandh. 1999. "Towards a Sociological Understanding of Mental Well-Being among the Unemployed: The Role of Economic and Psychological Factors." *Sociology* 33(3): 577–97.

Occhipinti, Laura. 1996. "Two Steps Back? Anti-feminism in Eastern Europe." *Anthropology Today* 12(6): 13–18.

Ockenga, Edzard. 1997. "Trade Unions in Romania." *Transfer: European Review of Labour and Research* 3(2): 313–28.

Ogoreanu, Ion Gavrilă. 1995. *Brazii se Frâng, Dar nu se Îndoiesc: Rezistenţa Anticomunistă în Munţii Făgăraşului.* 2 vols. Timişoara: Editura Marineasa.

Oldson, William O. 1996. "Background to Catastrophe: Romanian Modernization Policies and the Environment." *East European Quarterly* 30(4): 517–29.

Open Society Foundation. 2001. *Barometrul de opinie publică.* Cluj-Napoca: Metro Media Transilvania.

Oprea, Ion. 1970. *Istoria Românilor.* Bucharest: Editura Didactică şi Pedagogică.

Ortner, Sherry B. 1984. "Theory in Anthropology since the Sixties." *Comparative Studies in Society and History* 26:126–66.

———. 1996. *Making Gender: The Politics and Erotics of Culture.* Boston, Mass.: Beacon Press.

Orwell, George. 1937. *The Road to Wigan Pier.* London: Penguin Books.

Ost, David. 1993. "Labor in Post-Communist Transformations." Working paper 5.17, Center for East European Studies. Berkeley: University of California.

———. 2002. "Letter from Poland." *Nation* 275(18): 16, 18–20.

Ost, David, and Stephen Crowley. 2001. "Introduction: The Surprise of Labor Weakness in Postcommunist Society." In *Workers after Worker States: Labor and Politics in Postcommunist Eastern Europe,* ed. Stephen Crowley and David Ost, 1–12. Lanham, Md.: Rowman and Littlefield.

Pandolfi, Mariella. 2005. "From Violence to (In)security: The Paradox of the 'Permanent Transition.'" Newsletter, Specialist Group on Ethnopolitics. Spring.

Pasti, Vladimir. 1995. *România în Tranziţie: Căderea în Viitor.* Bucharest: Editura Nemira.

Pasti, Vladimir, Mihaiela Miroiu, and Cornel Codiţa. 1996. *România—Starea de Fapt.* Vol. 1: *Societatea.* Bucharest: Editura Nemira

Patico, Jennifer. 2000. "'New Russian' Sightings and the Question of Social Difference in St. Petersburg." *Anthropology of East Europe Review* 18(2): 73–78.

———. 2005. "To Be Happy in a Mercedes: Tropes of Value and Ambivalent Visions of Marketization." *American Ethnologist* 32(3): 479–96.

Pavlinek, Petr. 2004. "Regional Development Implications of Foreign Direct Investment in Central Europe." *European Urban and Regional Studies* 11(1): 47–70.

Pecican, Ovidiu. 1997. "Romanian Masculine Model." In *Women and Men in East European Transition,* ed. Margit Feischmidt, Enikö Magyari-Vincze, and Violetta Zentai, 201–12. Cluj-Napoca: Editura Fundaţiei pentru Studii Europene.

Perjovschi, Dan. 1999. "Mineri buni, mineri rai." *Revista* 22(3): 1–3.

Petrovic, Jasna. 2002. "Countering the New Masters: Central and Eastern European Workers Struggle to Hold Their Ground in Hard Economic Times; Interview with Jasna Petrovic." *Multinational Monitor* 23(5): 24–26.

Petryna, Adriana. 2002. *Life Exposed: Biological Citizens after Chernobyl.* Princeton: Princeton University Press.

Pine, Frances. 2002. "Retreat to the Household: Gendered Domains in Postsocialist Poland." In *Postsocialism: Ideals, Ideologies and Practices in Eurasia,* ed. C. M. Hann, 95–113. London: Routledge.

Pleşu, Andrei. 1996. "Post-totalitarian Pathology: Notes on Romania, Six Years after December 1989." *Social Research* 63(2): 559–77.

Pollert, Anna. 1999. *Transformation at Work in the New Market Economies of Central Eastern Europe.* London: Sage.

———. 2001a. "Gender Relations, Equal Opportunities, and Women in Transition in Central and Eastern Europe." *Labour Focus on Eastern Europe* 68:4–49.

———. 2001b. "Labor and Trade Unions in the Czech Republic, 1989–2000." In *Workers after Workers' States: Labor and Politics in Postcommunist Eastern Europe,* ed. Stephen Crowley and David Ost, 13–36. Lanham, Md.: Rowman and Littlefield.

Popa, Aron, Ilie Rotunjeanu, et al. 1993. *Exploatări Miniere.* Bucharest: Editură Didactică şi Pedagogică.

Popescu, Adrian. 1999. "La Făgăraş strugurii se vând cu 500 lei . . . bobul." *Adevărul,* July 26, p. 8.

———. 2005. "Pâinea disperării"– la Nitramonia Făgăraş." *Gândul* 1:109 (September 7).

Popescu, Razvan. 1996. *Prea Tîrziu.* Bucharest: Humanitas.

Pospai, Mircea. 1978. *Amintiri din Valea Luminii: Viaţa şi Activitatea Minerilor din Oltenia.* Craiova, Romania: Scrisul Românesc.

Prisăcaru, Corneliu. 1996. *Pensionarii în perioada 1990–1995.* Bucharest: Institute for Research on the Quality of Life of the Romanian Academy.

Rausing, Sigrid. 2002. "Re-constructing the 'Normal': Identity and the Consumption of Western Goods in Estonia." In *Markets and Moralities: Ethnographies of Postsocialism,* ed. Ruth Mandel and Caroline Humphrey, 127–42. Oxford: Berg.

———. 2004. *History, Memory, and Identity in Post-Soviet Estonia: The End of a Collective Farm.* London: Oxford.

Reed-Danahay, Deborah. 2005. *Locating Bourdieu.* Bloomington: Indiana University Press.

Rey, Violette. 1997. "L'étonnant retour paysan en Roumanie." *Papers of the French Agricultural Academy* 83(8): 17–28.

Ries, Nancy. 1997. *Russian Talk: Culture and Conversation during Perestroika.* Ithaca, N.Y.: Cornell University Press.

Rivkin-Fish, Michelle. 2003. "Anthropology, Demography, and the Search for a Critical Analysis of Fertility: Insights from Russia." *American Anthropologist* 105(2): 289–301.

Rodina, Vladimir. 1994. "Romania: Unions Running Out of Steam." *Warsaw Post,* June 26. Lexis-Nexis European News Service.

Rogers, Susan Carol. 1975. "Female Forms of Power and the Myth of Male Dominance: A Model of Female/Male Interaction in Peasant Society." *American Ethnologist* 2(4): 727–56.

Roman, Denise. 2001. "Gendering Eastern Europe: Pre-feminism, Prejudice, and East-West Dialogues in Post-Communist Romania." *Women's Studies International Forum* 24(1): 53–66.

Romania. Government. 1992. "Romanian Articles on Collective Labor Contract at National Level of 1/92." Springfield, Va.: National Technical Information Service. Translated from *Adevărul,* January 23, 1992, pp. 3–5.

———. 1997a. Legea Asigurărilor Sociale de Sănătate. *Monitoru oficial al României* 9(178) (July 3).

———. 1997b. Ordonanţa Nr. 22/1997 Privind unele măsuri de protecţie ce se acordă personalului din industria minieră şi din activităţile de prospecţiuni şi explorări geologice. *Monitorul oficial al României* 200(20) (August 20).

———. 1998. Ordonanţă de urgenţă privind regimul zonelor defavorizate. *Monitorul oficial al României,* part 1, no. 378 (October 2).

———. 1999a. Contracte colective de Muncă. *Monitorul oficial al României.* 3(10) (July 18).

———. 1999b. Memorandum în legătură cu negocierile privind lista de revendicări comune pe temen scurt convenite la întâlnirea Primului-ministru Radu Vasile cu confederaţiile sindicale Cartel Alfa, BNS, CNSLR-Fraţia, şi CSDR la data de 21 aprilie 1999. Bucharest: Comisia de Monitorizare.

Romania. Parliament. 1991a. *Law on the Settlement of Collective Labor Conflicts.* Springfield, Va.: National Technical Information Service.

———. 1991b. Trade Union Act. Law 54/1991. Buletin Oficial no. 164, August 7.

Rompres. 1998. "Women Make Up Nearly 50 Percent of Unemployed in Romania." BBC Summary of World Broadcasts, part 2, Central Europe, October 8.

Rose, Richard. 1997. "How Patient Are People in Post-Communist Societies?" *World Affairs* 159 (3): 130–44.

Rubin Meyer Doru and Trandafir. 2003. "Labor Lost: The New Romanian Labor Law." *Romanian Digest* 8(3): 1–7.

Rus, Alin. 2002. "Relaţiile de gen din Valea Jiului—între trecut şi prezent." Working paper, typescript.

———. 2003. *Valea Jiului-O Capcană Istorică.* Vulcan, Romania: Editura Realitatea Romanească.

Sabel, Charles F., and David Stark. 1982. "Planning, Politics, and Shop-Floor Power: Hidden Forms of Bargaining in Soviet-Imposed State Socialist Societies." *East European Politics and Societies* 2(4): 439–75.

Said, Edward. 1975. *Orientalism.* Chicago: University of Chicago Press.

Sampson, Steven. 1984. *National Integration through Socialist Planning: An Anthropological Study of a Romanian New Town.* New York: East European Monographs.

———. 1987. "The Informal Sector in Eastern Europe." *TELOS* 66:44–66.

———. 1996. "The Social Life of Projects: Importing Civil Society to Albania." In *Civil Society: Challenging Western Models,* ed. Chris Hann and Elizabeth Dunn, 121–42. London: Routledge.

———. 2002. "Weak States, Uncivil Societies, and Thousands of NGOs: Benevolent Colonialism in the Balkans." In *The Balkans in Focus: Cultural Boundaries in Europe,* ed. Sanimir Resic and Barbara Törnquist-Plewa, 27–44. Lund, Sweden: Nordic Academic Press.

———. 2005. "Integrity Warriors: Global Morality and the Anticorruption Movement in the Balkans." In *Corruption: Anthropological Perspectives,* ed. Dieter Haller and Cris Shore, 103–30. London: Pluto Press.

Sapolsky, Robert M. 1997. *"The Trouble with Testosterone" and Other Essays on the Biology of the Human Predicament.* New York: Simon and Schuster.

Satter, David. 2003. *Darkness at Dawn: The Rise of the Russian Criminal State.* New Haven: Yale University Press.

Scheper-Hughes, Nancy. 1992. *Death without Weeping: The Violence of Everyday Life in Brazil.* Berkeley: University of California Press.

Scheper-Hughes, Nancy, and Margaret M. Lock. 1987. "The Mindful Body: A Prolegomenon to Future Work in Medical Anthropology." *Medical Anthropology Quarterly* 1(1): 6–41.

Schneider, Jane C., and Peter T. Schneider. 1996. *Festival of the Poor: Fertility Decline and the Ideology of Class in Sicily, 1860–1980.* Tucson: University of Arizona Press.

Scott, James C. 1985. *Weapons of the Weak: Everyday Forms of Peasant Resistance.* New Haven: Yale University Press.

Segal, Jerome M. 1991. *Agency and Alienation: A Theory of Human Presence.* Lanham, Md.: Rowman and Littlefield.

Şelaru, Vasile. 2004. "Faith Kesser a Distrus 'Colorom' şi 'Nitramonia,' după care a Dispărut." *România Liberă,* August 10, p. 6.

Şerbanescu, Florina, Leo Morris, Paul Stupp, and Alin Stanescu. 1995. "The Impact of Recent Policy Changes on Fertility, Abortion, and Contraceptive Use in Romania." *Studies in Family Planning* 26(2): 76–87.

Shafir, Michael. 2001. "Romanian President Rejects Miners' Leader's Pardon Request." *RFE/RL Newsline* 4(167), part 2 (September 4).

Shilling, Chris. 1993. *The Body and Social Theory.* London: Sage.

Silverman, Marilyn. 2001. *An Irish Working Class: Explorations in Political Economy and Hegemony, 1800–1950.* Toronto: University of Toronto Press.

Słomczyński, Kazimierz, and Tadeusz Krauze, eds. 1978. *Class Structure and Social Mobility in Poland.* White Plains, N.Y.: M. E. Sharpe.

Słomczyński, Kazimierz, and Goldie Shabad. 1997. "Systemic Transformation and the Salience of Class Structure in East Central Europe." *East European Politics and Societies* 11(1): 155–89.

Smith, Martin Cruz. 1996. *Rose.* New York: Ballantine Books.

Snyder, Tim, and Milada Vachudova. 1997. "Are Transitions Transitory? Two Types of Political Change in Eastern Europe since 1989." *East European Politics and Societies* 11(1): 1–35.

Spencer, Jonathan. 2000. "On Not Becoming a 'Terrorist': Problems of Memory, Agency and Community in the Sri Lankan Conflict." In *Violence and Subjectivity,* ed. Veena Das, Arthur Kleinman, Mamphela Ramphele, and Pamela Reynolds, 120–40. Berkeley: University of California Press.

Stănculescu, Manuela Sofia, and Ionica Berevoescu. 2002. "Literature Review: Romania." In *HWF Research Report #1: Critical Review of Literature and Discourses about Flexibility,* ed. Claire Wallace, 189–255. Vienna: HWF Research Consortium and the Institute for Advanced Studies.

Stark, David, and László Bruszt. 1998. *Postsocialist Pathways: Transforming Politics and Property in East Central Europe.* Cambridge: Cambridge University Press.

Ştefan, Ilie. 1997. "Putere de cumpărare a populaţiei se deteriorează pe zi ce trece." *Adevărul,* June 30, p. 5.

———. 1999. "Românii cheltuiesc tot mai mult, dar coşniţa zilnică este tot mai goală." *Adevărul,* August 9, p. 6.

Stewart, Michael. 1997. *The Time of the Gypsies.* Boulder, Colo.: Westview.

Stone, Richard. 2000. "Stress: The Invisible Hand in Eastern Europe's Death Rates." *Science* 288:1732–33 (June 9).

Straussner, Shulamith, Lala Ashenberg, and Norma Phillips. 1999. "The Impact of Job Loss on Professional and Managerial Employees and Their Families." *Families in Society* 80(6): 642–48.

Sturdza, Mihai. 1990. "The Labor Movement." *Report on Eastern Europe,* Radio Free Europe, July 27, pp. 36–44.

Svendsen, Mette Nordahl. 1996. "The Post-Communist Body: Beauty and Aerobics in Romania." *Anthropology of East Europe Review* 14(1): 8–14.

————. 1997. "The Body as a Business Card: How to Become a Modern Woman in Urban Romania." In *Women and Men in East European Transition,* ed. Margit Feischmidt, Enikö Magyari-Vincze, and Violetta Zentai, 135–43. Cluj-Napoca: Editura Fundaţiei pentru Studii Europene.

Synovitz, Ron. 1997. "The East: Labor Leader Says Unreformed Unions Fail Workers." *RFE/RL Newsline,* December 2.

Szelényi, Ivan, et al. 1988. *Socialist Entrepreneurs: Embourgeoisement in Rural Hungary.* Madison: University of Wisconsin Press.

Szelényi, Ivan, Éva Fodor, and Eric Hanley. 1997. "Left Turn in Post-Communist Politics: Bringing Class Back In?" *East European Politics and Societies* 11(1): 190–224.

Słomczyński, Kazimierz, and Tadeusz Krauze. 1978. *Class Structure and Social Mobility in Poland.* White Plains, N.Y.: M. E. Sharpe.

Tambiah, Stanley. 1990. "Presidential Address: Reflections on Communal Violence in South Asia." *Journal of Asian Studies* 49(4): 741–60.

Tchernina, Natalia. 2000. "Rising Unemployment and Coping Strategies: The Case of the Novosibirsk Oblast in Russia." In *The Mortality Crisis in Transitional Economies,* ed. Giovanni Andrea Cornia and Renato Paniccia, 151–73. London: Oxford University Press.

Thompson, E. P. 1963. *The Making of the English Working Class.* New York: Vintage.

Ţic, Nicolae. 1977. *Roşu pe Alb.* Craiova, Romania: N.p.

Tilly, Charles. 1999. *Durable Inequality.* Berkeley: University of California Press.

————. 2001. "Social Class." In *Encyclopedia of European Social History from 1350 to 2000,* ed. Peter N. Stearns. 3:3–17. New York: Charles Scribner's Sons.

Tintori, Karen. 2002. *Trapped: The 1909 Cherry Mine Disaster.* New York: Atria Books.

Tismaneanu, Vladimir. 1998. *Fantasies of Salvation: Democracy, Nationalism, and Myth in Post-Communist Europe.* Princeton: Princeton University Press.

Toth-Gaspar, Margareta. 1964. "Condiţiile de Munca şi Viaţa ale Minerilor din Valea Ji-ului şi Luptelelor Greviste pînă la Sfârşitul Secolului al XIX-lea." *Acta Musei Napocensis,* 255–85. Cited in Friedman 2003.

Tsantis, Andreas C., and Roy Pepper. 1979. *Romania: The Industrialization of an Agrarian Economy under Socialist Planning.* Washington, D.C.: World Bank.

Tulbure, Ildiko, and Ioan-Iulian Irimie. 1995. "Socio-dimensions of Environmental Pollution in a Coal Mines Region of Romania." In *Proceedings of the First World Mining Environment Conference,* 173–82. Rotterdam: A. A. Balkema.

United Nations Development Program. 2000. *Femeile şi Bărbaţii în România.* Bucharest: UNDP.

Vasi, Ion Bogdan. 2004. "The Fist of the Working Class: The Social Movements of Jiu Valley Miners in Post-Socialist Romania." *East European Politics and Societies* 18:132–57.

Velica, Ion. 1999. *Lupeni '29: Blestemul Cărbunului.* Petroşani, Romania: Romsver.

Velica, Ion, and Carol Schreter. 1993. *Călătorie prin Vârstele Văii Jiului: Istoria în date a Văii Jiului.* Deva, Romania: Editura Destin.

Velica, Ion, and Dragoş Ştefan Velica. 2002. *Lupeni '77: Laboratorul Puterii.* Deva, Romania: Editura Polidava.

Verdery, Katherine. 1996. *What Was Socialism, and What Comes Next?* Princeton: Princeton University Press.

————. 1998. "Transnationalism, Nationalism, Citizenship and Property: Eastern Europe since 1989." *American Ethnologist* 25(2): 291–306.

————. 1999. *The Political Lives of Dead Bodies: Reburial and Post-Socialist Change.* New York: Columbia University Press.

————. 2002. "Whither Postsocialism?" In *Postsocialism: Ideals, Ideoogies and Practices in Eurasia,*ed. C. M. Hann, 15–28. London: Routledge.

———. 2003. *The Vanishing Hectare: Property and Value in Postsocialist Transylvania.* Ithaca, N.Y.: Cornell University Press.

Verdery, Katherine, and Gail Kligman. 1992. "Romania after Ceauşescu: Post-Communist Communism." In *Eastern Europe in Revolution,* ed. Ivo Banac, 117–47. Ithaca, N.Y.: Cornell University Press.

Vrânceanu, Ovidiu. 2004. "Ultimul Pui UPRUC, Scos la Licitaţie." *Buna Ziua Braşov,* August 13, p. 4.

Wahler, H. J. 1968. "The Physical Symptoms Inventory: Measuring Levels of Somatic Complaining Behavior." *Journal of Clinical Psychology* 24:207–11.

Watson, Peggy. 1993. "The Rise of Masculinism in Eastern Europe." *New Left Review* 198:71–82.

———. 1995. "Explaining Rising Mortality among Men in Eastern Europe." *Social Science in Medicine* 41:923–34.

Wedel, Janine. 1998a. *Collision and Collusion: The Strange Case of Western Aid to Eastern Europe, 1989–1998.* New York: St. Martin's.

———. 1998b. "The Harvard Boys Do Russia." *The Nation,* June 1, pp. 1, 4.

Weidner, Gerdi. 1998. "Gender Gap in Health Decline in East Europe." *Nature* 395:835 (October 29).

Weiner, Elaine S. 2005. "No (Wo)Man's Land: The Post-Socialist Purgatory of Czech Female Factory Workers." *Social Problems* 52(4): 572–92.

West, Barbara A. 2002. *The Danger Is Everywhere: The Insecurity of Transition in Postsocialist Hungary.* Prospect Heights, Ill.: Waveland Press.

White, Paul, and Deborah Sporton. 1995. "East-West Movement: Old Barriers, New Barriers?" In *Europe's Population: Toward the Next Century,* ed. Ray Hall and Paul White, 142–60. London: UCL Press.

Williams, Raymond. 1976. *Keywords: A Vocabulary of Culture and Society.* New York: Oxford University Press.

World Bank. 2004. *The Jiu Valley Region: Multi-dimensional Assessment.* Washington, D.C.: World Bank.

Zanca, Russell. 2000. "Intruder in Uzbekistan: Walking the Line between Community Needs and Anthropological Desiderata." In *Fieldwork Dilemmas: Anthropologists in Postsocialist States,* ed. Hermine G. DeSoto and Nora Dudwick, 153–71. Madison: University of Wisconsin Press.

Zderciuc, Boris. 1972. "Combinatul Chimic Făgăraş, factor de transformare socială." In *Combinatul chimic Făgăraş: Cincizeci ani de înfiinţare,* ed. Train Herseni et al., 277–302. Sibiu, Romania: Intreprindera Poligrafica.

Zerilli, Filippo M. 1998. "Identité et propriété en milieu urbain: Locataires et propriétaires dans la Roumanie contemporaine." *Yearbook of the Romanian Society of Cultural Anthropology* 1:165–70.

———. 2000. "Property Sentiments and/as Property Rights: On Conflicts between Tenants and Landlords over House Property Restitution in Romania." Paper presented at the sixth biennial conference of the European Association of Social Anthropologists. Cracow, Poland, July 26–29.

———. 2005. "Corruption, Property Restitution, and Romanianess." In *Corruption: Anthropological Perspectives,* ed. Dieter Haller and Cris Shore, 83–99. London: Pluto Press.

Index

Italicized page numbers indicate illustrations.

New Anthropologies of Europe

Daphne Berdahl, Matti Bunzl, and Michael Herzfeld, founding editors

David A. Kideckel is Professor of Cultural Anthropology at Central Connecticut State University. His books include *The Solitude of Collectivism: Romanian Villagers to the Revolution and Beyond*, *East European Communities: The Struggle for Balance in Turbulent Times*, and *Neighbors at War: Anthropological Perspectives on Yugoslav Ethnicity, Culture, and History* (with Joel M. Halperin).

For those interested in further exploring the lives of the Jiu Valley miners, a companion fifty-two-minute video documentary is available from the author at kideckel@ccsu.edu. *Days of the Miners: Life and Death of a Working Class Culture* begins at a memorial service for fourteen miners killed at the Vulcan mine in 2001, and continues with scenes and interviews illuminating the social and economic difficulties faced by miners in postsocialism. It describes the development of the mining way of life from the mid-nineteenth century through socialism to the present, highlighting strikes and political violence. A segment then follows miners through a typical work day, emphasizing cohesion in the underground, the difficulty of mine labor, and miners' opinions on life and work, and then returns to a discussion of the Vulcan mine accident and the fourteen miners' fate. The film closes with scenes of neighborhood life and celebration, suggesting that despite danger, death, and decline, the Jiu Valley mining way of life still survives.